Palgrave Executive Essentials

Today's complex and changing business environment brings with it a number of pressing challenges. To be successful, business professionals are increasingly required to leverage and spot future trends, be masters of strategy, all while leading responsibly, inspiring others, mastering financial techniques and driving innovation.

Palgrave Executive Essentials empowers you to take your skills to the next level. Offering a suite of resources to support you on your executive journey and written by renowned experts from top business schools, the series is designed to support professionals as they embark on executive education courses, but it is equally applicable to practicing leaders and managers. Each book brings you in-depth case studies, accompanying video resources, reflective questions, practical tools and core concepts that can be easily applied to your organization, all written in an engaging, easy to read style.

John Colley

The Unwritten Rules of M&A

Mergers and Acquisitions that Deliver Growth—Learning from Private Equity

John Colley
Warwick Business School
University of Warwick
Coventry, UK

ISSN 2731-5614   ISSN 2731-5622 (electronic)
Palgrave Executive Essentials
ISBN 978-3-031-68367-1   ISBN 978-3-031-68368-8 (eBook)
https://doi.org/10.1007/978-3-031-68368-8

© The Editor(s) (if applicable) and The Author(s), under exclusive license to Springer Nature Switzerland AG 2024

This work is subject to copyright. All rights are solely and exclusively licensed by the Publisher, whether the whole or part of the material is concerned, specifically the rights of translation, reprinting, reuse of illustrations, recitation, broadcasting, reproduction on microfilms or in any other physical way, and transmission or information storage and retrieval, electronic adaptation, computer software, or by similar or dissimilar methodology now known or hereafter developed.
The use of general descriptive names, registered names, trademarks, service marks, etc. in this publication does not imply, even in the absence of a specific statement, that such names are exempt from the relevant protective laws and regulations and therefore free for general use.
The publisher, the authors and the editors are safe to assume that the advice and information in this book are believed to be true and accurate at the date of publication. Neither the publisher nor the authors or the editors give a warranty, expressed or implied, with respect to the material contained herein or for any errors or omissions that may have been made. The publisher remains neutral with regard to jurisdictional claims in published maps and institutional affiliations.

Cover credit: artvea

This Palgrave Macmillan imprint is published by the registered company Springer Nature Switzerland AG
The registered company address is: Gewerbestrasse 11, 6330 Cham, Switzerland

If disposing of this product, please recycle the paper.

Foreword

Deal Fever. That's what they call it. You have someone telling you that your business is worth multiples of its current value, and they are willing to give you every penny for it. They confirm all the positive biases you had about your business, appear to share a common vision for its future and are prepared to brush aside the potential limitations which have been nagging you for years. On top of this, the money involved can be life-changing and, depending on your personal situation, might finally mean a tidy exit from the business that had become something of a burden. It all sounds too good to be true. As the buying process progresses, you dismiss the warning signs, or in fact anything that might compromise the deal going through. This is too lucrative a deal to ignore, you tell yourself, 'Let's just get it over the line.'

And that is how it happens; you've been infected with the phenomenon of deal fever.

That is not to say that all deals are bad or impulsive, nor that all actors in M&A deals are out to take advantage of you, but a look at the literature plainly shows that the overwhelming majority of acquisitions destroy value. In order to make an acquisition work for you and your company, you need to go into it with your eyes wide open.

The problem is that the deck is stacked against you. Perhaps this is the first time that you are selling a company you own or manage, and as yet, you don't even know 'what you don't know' about the complex process you have initiated. Instead, you will have to learn the rules of the game as you go, and even to most experienced businesspeople, you will be surprised at how little you actually knew.

A novice to M&A might presume that due diligence is akin to someone looking under a few rocks to check over your figures. In fact, it can be a rigorous, forensic evaluation of *their* data about your business, which you must then defend. Prepare for each loose thread to be tugged to the extreme, in fact, to the point where you begin to question if you have it all wrong. On top of this are the complexities of the game itself, which involves multiple external parties, including lawyers, bankers, advisors and consultants, all with exacting demands that are far from the simple, friendly handshake with which you hoped to close the deal.

Each of these parties has its own intentions and incentives that are seldom aligned solely with what is best for you, and each of these players has a single focus: the deal. You, on the other hand, are still trying to attend to the running of the business which—with the distracting interrogation of the due diligence—may not be performing as well as it might. This is soon to be a point of weakness, exploited as the deal makers ratchet up the speed of the process to the point where you may feel overwhelmed and are losing control. Your confidence is low, stress levels high and time is running out. Eventually, you may agree to a deal—*any* deal—just to restore a sense of normality.

So, should deals be avoided at all costs? No, this benefits few in what may be a prolonged period characterised by no or slow business growth. Going it alone can be risky, and joining a larger group can bring stability and access to new markets and resources. Small business owners always have the risk of cash flow running out, and this can take its toll over the years. There is a way forward, but it relies on you understanding the process of a deal, retaining a sense of control and protecting the inherent value of your business.

My first exposure to an acquisition deal during my career happened in my first tenure as MD. I was running a highly profitable technology company and my shareholders decided to put the business up for sale. Fortunately, I had already received some training in this area. Several years earlier, I had attended a Business School where John Colley was lecturing and later completed my dissertation on M&A with John as my supervisor. Whilst the course I was doing gave a comprehensive account of M&A, the theories in those textbooks did little to prepare me for what was to come.

John and I stayed in touch after my dissertation, and over a period of two years, we had multiple conversations and discussions on how I should approach my situation, as each deal has its own set of unique peculiarities. John was able to offer his advice and experience from his years in business and handling multiple acquisitions. As one of only a handful of 'professors of practice' at Warwick University, he had unique insights into the academic context of how a deal should be run yet was also able to offer the real-world context of what *actually* happens. Whilst my deal may not have gone perfectly, and certainly there were bumps along the way, I was able to navigate them with this vital independent advice from John.

To give a little more personal background to John Colley, he has been a Professor of Practice studying M&A and private equity for many years. He has previously been Group Managing Director at a FTSE100 company and Executive Managing Director at a French CAC40 business. He has chaired many companies, including listed, private equity and family-owned businesses. As a consequence, he has significant practical experience in M&A and draws heavily on example cases he has experienced first-hand as well as those studied from his academic position.

Of course, not everyone will have an M&A professor and deal expert in their corner when their time comes to step into the M&A ring. That's why this book is so important. There are numerous dry academic textbooks out there on the subject that outline integration plans, deal legalities and synergies, but none that are written with the business owner in mind. This book is unique in its practitioner's perspective and a useful guide to anyone wishing to reduce risk and improve their knowledge about what exactly they are signing up for. I certainly wish I had read this book before I stepped into the real world of M&A.

You will note that there are numerous points at which private equity-funded ventures are compared directly to corporate activity. Whilst there are mixed views on the private equity buy–improve–sell model, there is much to be learnt from their approach which John's book argues well.

Each chapter is full of case studies demonstrating key issues and relevant research findings. I found this encouraged me to reappraise some of the biggest M&A deals of recent years and identify with more clarity their costs, benefits, motives and methods. Asking 'what would I have done?' is the self-reflective approach necessary to avert rash decisions and hubris-driven deals. To give any deal you might be involved with now, or in the future, an element of objectivity and rational thinking, the advice that follows is valuable reading.

Coventry, UK
Conor McCarthy, PhD MBA
Managing Director

Preface

Why write a book on M&A? There are plenty of other informative and interesting books on the subject, however, I am yet to find one which genuinely integrates the major research findings with practical insight. In my experience, many of the people who instigate deals as principals know remarkably little about how to create value and more importantly, how it is lost. Indeed, lost for the most part. They learn from experience, and that takes time and can be accompanied by much value destruction. My motivation is to help those involved in instigating growth through deals and integration to avoid the many pitfalls of M&A.

My career path to date has been somewhat unusual. I progressed through a finance background to become Finance Director and Managing Director of large businesses, then later Group Managing Director at an FTSE 100 business. I then moved on to become Executive Managing Director at a large French-owned CAC30 business.

During this time, we bought a significant number of businesses with varying degrees of success. Internally, we never openly accepted this to be the case nor, as long as acquisitions were consistent with our strategy, did we worry too much. We had the usual belief that they would turn out all right in the long run. Strategy ruled and within that framework almost anything went. When appropriate businesses became available, we paid what was necessary and accepted share price dilution. As our approach was generally 'light touch,' we tended not to destroy too much value through integration, yet our acquisitions were often poorly timed, acquiring at the top of the market only to have to nurse these acquisitions through difficult downturns. Performance was often disappointing and rarely achieved the planned returns which formed the basis for internal and in some cases shareholder approval.

I managed some of our successes and mistakes myself. The entire process for all of us, including corporate development, was one of learning from experience. As we were spending many millions on acquiring businesses our learning and development over those years could be a costly affair. Frankly, writing off 50 Ferraris would have been cheaper.

We were eventually bought out in a hostile bid and at a high price from which the acquirer never truly recovered. Indeed, their acquisition strategies reflected ours, frequently destroying value and subsequently dumping acquisitions.

With a far wiser head than two decades earlier, this seemed the prime opportunity to transition into the academic arena and begin investigating some of the questions my career had raised. I retired from full-time major leadership jobs in vast corporates and undertook a Ph.D. in business strategy, going on to teach MBA and executive students at various major business schools. At the same time, I took positions as Non-Executive Chairman and enjoyed a dual role both academic and practical. The insight I had gained gave me a new perspective, and my success rate improved dramatically in buying and selling businesses. The fact that a significant amount of my own money was involved seemed to have helped with improving the success rate, although not always!

I became only more interested in M&A over the years and had seen first-hand what the research consistently finds—most, or at least 60–80% of acquisitions fail to deliver on their proposals, and the majority *destroy* value. This raises a whole series of questions: why are so many M&As undertaken when the chances of success are so low? Why are proposals rarely achieved and should boards not kick back and demand more realistic figures? In short, why do so many go so wrong?

Working with private equity (PE) in both buy-outs, chairing businesses owned by PE, and as an industry expert made me realise how professional and thorough they are at every stage of the process. In effect they make major returns consistently over the years through very similar activities to those we see corporates struggling with. What do they do differently and is there anything for corporates to learn from their approach?

I go on to explore the kinds of PE strategies which do appear to work, from identifying viable integrations and sources of value creation to optimising benefits without risking entire ventures. I also explain why corporates often unnecessarily pay too much or unwittingly destroy value.

You may argue that for the inexperienced there are advisors only too eager to help with all of the above processes. Certainly, these are helpful, and in some areas entirely necessary, however, it's easy to forget that consultants and advisers are not solely driven by helping you but also by maximising their fees. This nearly always means pushing the deal, and they may not be as transparent with you about prospects for success as they might. During a negotiation, you are almost always having to negotiate with your own advisors first as they attempt to draw you into considering substantial compromises to accelerate deal completion. Once the deal is completed then the consultants disappear, and the consequences and responsibility are yours alone.

Researchers attempt to categorise the potentially problematic stages, focusing on strategy, integration and pricing. But few conclude how and why these are so problematic. They are often put down to deal heat or the excitement of getting a deal done. Experiencing, learning and then studying how expensive such underperforming M&A can be has lent more force to my core question: Can such a costly learning curve be avoided? As with all business ventures, there are no quick fixes or simple solutions. There are, however, words of experience, the facts and case studies to explain them and suggestions throughout each chapter on how to navigate the complexities of M&A with the best possible outcome.

Coventry, UK   John Colley

Acknowledgements

Many senior business people are aware of the risky nature of M&A and the likelihood of value destruction and failure. However, few can tell you why or what can be done about it. Others view it as a specialist activity to be left to advisors. Some also consider it as a rare event which is unlikely to trouble them during their careers. From my discussions with classes of executive students over the many years and acting as informal advisors to some as their careers subsequently develop into more senior roles, it has become increasingly clear how much this book is needed. It is to these many students that my thanks go for their candid input and open discussion.

M&A is a frequent event for larger organisations which affects many of their people in terms of strategy, due diligence and integration. Failure can be avoided, and this book draws on students' experiences to identify the key areas of failure and how these can and should be remedied. Research allied to my own extensive practical experience provides real insight into the process from a management and leadership perspective.

I would also like to thank the many colleagues and advisors I have worked with over the years who have lent me their practical experience and insight. There is always something to be learnt from every situation and, during a very lengthy career as a senior business person and an academic, I have found you never stop learning. When you do think that, then it is time to do something else.

I am sincerely grateful to Warwick Business School for creating a learning environment in which ideas can flourish and offering the opportunity to meet so many talented academics and students, whose differing perspectives provide challenge and development of thought.

I am particularly thankful to Rosemary Morrison for her patience and persistence in overseeing this project to completion. Her role and work as a development editor has been critical in keeping the project on track. Special thanks also go to Seethalakshmi Vijayasarathy and both Liz Barlow and Stephen Partridge at Palgrave MacMillan.

My thanks also go to my daughter, Lauren Colley, for her meticulous approach to the editing of the text and for creating the many diagrams. Her patience, time and hard work have been invaluable to the project.

Lastly, I would like to express my appreciation to my wife, Jackie Colley, for her unwavering support throughout this project.

John Colley

Contents

Part I Introduction

1 Getting M&A Right   3
  Could the Private Equity Model Be the Antidote to Poor
  Performance?   4
  The Attractions and Risks of M&A   4
  Growing a Business   5
  Learning from Private Equity   6
  Growth in Mature Markets   7
  Internationalise   8
  Diversification   8
  Acquisition   9
  The Problems with M&A—Illustrative Case Studies
  and Commentary   9
    Case Study: Carlos Brito at AB InBev   9
    Comment   10
    Case Study: Bayer's $67bn Acquisition of Monsanto in 2016   11
    How Did It Happen?   12
    Case Study: AOL and Time Warner—How History
    Repeats Itself   13
  What Goes Wrong?   14
    Paying Too Much   15
    Ineffective Strategy   16

Integration	18
Why Do They Do It?	20
Multiple Arbitrage	21
Types of Multiple Arbitrage	22
Differences Between Public and Private Companies	24
Stakeholder Analysis: Who Wins and Who Loses in Horizontal Mergers	25
Acquiring Shareholders	25
Target Shareholders	25
Acquiring Boards	26
Target Board	26
Target Employees and Management	26
Customers	27
Suppliers	27
Competitors	27
Governments	27
Conclusions	27
References and Recommended Readings	28

Part II M&A: Strategy, Pricing and Integration

2	**Strategic Growth Options and Respective Risk Profiles**	**33**
	Introduction	33
	Integration—The Problem	34
	Comment	35
	Strategic Options	37
	Strategy 1: 'Bulking Up'	37
	Strategy 2: 'Reinventing the Business Model'	39
	Strategy 3: Product and Market Extensions	40
	Strategy 4: Unrelated Diversification	40
	Case Study 1: Hewlett Packard's M&A Travails	41
	Strategy 5: Mergers of Equals	42
	Case Study 2: Daimler Chrysler, a 'Merger of Equals'?	43
	Case Study 3: Aberdeen Asset Management and Standard Life 'Merger of Equals'	44
	Comment	44
	Strategy 6: Vertical Integration	45
	Deal Size Does Matter	47
	The Synergy Trap	47
	References and Recommended Readings	49

3	**Improving Integration Performance and Synergy Extraction**	51
	Introduction	51
	Why Does Integration Often Fail?	52
	The Deal Team	53
	In the Dark	53
	Integration by Consultants	54
	Dimensions of Integration	55
	Speed and Depth	55
	Available Synergies and Management Autonomy	55
	A Typology of Strategy and Consequences for Integration	56
	Integrating Management: To Change or Not to Change?	58
	Integration Learning	59
	Comment	61
	Silver Linings?	62
	Risk Assessment and Monitoring	62
	Culture	63
	Experiencing Integration	63
	Essentials for Effective Integration	64
	A Detailed Plan	64
	Communication	65
	Team	65
	Consequences for Strategy	66
	Hostile Bids	67
	Defence and Attack	68
	The First Dinner	69
	Integration	69
	Postscript	70
	10 Lessons for Better Integration	70
	Comment	72
	References and Recommended Readings	73

Part III   M&A: The Private Equity Way—What Is There to Be Learnt?

4	**Private Equity: A Rising Power**	77
	Introduction—Why Study Private Equity?	77
	Philosophy and Strategy	78
	Do KPIs Improve EBITDA?	79
	Governance and the Problem of Agency	80
	Satisficing: A Decision-Making Strategy?	82
	The Exit	83

xviii Contents

PE Incentives	83
How Does Private Equity Create Value?	85
Exit Multiple	88
M&A Cycle	89
Industry Cycle	91
Multiple Arbitrage—Size and Public/Private	92
Growth	93
Industry Categorisation	93
Managing Cash Efficiency	94
Leverage	94
Motivation Provided by Expensive Debt Funding	95
Summary	96
References and Recommended Readings	97
5 Comparing Private Equity and Corporate Approaches to M&A	**99**
Introduction	99
How Corporates and PE Differ in Approach to M&A	100
Philosophy and Objectives	100
References and Recommended Readings	110
6 The Future of Private Equity	**111**
Introduction	111
Recent Developments	112
Performance	112
Inflation, Interest Rates, Recession and Closed Markets	118
PE as Conglomerates?	120
Expertise and Focus	121
References and Recommended Readings	122

Part IV Valuation, Process, Governance and Case Studies

7 Business Valuation, Process and Negotiation	**127**
Introduction	127
Strategic Vs. Private Equity Buyers	128
Which Advisors?	130
Why Value a Business?	131
Valuation Methods	132
Timing	133
Process Stages	134
Strategy	134
Intelligence	135

	Negotiation	135
	Due Diligence	136
	Distraction	137
	The Pass	137
	Management Buy Outs (MBOs) and Conflicts of Interest	138
	'Skin in the Game'	139
	Incentivisation	140
	Divestments: Exclusive Sale or Market the Business?	140
	Private Equity Tactics	142
	PE Charm Offensive	143
	Earnouts	144
	Conclusions	144
	References and Recommended Readings	145
8	**Effective Governance and M&A**	147
	Introduction	147
	Personal Interest	148
	Analysis	150
	Analysis	152
	Analysis	153
	Risk and Due Diligence	153
	Growth: Earnings or Size	154
	Is Previous Success a Liability?	155
	Deal Success or Failure, and for Whom?	155
	Dealing with the Fallout	156
	The Proverbial Hockey Stick	157
	Governance Failures	158
	Why Don't the NEDs Do More to Stop These Deals?	159
	Effective Models of Governance	160
	Agency Theory	160
	Family Businesses	161
	Private Equity	162
	Eclipse of the Corporation?	163
	NEDs: How Effective Are They?	164
	Jensen on PE	165
	Incentives	165
	Active Board Management	166
	Governance	166
	References and Recommended Readings	167

9 Case Studies — 169
Introduction — 169
Case 1: Rawlplug: Stick to the Strategy — 170
  Making a Decision — 171
  Integration — 172
  Failed Synergies — 172
  From Bad to Worse — 172
  Another Phone Call — 173
Lessons — 173
  Summary — 175
Case 2: Twitter: Money-Maker or Mistake? — 176
  Paying Over the Odds — 176
  Tesla the Loser? — 177
  Musk's Strategy — 178
  Threads—More Challenges Ahead — 178
  Ask Yourself the Following: — 179
  Analysis: Musk's Mutating Strategy — 180
Case 3: The Rise of PE and the Fate of the Grocery Market's 'Big Four' — 181
  The 'Big Four' — 181
  Less Is More — 182
  The Online Grocery Market — 183
  An Industry Under Pressure: The Response of the 'Big Four' — 183
  Asda — 184
  The Reign of Amazon — 184
  A Failed Merger — 184
  PE Buy Asda for £7.2bn — 185
  Morrisons — 186
  Questions — 187
What Might PE Do in the Case of Asda and Morrisons? — 187
  Are There Benefits to Owning These Businesses or the Property They Operate From? — 188
  How Much Property Do Asda and Morrisons Need to Own in Order to Operate an Efficient Business Model? — 188
  What Happened? — 188
  Some Options to Consider — 189
  Risks — 189
  Outcomes for Asda — 189
Morrisons — 190

The Iceberg of Floating Debt	190
Case 4: Garrett Motion—Turbulent and Transient Industries	191
Introduction	191
The European Car Industry	191
Garrett Motion	192
The Theory of Turbulent and Transient Industries	193
Turbulent Industries	193
Transient Industries	194
From Traditional to Transitional: Garrett Motion Strategy	197
Management Reflections on Ownership Change to PE	198
References and Recommended Readings	199

Part V   Conclusions

10 Ten 'Rules' to Improve Your M&A Performance   203

Pricing	204
Integration	204
Private Equity	205
Governance	205
Conclusions	206
The Rules	207
Strategy	207
Pricing	209
Integration	210
Conclusions	211
References and Recommended Reading	212

Index   213

About the Author

John Colley is Professor of Practice and Associate Dean at Warwick Business School teaching MBA and executive education students. From Finance Director and Managing Director at British Gypsum, John rose through leadership roles to become Group Managing Director at a FTSE 100 business and Executive Managing Director at a French CAC 40 business. Having chaired a listed business and a number of privately owned businesses, including private equity and family owned, he remains sought after for advice at board level. He has conducted corporate transactions throughout his career and studies and teaches strategy, M&A and private equity. Entering academia with a PhD from Nottingham University, Professor Colley has unique business insight that bridges practise and theory. He is highly quoted for his expertise and has written for the international press and popular business journals.

List of Figures

Fig. 1.1	The reinforcing power of network effects	6
Fig. 1.2	Why do acquisitions fail to meet expectations?	14
Fig. 1.3	The core elements of successful M&A	20
Fig. 1.4	Why business size and public or private status matter	22
Fig. 2.1	Employee concerns on hearing news of integration	34
Fig. 2.2	Six strategic options for growing a business by M&A	38
Fig. 2.3	Biggest global M&A transactions worldwide as of December 2022	48
Fig. 3.1	Improving integration performance	52
Fig. 3.2	The relationship between strategy and integration approach (adapted from Haspeslagh & Jemison, 1991)	56
Fig. 3.3	John Kotter's 8-step change management model	58
Fig. 4.1	Private equity's simplicity of focus	84
Fig. 4.2	Simplifying the key elements determining the exit proceeds	84
Fig. 4.3	Common measures taken to improve EBITDA	86
Fig. 4.4	Key factors determining the exit multiple	89
Fig. 4.5	M&A waves: global M&A activity 1985–2022	90
Fig. 4.6	How private equity reduce high-cost debt levels	95
Fig. 5.1	Value of private equity dry powder globally 2003–2022	100
Fig. 6.1	Growth expectations of private equity M&A in Europe 2023 (by industry)	113
Fig. 6.2	Consumer goods/FMCG global average multiples by sector	114
Fig. 8.1	The virtuous circle: higher multiples following acquisition-fuelled growth	151

Part I

Introduction

1

Getting M&A Right

Whilst its roots may lie in theory, this book is a practise-based guide to the processes of M&A and how, where successful, they can provide a means of lowering operating costs, increasing market influence, gaining knowledge and developing technologies, all of which might enable businesses to break into new markets with high entry barriers.

This contextualising chapter identifies the key areas fundamental to optimum performance in M&A. It offers advice and recommendations as to how major pitfalls might be avoided that boost your chances of being amongst the conspicuously low success rate for deals.

Whilst recent publications observe many bleak statistics in regard to M&A, they suggest few remedies (Christensen et al., 2011; Martin, 2016). Here we look at the approach of private equity (PE) as a means of informing more successful M&As. Whilst PE has different objectives, it has similarities in approach and a much higher success rate.

In structure, short examples are highlighted in grey, whilst more extensive case studies are not. The intention is to identify elements of M&A that are commonly difficult, and the cause of value destruction.

Hopefully, you will find value in the reflections of a practitioner whose career has seen many successes as well as some failures, and who provides advice that might mitigate the steep and costly learning curve towards successful M&A.

Could the Private Equity Model Be the Antidote to Poor Performance?

As a theoretical framework for this book, we review the acquisition process alongside the rather different business model of private equity (PE) which, as we discuss, has been shown to regularly far exceed expectations associated with M&A outcomes for corporates. Private equity uses funds raised from private investors to buy, improve and sell businesses, usually over a period of 3–5 years. PE regularly outperforms the major stock market indices with a model that proves highly successful in the very areas where so many businesses fail.

As the economic climate exists in a constant state of flux, much can be learnt from the PE approach that is as relevant to the experienced acquisitor and seller as it is to those less familiar with the 'unwritten rules' with which this book is chiefly concerned. Although theory necessarily underpins much of its advice, its examples of both success and failure are real world and current.

The Attractions and Risks of M&A

2021 proved to be a record year for acquisitions, with around $5.8 Trillion of transactions taking place globally. In that year alone, investment banking fees exceeded $157bn, a volume fuelled by cheap, available money and the huge amounts of quantitative easing funds that governments were forced to produce in the aftermath of Covid-19. By far one of the most significant deals was the $132bn merger of Time Warner with Discovery, listed in 2022. This was a consequence of the abortive acquisition of Time Warner for $85B by AT&T in 2018. The subsequent performance of such an acquisition destroyed both the share price and results of AT&T, rapidly bringing the event to a close.

This is one of a catalogue of failed deals. In fact, research suggests that 60 to 80% of acquisitions materially fail to meet expectations (Christensen et al., 2011; Martin, 2016). Furthermore, approximately 60% destroy value, and half are sold off within 5 years. Indeed, evidence suggests that, like the case of AT&T, the larger the acquisition, the more likely it is to fail, often with catastrophic outcomes for the acquirer. Few businesses are immune to this risk; acquisition strategies may provide rapid growth but usually at a high cost. There are few sources that offer a balanced and experience-based guide to the complexities of M&A that this book intends to cover. The good news is that there are acquisition strategies which do have better outcomes, and we will discuss these in due course.

Growing a Business

The traditional means of growing a business by gradually extending activities is known as 'organic growth,' and by and large constitutes a low-risk approach when implemented. This approach allows investment to support growth with reliable efficiency. However, it has been established that businesses exceeding 500 employees predominantly grow by acquisition (Lawver, 2023). In effect, organic growth is too slow for many, and those with the resources to acquire and integrate rely broadly on M&A.

Evidence suggests that such M&A strategies involving consistent acquisition policies focused on smaller companies, are successful for a variety of reasons (Giersberg et al., 2020). They expedite growth rates whilst building capabilities to acquire and integrate businesses. They also benefit from 'multiple arbitrage' which we will explore later in the book. In this chapter we will explore major acquisitions which, at the time of the deal, attract much in the way of media cover, most of which will be positive. There is an immense and lucrative industry employed in facilitating and managing such deals, and that are the main focus of this media attention. A more objective, long-term appraisal, however, does not make such optimistic reading.

In recent years, attitudes have changed and speed of growth has become paramount in some industries, most notably in the technology sector. In the quest to achieve 'network effects' newer businesses attempt to raise as much investor money as rapidly as possible to boost growth rates before competition closes in. 'Network effects' work on the basis that the more customers a business can attract, the more appealing it will be to suppliers. More suppliers create an increase in both responsiveness and choice, which in turn attracts more customers; the result is one of 'winner takes all.' Recent years have seen this mechanism played out in the gig economy with the extension of ride hailing, takeaway food deliveries, rapid grocery delivery, online marketplaces and social networks (Fig. 1.1).

> **Example: Uber**
> The main and valid concern is the rate at which copies proliferate, limiting the rate at which the first mover can expand. Uber, for instance, is believed to be the first mover in the ride-hailing industry. Starting out in San Francisco, their

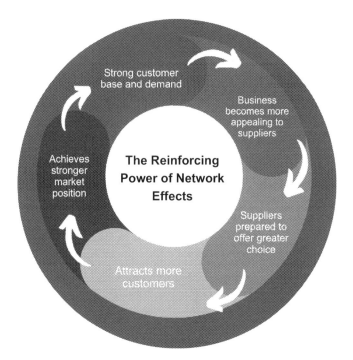

Fig. 1.1 The reinforcing power of network effects

> technology and convenience rapidly spread to most large US cities, followed soon after by Europe, Russia, India, Southeast Asia and China, all by organic growth. However, competitors were quick to arrive on the scene, copying propositions and resulting in high losses for Uber in some countries. The company was effectively forced out of the market in others, notably China, Russia and Southeast Asia. In the takeaway food delivery market, Uber was a late entrant and is now having to buy competitors to develop a competitive position.

Learning from Private Equity

As the introductory section sets out, there are lessons to be learnt from private equity which can inform M&A activity to good effect. Over the last 20 years, public company numbers have more than halved in both the USA and the UK, whilst private equity has multiplied in both size and number of transactions. In 2021 almost a third of all transactions involved PE. The four largest

PE businesses have increased assets under management fivefold over the last 10 years, and PE transactions continue to grow rapidly.

The buy, improve and sell model is outpacing public companies in performance and raising investment capital with 'dry powder' in 2022 standing at $3.7 Trillion. The approaches employed by PE have elicited varied, and at times provocative, criticism from its opponents that cite those involved as 'barbarians,' 'people without morals,' 'asset strippers' and 'cost cutters' that leave only 'excessive debt' in their wake. However, PE is a broad church in which leverage and cost-cutting are only part of the story; behaviour and approach admittedly vary across the PE community.

PE ownership frequently generates new ideas around running a given business, identifying potentially lucrative growth markets and managing change at a rapid pace. This raises the obvious question as to why the previous management could not have achieved the same, and subsequently whether a particular firm or owner is the right match for some of its businesses; these questions are addressed in the central sections of this book.

The previous management may retain their positions in a PE acquisition but with a new plan, guidance and reoriented incentives that only pay out once new value is created; many employees find these changes too challenging to remain with the business.

There are further steps taken towards higher levels of performance, and we later compare and contrast the PE approach with that of public companies, exploring how they achieve such returns when public companies are so prone to failure in the M&A arena.

Growth in Mature Markets

As markets mature, barriers to entry in terms of brands, reputation, scale economies, know how and technology expand, rendering the possibility of new entrants increasingly difficult. Late entrants and those wishing to gain a foothold in given markets are far more likely to have to make mergers or acquisitions to be successful. In some cases where late organic entry is possible, it often comes with falling prices and over capacity. In such cases the worst affected are usually the new entrants, who, unless they have a superior product and strong marketing campaign, may find vast investment is required.

To add to this, the matured markets tend to see a fall in growth rates and incumbents see lower levels of development. The resultant fall in business valuation leaves businesses with several options—to internationalise, diversify or invest in the acquisition of direct competitors. The next section outlines the benefits and limitations of each strategy.

Internationalise

One option is internationalisation, provided the source of competitive advantage is attractive in other markets. This is often not the case with foodstuffs which tend to reflect historical, cultural and traditional tastes. The UK's fish and chips industry, for example, has not found entry to overseas markets, nor indeed has Yorkshire pudding, black pudding or Scotland's penchant for haggis. Supermarkets such as Walmart and Tesco have also struggled to internationalise successfully, as extensive and efficient supply chains tend not to cross borders.

Beyond that of national tastes, the chief difficulty is that their sources of competitive advantage are routed in store locations and efficient supply chains, neither of which are readily transferable in other countries. Furthermore, if a product has been successful in one market, there are always enterprising businesses primed to replicate its model, as we have seen in the case of Uber.

Diversification

Diversification is the move into associated markets such as selling a similar product into different markets or, indeed, selling different products to the same customer base. Supermarkets typically employ this latter approach, although not always successfully. For example, a visit to a supermarket not only encompasses food but now may include alcohol, clothing, homeware, electrical goods, phones, petrol and financial products. Technology can sometimes be used to produce other products which can be sold into quite different markets, as is often the case with plastics that appear in many markets, such as packaging, building materials and other related uses. Most research evidence suggests that unrelated diversification in which new products do not share either markets, products or technology with the core business is likely to be far less successful (Palich et al., 2000).

Acquisition

Growth by acquisition—the strategy of buying direct competitors—can have the advantage of removing competition either current or future. It is rapid, the whole transaction taking an average of six months to a year to complete, unless competition clearance extends the process. Acquisition can be used to speed internationalisation or diversification and is a device able to gain technology, know-how and market position rapidly.

The downside is that it can be costly, high-risk and with much that can go wrong. In the case examples of AB InBev and SABMiller and Bayer and Monsanto, the industries had reached maturity and growth had drastically slowed, prompting the decision to identify and acquire competitors. In both cases the lack of effective options to buy forced a high acquisition price. In addition, Bayer chose to overlook the due diligence in its desperation to buy Monsanto, principally because it was the only remaining viable option.

The Problems with M&A—Illustrative Case Studies and Commentary

Case Study: Carlos Brito at AB InBev

Headquartered in Belgium, AB InBev is currently the world's largest brewer of beer with a global market share of 28% (Statista, 2023). CEO, Carlos Brito, had consistently managed to 'beat the odds' with his acquisition strategy. Indeed, AB InBev was built by acquiring major brewers worldwide, extracting substantial cost savings and merging with their mainstream business. In reality, all AB InBev wanted from acquisitions were the brands, breweries and distribution in terms of outlets such as bars, restaurants and sporting and concert venues. Regional, functional and top management could be dispensed with. Brewing could be focused on the large, efficient breweries near to high demand, thereby reducing manufacturing and distribution costs. AB InBev had strict control of its supply chain, allowing raw material costs to be reduced. In effect they had an acquisition model which worked well. With such a long history of successful acquisitions, Carlos Brito was tempted by the second largest global brewer—South African-based SABMiller, then listed on the London Stock Exchange. If the acquisition succeeded, then the new business would produce almost a third of the world's beer.

Carlos, however, had met his match in the obdurate SABMiller. In October 2015, nine years into his successful tenure, he made his most ambitious move yet. This was to be the beginning of the end for his reign. It took four bids to persuade the SABMiller shareholders to accept with an enormous price of $107bn. This amounted to 17 times the earnings of SABMiller, which was viewed by many as steep in view of the many ex-growth markets which the number two producer occupied. Carlos knew that he would have trouble with the various competition authorities; the level of owner concentration would be viewed as excessive and contrary to the interests of the consumer. Ultimately, the various authorities forced him to sell all his acquired assets in North America, Europe and China. After paying a high price to buy them, he was then forced to sell them rapidly for whatever he could get to achieve the overall deal. Buying at a high price and selling at a lower price inevitably forced the earnings multiple up to 23 for the remainder of SABMiller, which is reasonable for rapid growth markets, but this is beer!

Comment

Typical of many mature markets, beer had largely plateaued in the West, with Europe and North America preferring other beverages such as spirits, cocktails and wine. To generate growth, acquisitions were needed, particularly positioned in growing markets such as Africa. SABMiller had a significant presence in both North America with Molson Coors and Europe with its Grolsch and Peroni brands, but also had a strong presence in the growing markets of Africa and China.

Ultimately, overconfidence played a significant part and with a high price already agreed, there was little prospect of making the acquisition work. AB InBev shareholder value was destroyed: the business was worth in excess of $110bn immediately before the deal and by 2021 was worth only $52bn, including SABMiller for which they paid $107bn. In the order of 30,000 people lost their jobs in the cost-cutting, virtually all senior management left and customers ended up with less choice as the new owners rationalised their product range. The SABMiller shareholders were the main benefactors from the high price, along with the various advisors earning around $2bn in fees. M&A is far more lucrative to advise on than to be a key player in. For Carlos and his shareholders SABMiller had been a 'bridge too far.'

The deal was closed a year later leaving AB InBev saddled with around $106bn of debt which weighed heavily on the balance sheet. Results declined and AB InBev came under pressure from banks and shareholders to reduce the debt which meant selling more assets. This involved halving the dividend and floating Southeast Asian assets on the Hong Kong stock market. One by one the board was changed culminating in Carlos Brito leaving in 2021. In the last year before the bid (2014) AB InBev made $11.3bn of net income, by 2018 this was down to $5.7bn for the newly enlarged business. Markets had declined, AB InBev had made too many promises on maintaining employment, they had paid too much and very likely underestimated the response of the competition authorities which ultimately unfolded as their worst fears were confirmed.

Case Study: Bayer's $67bn Acquisition of Monsanto in 2016

At much the same time as AB InBev was breaking the record for size of acquisition on the London Stock Exchange, Bayer, the German pharmaceuticals and agribusiness conglomerate, was also breaking new financial ground in German records in paying $66bn for Monsanto the US-based agribusiness. This remains a record for German corporate acquisitions considered historically to be both conservative and cautious.

Agribusiness consists of pesticides, herbicides, seed technology and fertilisers. In recent years there has been food overproduction culminating in farmers cutting back on their most expensive input costs which are the pesticides/fertilisers. The consequence is lack of growth for agribusiness producers. Producers then look to growth through acquisition of competitors which would lower costs and increase market influence.

The top six global agri-business producers are Bayer (Germany), Syngenta (Swiss), Du Pont, Dow Chemicals, Monsanto (all USA) and Chem China. Chem China set the ball rolling by acquiring Syngenta for $40bn. This was immediately followed by Du Pont and Dow Chemical's merging in a $130bn share exchange deal. This left Bayer and Monsanto. Bayer was concerned that the other global players were all increasing their market power, lowering their costs and that they would be marginalised. Monsanto might also be acquired by someone else which would have meant the opportunity may have gone for good. Bayer felt they had little choice but to acquire Monsanto.

Monsanto had developed something of a dubious record after reported associations with Genetically Modified crops (GMs) which in recent years had built up a significant body of environmental opposition.

Nevertheless, Bayer started bidding for Monsanto in 2016 and only closed in 2018 after achieving the various competition authority clearances. The price of $66bn was undoubtedly steep at 16 times the earnings for a business in an ex-growth industry.

Not only did Bayer pay too much but they were soon to run into another major difficulty regarding the weedkiller marketed as 'Roundup.' Just two months after the deal closed, a US court ordered Monsanto to pay $289mn to a groundsman and his wife who had both contracted non-Hodgkins Lymphoma after regularly using the weedkiller. Although the settlement was reduced by appeal, it still cost the company $21.5mn. Following this payout over 10,000 claims emerged requiring more than $12bn to resolve. The share price plummeted and, following major losses, Bayer was worth just €44bn at the end of 2021. By 2024 the overall value had sunk further to less than $28bn. Prior to the deal Bayer was priced in excess of 140bn. This qualifies as one of the worst deals ever. Strangely the CEO Werner Baumann, who did the deal in 2016/18, is still there in 2021. There is often a view that CEOs ought to clean up the mess they made before duly leaving; this mess might take some time to fix.

How Did It Happen?

Due diligence is the process whereby a potential acquirer can explore risks and potential liabilities prior to finalising a deal. It can be done by one's own people but usually firms hire specialist accountants, lawyers and consultants to undertake the review. They submit independent reports and are liable on their findings if they fail to spot key issues.

CEOs and boards usually use any adverse findings to 'chip' the price downwards rather than using it as a 'deal-breaker' as PE might. So, the decision to go with the deal despite the due diligence findings is likely to have been made by the CEO and board.

This is often the case; anxiety and determination to get the deal done have the potential to obscure any objective analysis. The consequences are that first, buyers pay too much and secondly that they disregard the risks of the deal. In this case, the two years spent negotiating and navigating the deal past the many competition authorities dimmed the board's ability to make objective decisions, and the price paid fell to both the shareholders and the board.

Businesses such as Bayer's Dr. Scholl and Coppertone must then set substantial cost-saving targets, including the removal of over 12,000 jobs. Baumann's contract is set to run until 2024.

Of course, there is always the possibility that issues may be deliberately concealed by the sellers, and the fact that Bayer does not appear to be suing anyone after buying 'Round Up,' suggests that potential liabilities may have been raised with the board prior to purchase. Bayer's acquisition of

Monsanto, therefore, demonstrates the potentially drastic consequences of disregarding prior analysis.

Case Study: AOL and Time Warner—How History Repeats Itself

As we have seen, there can be a high level of competition in the acquisition process. By far the worst deal ever to be done in my living memory occurred in 2001 when AOL (originally America Online), a dial up internet provider merged with Time Warner, a content business. Time Warner, including Warner Bros, HBO, CNN and a host of other content providers, was valued at $164bn, making up 45% of a new business valued at $364bn.

Clearly, one objective was to use the high-quality content to drive trade through the internet business. According to Bob Pitman, then COO of AOL, the growth of Time Warner would take off at internet speed as a consequence of the merger. Sadly, two years later, the value of the new business had slumped to $20bn as AOL's dial up network was outstripped by high-speed broadband provision. The joint board had not worked well for some time, due to the complexities of running an infrastructure provider with the rather different management required for a content business.

Regrettably, the strategic rationale for the deal had been more rhetoric than practicable proposition. High-quality content production is so expensive that it requires extensive distribution and cannot be restricted to one provider. It needs to find both as wide an audience as possible and also one willing to pay the high costs. In addition, Time Warner consisted of a collection of fiefdoms in which the CEOs had complete control and failed to work together effectively, even with AOL executives. The dot.com crash of 1999 only added to these mounting obstacles. Even the enormous value destruction was not enough to prevent its recurrence as we shall see.

Roll on 2016 when AT&T, a telecom, broadband and fixed line provider, announced their own intention to buy Time Warner for the rather diminished value of $85bn. Many similarities to the AOL deal may ring alarm bells, in that the Time Warner content would again be used to drive trade through the AT&T infrastructure. Once again this would mean an infrastructure provider would run a 'sexy' content producer of which it had little knowledge or experience.

In this case, the rhetoric was more subdued, but the problem of uncooperative fiefdoms remained a strong internal culture of Time Warner which was, in effect, a loose collection of independent businesses. Culturally Time Warner would always be difficult to manage or indeed integrate. It had a 'showbiz' culture with parties and all that goes with content production, whilst AT&T was a highly efficient centralised organisation. The plan was for $1.5bn of cost savings which was always likely to end in a wholesale loss of talent. There was also an ambitious plan of $1bn of revenue benefits. The intention was to remove the top management and then set about altering the 'high-cost' culture; this would be a challenging feat.

Immediately before the deal in 2017, AT&T's net income was $29.8bn falling rapidly to $13.9bn in 2019. The share price had also fallen over 40% since the acquisition. The declining results, although not necessarily due to the deal, meant the loss of over 20,000 jobs. Debt had reached $200bn, partly due to the Time Warner acquisition. Under pressure from activist shareholder Elliott Management, divestments and cost-cutting were to commence.

Closure of the deal was delayed until 2018 as a number of US institutions raised opposition on various grounds. CNN had been a consummate critic of Donald Trump, recently elected US President, and therefore far from well-disposed to Time Warner. Ultimately, the courts determined that the deal should be allowed. A variety of senior Time Warner executives left the business in the years following the merger, and in 2021, AT&T announced that Time Warner was to be merged with Discovery Inc. and spun off—the deal closed in April 2022 and the business began trading as Warner Bros. Discovery.

What Goes Wrong?

See Fig. 1.2.

Fig. 1.2 Why do acquisitions fail to meet expectations?

Paying Too Much

As later chapters address, it is not difficult to value a business. Typically, privately owned businesses are valued on the basis of their earnings multiples, whilst public listed businesses are effectively valued by daily pricing in the stock market. This means an acquirer has a fair idea if they are paying too much. In terms of a public listed business, it usually takes a bid of 30–50% above the previous market valuation or 'undisturbed' share price—a substantial premium which has to be justified through 'synergies,' the increased benefits that should accrue by owning that business. These are often cost-based, as a newly merged business will no longer require two head offices, two functional management teams or two sets of systems. Supply chain benefits can usually be achieved through the rationalisation of suppliers and driving greater volume and lower prices to those retained suppliers. There may well be further market-based benefits in achieving a greater market share including higher prices and greater influence in their market.

> **Example:**
> On occasions, that bidding premium can run to 100% as in the case of Comcast's purchase of Sky's European cable business for almost £30bn in 2018 after a period of fierce bidding from Disney. When two bidders are determined in their acquisition pursuit, price can become irrelevant. What this fails to take into account is that the debt will weigh heavily long into the future, and the pressure to demonstrate some sort of return becomes increasingly remote.

Excessive prices are paid for several reasons; however, many stem back to one source—a lack of real buying options. Public listed businesses have a strategy and need certain pieces of a jigsaw to realise their vision. When these become available there is a temptation to pay whatever is necessary to secure the stepping stones. A way to avoid this is to have plenty of strategic options. A good example is the strategic pivot Dow Chemicals made from bulk chemicals to speciality chemicals due to perceived lower competition, more defensible niches and higher margins. Speciality chemicals offer returns to investment in research and development, whilst bulk chemicals are highly commoditised, and the players are price takers. In effect the prices tend to move up and down with oil prices. The difficulty for Dow is that there are not so many options in the speciality chemicals industry to buy and as one is acquired, it forces the prices of the remaining players still higher. This is called a 'roll-up' strategy.

Paying too much is the most common result of 'deal heat.' The acquisition team and CEO have invested too significant amounts of time and money in developing the bid to back out even as the price rises unfeasibly high. It is easy to develop excessive focus on pursuing the deal irrespective of whether it still makes sense or not.

This is not helped by the many advisors; investment banks and other intermediaries are usually on 'win only' fees, to be paid out only if the deal is successful. Clearly, their advice may lack objectivity in the context of their fee incentives. The advisor fees for the AB InBev acquisition of SABMiller alone are believed to be over $2bn. Between 2001 and 2018 Jeff Immelt was CEO of GE, the US-based conglomerate, and over the 17 years is believed to have spent in the region of $7bn with advisors on acquisitions, disposals and reconstructions.

> **Example: Sainsbury's**
> If a CEO does pull out of a major deal after having spent much time persuading the board and shareholders of the merits of the deal, it may well be viewed as a failed strategy. CEOs may have a price to pay for that. Mike Coupe, CEO of the UK grocery chain Sainsbury's, provides a clear example of this in his attempt to engineer a £12bn merger with Asda in 2018, another UK grocer of similar size. The merged business would have been responsible for around 30% of all UK grocery sales in the UK. Competition and Markets Authority (CMA) expressed an interest and spent almost a year reviewing the expected impact on customers and other parties. In the end, they prevented the merger which was announced in April 2019. Sainsbury's had spent over £50mn on the merger and had lost market share during the year of continuing CMA deliberations. Management is often distracted by major corporate activity which results in market share decline. Somewhat inevitably, Mike Coupe left Sainsbury's soon after.

Ineffective Strategy

In the case of the original merger between AOL and Time Warner in 2001, the Chairman of AOL issued a great deal of rhetoric as to how they would be able to 'turbo charge' the rate of production at Time Warner. He implied that digital technology would have some role to play, yet a plan of action remained unclear, and as became evident, results failed to materialise. In the merger between AT&T and Time Warner in 2018 more promises abounded that Time Warner's content would widen with the additional use of AT&T's infrastructure. Again, this failed to emerge.

Merger strategies are often about cross-selling each other's products or sharing a single supply chain. The merger between US pharmaceuticals/convenience chain Walgreens and UK pharmaceuticals chain Boots has produced little in the way of mutual benefits, and an announcement was made at the end of 2021 that strategic options were being investigated to dispose of Boots. The Atlantic separated the two supply chains which remained separate, and US customers often have different tastes to those in the UK. In reality, it is unclear whether there had been any real synergies between the businesses. However, that is not necessarily the tale given to shareholders to justify the deal in the first place.

> **Example: Personal Experience Rawlplug Case**
> My own strategic failure story occurred whilst I was Group Managing Director of a major public business and decided to acquire another business. My belief was that we could incorporate the products of this business into our specified systems which had performance test certificates. This would 'pull through' sales of the newly acquired products. The strategy failed when customers refused to use the new components and we ended up selling off the business less than three years later. Fortunately, we just about returned the original purchase price by selling the land and buildings separately to the business and retaining the working capital which we collected separately. An extended version of this case study with learning points appears in Chapter 9.

Time and again such impressive sounding strategies simply do not work. Take the $36bn Daimler Chrysler merger of 1998. This was supposed to marry the known German engineering excellence of Mercedes with Chrysler's marketing prowess which had been outstandingly successful predominantly in the USA. There were expected to be supply chain benefits from sharing and use of standard platforms to rationalise spares and allow more than one model to be made on a line. None of these objectives were achieved as cultural differences became a major impediment to cooperation. Chrysler was eventually sold off for $6bn after dragging both companies into losses. The 'merger of equals' suffered with indecision and an unwillingness for either party to talk with each other. The strategy was neither credible nor workable.

In 2016 Microsoft purchased the 'professional' social network LinkedIn for $26bn. The strategy was never announced or understood by investors. It is also unclear to what extent either Microsoft or LinkedIn benefitted from the acquisition.

An effective strategy does need to produce synergistic benefits whereby both businesses benefit from the merger. These can be rare. One can see that horizontal mergers such as AB InBev and SABMiller will have plenty of mutual benefits provided the price paid does not hand all the benefits to the SABMiller shareholders before any synergies are developed. There may have been synergies from the Bayer/Monsanto merger but again the price paid and the ineffective use of due diligence meant that these were dwarfed by other bills.

There is research (Mankins et al., 2017) to suggest that horizontal M&A within the same industry creates deals based predominantly on cost savings, the new combined business often struggles to grow after three years. Indeed, growth is usually below average as the internal focus on cost reduction limits the ability to grow. The acquisition by US food producer Kraft of another US food producer Heinz in 2015 was initially viewed as successful due to the extent of cost savings. Net income achieved $11bn in 2017 but rapidly crumbled to $1bn in 2020 whilst the share price halved. The ability to create organic growth appeared to be lost in the aftermath of the merger.

Integration

Integration is an uncertain and understandably anxiety-provoking process for employees of an acquired business. Personnel know that there will be cost savings and a merger of management equating to significantly less jobs than at the time of the merger. The management of the acquired business will also believe that the acquiring business is likely to favour their own people when it comes to making decisions about who is retained. The younger element, those without much in the way of pension plans or years of service towards a termination package, are likely to choose to remain 'masters of their own destiny' and find an appropriate career elsewhere. Many key people and senior management of the future leave this way. An example is when AB InBev bought SABMiller and created a senior committee to oversee the merged business. There were 19 on the committee of which only one remained from SABMiller. Around 35,000 employees left the business following the acquisition.

> **Example: Personal Experience**
> I have been on the difficult end of both acquisition and integration—processes that were steep learning curves and which, for all the reasons given above, I left soon after. It can be an unpleasant experience in which power, status and position change and are not necessarily for the better. This is discussed in greater detail in Chapter 3 which focuses on integration. In an acquired business all the executive committee left, except for two positions which were filled by previous management, whilst those a layer below also left. Many were offered jobs in the new merged entity, but few wished to stay, as clearly, the future would be one of change and uncertainty and rather disconnected from the past.
>
> The acquirers had paid over £4bn for the privilege of running the business, and no doubt would do that. Those remaining would not have the same power or authority as they had in the past. Most decisions had to be passed up to the new head office for approval. The acquirer was centrally organised so that there was much less in the way of devolved power. Those who left were predominantly highly talented individuals who would be welcomed into senior jobs elsewhere.

In this way, integration is a profoundly inward-looking process—an internal battle for jobs and an uncertainty as to what those jobs might now entail. It is not unusual at this point for the acquired business to lose market share. For one, employees are distracted, the sales employees are focused on who will have jobs going forward and customers grow apprehensive as to the new owners and their motives (Fig. 1.3).

In the case of a merger within the same industry the business will now be buying from a new supplier—not necessarily the one they wished to buy from or had previously. Customers with contracts often have change of control clauses which means they can terminate the contract if they aren't satisfied with the acquirer. In the case of the 2016 merger of two UK fund managers, Standard Life and Aberdeen Asset Management, a large customer of Aberdeen, Scottish Widows, chose to leave on the basis of such a clause. They accounted for around 15% of Aberdeen's sales. Ultimately both the co-CEOs and the Chairman had to leave due to the botched merger integration. Research has suggested that average market share losses are normally in the range of 2 to 5% of the combined turnover (Christofferson et al., 2004).

Many integration processes are actually change management projects but performed under the stress of an acquisition, and with a likely high number of job losses; these rarely go as planned. There are decisions to be made as to what extent there should even be an integration and at what speed.

Fig. 1.3 The core elements of successful M&A

A rapid integration, though difficult, at least clears uncertainty faster, but a slower option allows for all to learn as they go. Inevitably, however, the latter means a protracted period of ambiguity which is likely to result in more underperformance and despondent employees.

Clearly, these questions depend on the nature of the strategy taken in the first place. Horizontal measures usually yield significant savings and are best performed rapidly to achieve the savings as quickly as possible. Indeed, the backers (such as the board and shareholders) will be expecting this. If you are buying technology or know-how or entering unknown markets, then you will need to preserve the capabilities of the business. 'Light touch' integration is usually appropriate in those circumstances, and in a later chapter, we consider the process of integration and various models for its approach.

Why Do They Do It?

Clearly, CEOs and boards do not enter into transactions in which they expect to destroy value. Evidence shows, however, that 'strategic' acquisitions viewed as important to the future of the business often do. The issue is the extent of share dilution and how long it will last, that is, the extent to which the shares are calculated to be worth less as a consequence of the deal, even before the deal is done. Dilution occurs because a higher multiple of earnings is being paid for the acquisition than the acquirer's shares are traded. In effect, it is a form of negative multiple arbitrage (see the section on multiple arbitrage for a more detailed explanation).

Whilst at the time, dilution might be an inescapable fact, it is the future performance of the acquired business which is critical. Acquirers will normally assume that under their custodianship the performance of the business will improve as synergies are developed. Typically, years 1 and 2 show dilution in share earnings but then the 'hockey stick' performance graph should hopefully show positive share gains. Most businesses are persuaded by the hockey stick approach when in reality it frequently fails to occur. At the very least it is dependent on a combination of a successful integration process and realistic estimates of benefits, both of which are uncommon.

Typically, proposals to boards and shareholders are based on the best case which might be achieved. Clearly a strong case is necessary in order to gain board or shareholder approval, and without a convincing proposal there would be little point in submitting a case. In view of the proposal being at the upper end of the range there is a significant prospect of not achieving it, although seldom would anyone admit to such an approach.

For boards and shareholders, they may query certain assumptions, but ultimately a major acquisition backed by the CEO is difficult to argue with without appearing as a vote of no confidence in the CEO. Whilst boards and shareholders go along with big deals, should it then become apparent that it has destroyed significant value, their tenure is likely to be under question.

Shareholders may, on occasion, express their negative views to the CEO and Chairperson regarding a significant acquisition. The CEO would be wise to find a way of withdrawing from the deal without loss of face, however, with enough shareholder support to see it through they should be prepared for a backlash if the deal goes badly.

Multiple Arbitrage

All too many acquisitions are based on strategies which ultimately destroy value by way of the simplest errors, such as paying too much or failing to acknowledge and respond appropriately to the economic climate and timing. Despite these inadequacies, many shareholders see merit in courses of action on the basis of 'multiple arbitrage.' This technical safety net often compensates for failures to meet planned expectations, which is a recurrent consequence of the acquisition process. It forms the basis for many private equity strategies such as 'buy and build' which involves buying multiple businesses in an industry with the sole objective of selling them at a higher multiple of earnings once the collection of businesses has greater market share and absolute size.

Why Business Size and Public or Private Status Matter

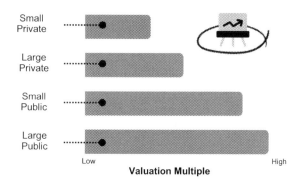

Fig. 1.4 Why business size and public or private status matter

The key to understanding the impact of multiple arbitrage lies in identifying the means of measuring success or failure. The benefits of an acquisition may fail to meet the expectations given in proposal form to the board. Indeed, Roger Martin in his 2016 article maintains that this is rarely achieved. The implication of this is that board members should treat the predicted returns with a realistic outlook and deduce that they may be significantly lower.

The next measure is Return On Investment (ROI). Will the outlay for the acquisition generate an acceptable return which exceeds the cost of capital for the business? Again, in many cases this is not practically achievable, and research suggests that 50–60% damage value.

Finally, shareholder returns can be measured as Total Shareholder Returns (TSR). This is the increase in share price over a period plus the dividends. The benefits of multiple arbitrage, therefore, are found in a process that means most smaller deals do increase shareholder value (Fig. 1.4).

Types of Multiple Arbitrage

In effect, there are two types of multiple arbitrage. Public companies usually enjoy higher valuations in terms of earnings multiples than private companies for reasons we will explore later. Secondly large private businesses have higher valuation multiples than smaller private businesses. Again, we will explore why that should be and how it can be leveraged to create additional value.

> **Example: Doing the Maths**
> Private business A has EBITDA of £4mn and is valued at 6 x EBITDA giving rise to an enterprise value of £24mn which, less the debt of £6mn, means the equity is worth £18mn. It is acquired by a much larger public business B which trades on a multiple of 10 x EBITDA.
>
> If A maintains the EBITDA at £4mn after acquisition, then the markets will increase the value of B by 10 x £4mn less the acquisition price and acquired debt of £24mn = £16mn.
>
> So, it is acquired for £24mn but now the market values the earnings at £40mn as a public company.

The argument is based on the premise that public listed firms usually enjoy much higher valuations than privately held businesses. The discount between the two can be as much as 30% to 50%. So a public firm valued on an EBITDA multiple of 10 buying a private business valued on, say, a multiple of 6 x EBITDA, then the value of the public firm will increase by 10 x EBITDA on the acquired earnings, whilst only having paid a multiple of 6. This assumes the earnings of the acquired business are unchanged before and after the deal. It also assumes both the acquirer and acquired operate in the same industry. So, this becomes a strategy which can be employed without any real strategic plan or integration process and still allows some scope for paying more than a business is worth.

However, badly the acquisition goes, the dice is loaded on the side of the public company. It allows substantial latitude for failure in terms of value-destroying integration but still benefit from the acquisition from the perspective of market valuation. Indeed, it may choose to perform only the most rudimentary of integrations to avoid value destruction. Of course, market sentiment can vary, and valuations of B will go up and down based on the market and how investors view the future of B and the industry it competes in.

Why are the valuations so different? Public companies have to comply with many rules about transparency and reporting of performance. They also have to comply with governance requirements demanding rigorous audits each year. It is easier for them to raise capital from the markets where shares are liquid and can be readily bought and sold. Financial public relations campaigns are employed to ensure that markets fully understand the positive features of the business.

Private companies tend to have minimal requirements in all these areas and critically the shares are normally restricted in terms of ability to trade.

Shareholder agreements often include pre-emption provisions which limit the extent to which the shares can be traded. Due to the lack of visibility and transparency, it may be difficult to identify a buyer for the shares or indeed an appropriate price. The earnings multiple calculation is usually where price negotiations start rather than conclude.

Differences Between Public and Private Companies

- More extensive and prescribed reporting requirements providing greater transparency to shareholders.
- Governance requirements are far more extensive in terms of ensuring shareholder interests are safeguarded through Non-Executive Directors (NEDs).
- Audit requirements are more extensive to ensure reporting accuracy.
- Ability to raise funds by issuing more shares through the stock market facilitates funding requirements.
- Shares are readily tradeable at a price which is transparent.
- Financial public relations are managed to ensure that shareholders both current and potential understand the strategy and performance of the business.
- Size (see below)

Multiple arbitrage operates on a lesser scale in terms of large compared to small firms, which can also contribute to the public listed premium. A larger private firm, say in excess of £100mn sales revenue, might trade on an earnings multiple of, say, 8, depending on the industry. Whilst smaller firms (with sales revenue up to £25mn) in the same industry might trade on, say 6 × EBITDA as they have much less market influence and lower scale and scope economies. This offers two options in that a roll-up strategy could be employed by buying a whole series of smaller businesses and then selling as a larger business so paying an EBITDA multiple of 6 to acquire but then selling at 8 without making any changes to the businesses. Typically, private equity does this (buy and build) as it avoids the value destruction of the integration process. Larger private businesses will also do this to arbitrage market value.

This arbitrage does form the basis of much acquisition activity. Clearly, when a large public company buys another such company then there is likely to be little or no arbitrage, which means that realising synergies become important and integration needs to be executed carefully to justify the price paid. Integration has a poor success record with some suggesting that between

60 and 80% end up destroying value. If there is little multiple arbitrage benefit, then the chances of destroying value through inept integration or a defective strategy are substantial.

Buying a major public business is likely to require a premium to the undisturbed share price of 30 to 50% simply to persuade enough shareholders to sell. Without arbitrage and with a poor prospect of successful integration there is little chance of justifying the price premium, unless the strategy is successful.

Stakeholder Analysis: Who Wins and Who Loses in Horizontal Mergers

So far, we have examined the deal process predominantly from the perspective of the board and shareholders. In an acquisition it is worth considering the impact on a wider set of stakeholders. For our analysis we have assumed a horizontal merger, which means two competitors in the same industry, form the parties to the acquisition, which makes up a significant proportion of acquisitions.

Acquiring Shareholders

As overpaying and underperforming appears to be the norm then acquiring shareholders are likely to see value destroyed on larger acquisitions. In terms of smaller acquisitions then the benefits of multiple arbitrage should help to create value despite performance falling well below expectations. This is provided the multiple of earnings paid remains below that of the acquirer. If it rises above that level, then value destruction becomes the odds-on favourite.

Target Shareholders

These are the main beneficiaries of any deal in that they exit with a good outcome. The premium paid to a 'normal' valuation is usually the extent of the benefit.

Acquiring Boards

Initially, they benefit from a larger business to run which usually results in higher pay, status and more power. The evidence suggests that board remuneration is more aligned with the size of business rather than performance. In 2021 the business which runs the London Stock Exchange (LSE) bought Refinitiv for £20bn. Refinitiv is a financial data business providing terminals on a subscription basis. The CEO of the LSE, David Schwimmer, announced a tripling of his remuneration package to almost £6.9mn on completion of the deal, predominantly due to his performance bonus achieved from an increased share price. Since then, the shares have fallen 30% as doubts gather about the acquisition performance. Performance targets are being revised backwards in time. The 'hockey stick' performance prediction is becoming shallower. When major deals ultimately fail to deliver, then the board including the chairman and CEO usually pay the ultimate price.

Target Board

Unless the deal is a 'merger of equals' then they are usually paid off which, with share options and contracts, can be a substantial sum of money. Despite this, many would have preferred to retain their jobs if given a choice. Boards battle hard to avoid takeovers even though it may be in the best interests of their shareholders. The argument is that they are trying to force a higher price when in reality, they are just attempting to preserve their jobs. In Europe, 'poison pill' defences are commonplace and involve increased voting rights in the event of a takeover bid. Certain shareholder classes (who might be viewed as loyal to management) develop multiple voting rights. A similar parallel is commonly found in Silicon Valley technology start-ups, in which founders are granted much higher voting rights, to the extent that they become very difficult to dislodge in the event of poor performance. Facebook, Google, Uber and many others had these founder provisions.

Target Employees and Management

For them uncertainty and job losses await as there are likely to be cost reductions and mergers of departments and closures of certain business streams. Those who retain their positions are largely unknown to the new owners, so their previous good work and reputation are effectively lost.

Customers

Customers are likely to see a reduced choice of product and supplier. Typically, ranges are rationalised as both businesses may well have competing products, and there might be price increases. Customers may start to look elsewhere if they don't like the new owners. Competition may be less as one competitor disappears from the market.

Suppliers

In a horizontal merger, supply chains are typically merged, and most supplies are put out to tender. The prize is that the winning bid will supply all, so reduced prices are expected and some suppliers will be shed. Suppliers are likely to end up with lower prices and some will lose the business altogether.

Competitors

Whilst there are now less competitors, the concern is that the merged competitor will have more market power and lower costs. Consequently, other competitors feel obliged to follow suit and negotiate similar acquisitions, as was the case with Bayer and Monsanto.

Governments

One objective of governments is to maintain high employment levels; as mergers are likely to result in job losses, they may be less supportive. A counter argument is that mergers should increase productivity and create scale economies that should drive down prices for customers. However, if competition is not adequate then the market players simply make more money.

Conclusions

Most of this chapter has been concerned with the very real risks which accompany the process of acquisition. Even the most professional acquirers with an organised, convincing strategy and careful preparation can make significant mistakes. The rest of the book will be concerned with how to minimise those risks and create value through the process of M&A.

Lessons
1. Most M&A does not achieve the returns promised in the prospectus that originally gained approval from boards and shareholders.
2. Value destruction is usually a consequence of failed strategy, ineffective integration or paying too much.
3. Large public companies buying other large public companies almost invariably destroy value.
4. Large private companies buying other large private or public companies are also likely to destroy value.
5. Many acquisitions destroy 'actual' value but create 'market' value through what is termed 'multiple arbitrage.'
6. As a direct consequence of multiple arbitrage, 'buy and build' (the acquisition of a number of smaller businesses in a similar industry) is often successful without recourse to any synergies through integrating the businesses.
7. Public companies buying private companies is often a successful strategy provided they are within the same industry.

References and Recommended Readings

Brady, C., & Moeller, S. (2014). *Intelligent M & A: Navigating the Mergers and Acquisitions Minefield* (2nd ed.). Wiley-Blackwell.

Christensen, C. M., Alton, R., Rising, C., & Waldeck, A. (2011). The Big Idea: The New M&A Playbook. *Harvard Business Review, 89*(3), 48.

Christofferson, S. A., McNish, R. S., & Sias, D. L. (2004). Where Mergers Go Wrong. *McKinsey Quarterly, 2*, 92–99.

DePamphilis, D. M. (2022). *Mergers, Acquisitions, and Other Restructuring Activities: An Integrated Approach to Process, Tools, Cases and Solutions* (11th ed.). Academic Press.

Dillon, K. (2011). I Think of My Failures as a Gift. *Harvard Business Review, 89*(4), 86.

Eccles, R. G., Lanes, K. L., & Wilson, T. C. (1999). Are You Paying Too Much for That Acquisition? *Harvard Business Review, 77*(4), 136–186.

Faelten, A., Driessen, M., & Moeller S. (2016). Why Deals Fail & How to Rescue Them. *The Economist*.

Giersberg, J., Krause, J., Rudnicki, J., & West, A. (2020). The Power of Through Cycle M&A. *McKinsey Insights, 4*(30/2020), 1–7.

Lawver, M. (2023, August). Acquisition as a Growth Strategy. *Quantive*.

Mankins, M., Harris, K., & Harding, D. (2017). Strategy in the Age of Superabundant Capital. *Harvard Business Review, 95*(2), 66–75.

Martin, R. L. (2016). MA: The One Thing You Need to Get Right. *Harvard Business Review, 94*(6), 42.

Meeks, G., & Meeks, J. G. (2022). *The Merger Mystery: Why Spend Ever More on Mergers When So Many Fail?* Open Book Publishers.

Palich, L. E., Cardinal, L. B., & Miller, C. C. (2000). Curvilinearity in the diversification-performance linkage: An examination of over three decades of research. *Strategic Management Journal, 21*(2), 155–174.

Statista. (2023). *Statista—The statistics portal*. https://statista.com

Part II

M&A: Strategy, Pricing and Integration

2

Strategic Growth Options and Respective Risk Profiles

Introduction

If there is anything to be learnt from this book, then it is that strategy and integration should go hand in hand. To anyone considering growing a business by acquisition, a clear strategy will determine the approach to integration which optimises synergistic benefits and reduces the risk of value destruction. One follows from the other.

Both practical logic and theory underpin the various recommendations made in the following two chapters. A wealth of examples is provided with commentary identifying decisions that might have increased the chances of success. You may ask how relatable these are if they only highlight the glaringly obvious mistakes. The truth is that, in these instances, the companies had little option but to admit to their mistakes. In reality, many more strategic and integration errors will be swept under the carpet. Corporates do not publicise their failures, unless the sheer scale of failure means they have to explain the numbers. Understanding these cases will help you to recognise and adapt your approach to avert these problems.

Good businesses are often plunged into crisis for years in the aftermath of major acquisitions and integrations. You may point out that most large businesses are the product of major acquisitions. This may be the case, but the amount of shareholder value lost in the process can be substantial but seldom divulged. Note: this is shareholder value and not CEO/board pay, status or power that is damaged. If it were their own money invested in some acquisitions they may have behaved quite differently.

This chapter first considers various approaches to and examples of acquisition strategy. The second part considers integration approaches and what constitutes best practice in addressing this topic.

Integration—The Problem

Have you ever been integrated? Is it an experience you never wish to repeat? For many this is the abiding memory of a period suffused with uncertainty. Everyone has questions about their own position: who will have continuing employment and who will be deemed surplus to requirements? What is the plan and what will the new structure look like? Will there be departmental mergers? How much are you being told? What has happened to your previous track record of achievement? What will your outlook for progression look like if the new management don't even know who you are? (Fig. 2.1).

This uncertainty and lack of job and status security prompts many to become 'masters of their own destiny' and choose to move elsewhere. Many key people leave, often to join the competitors. Those left are often waiting for a cheque or retirement. Whether the acquirer wants this outcome or not, it often happens.

Integrations are intense affairs with a strong internal focus. The acquirer may need few of the acquired staff, the thought of which causes collapsing morale and low productivity. This insecurity is often transferred to customers

Fig. 2.1 Employee concerns on hearing news of integration

via the salespeople, who are concerned that their contacts may change, and do not know the future strategy. Lost market share frequently accompanies this period of uncertainty.

Furthermore, competitors may take advantage of the distraction created by a significant acquisition to approach key employees with offers or remind customers that more attentive supply alternatives exist.

How can this carnage be prevented? How can we improve the odds? McKinsey research suggests that between 60 and 80% of integrations fail to achieve their post-acquisition objectives. Following a case study, we will consider how the integration process can be improved.

> **Example: Two Banks**
> A major retail bank chairman contacted me regarding briefing his board about a potential acquisition of another similar-sized retail bank. He had made a ten-figure bid which had not been accepted. Both banks had extensive branch networks. His strategy was to buy the other bank with debt, make substantial savings through the integration process and then float the now enlarged bank. His board was less keen on this strategy. His belief was the board did not understand the importance of growth, and as their ultimate owners were private equity then clearly, they would want some kind of eventual exit.
>
> I asked the Chairman about his bank's integration capabilities and previous experience in M&A. This acquisition would be a major integration challenge and, overpaying aside, that was where the major risks lay. He said he was sure the management would be able to sort it out. He considered that strategy and deals were the preserve of the board whilst integration was for management to organise and implement effectively. The bank had not made an acquisition for ten years as they had been repairing their balance sheet after incurring some major self-inflicted losses. Some cost reduction had been achieved, but an aggressive approach to costs was not consistent with either the culture or image of the bank.

What were the risks and benefits of the chairman's strategy? (Table 2.1).

Comment

The concept of a horizontal merger of two private companies makes good sense. The cost savings that typically follow a merger of businesses in similar markets and with comparable products can be significant. A stock market listing optimises multiple arbitrage in terms of size, and in moving from

Table 2.1 Benefits and risks of the Chairman's M&A strategy

Benefits	Risks
1. Provided he pays a lower multiple for the target than the likely float multiple, shareholders would benefit from the difference and the integration savings	1. The acquisition price may be far higher than envisaged
2. A much larger business would have greater market share and scale, plus, as a listed business it should have a significantly higher exit multiple than smaller private businesses	2. Integration may be much harder and cultural differences greater than the buyer thought. He also had limited experience of cost-cutting or integration
3. Listing normally brings with it higher valuations due to equity liquidity, greater transparency and higher standards of governance	3. There did not seem to be a detailed plan or designated team
	4. Most retail banks are reducing their branch networks; he may be buying a network of branches which he might later pay to close
	5. Acquisitions of similar sized businesses are unlikely to create value. Research is conclusive that the scale of integration, lack of multiple arbitrage and cultural differences destroy value (Giersberg et al., 2020)

private to public ownership, generates value. However, it should be questioned whether or not they have the capabilities to make this strategy work, and what risks may be attached to a merger of similar sized businesses both with long heritages. Strong individual cultures do not bode well for a successful merger (Table 2.1).

The practicalities of integration are often overlooked in acquisition planning, with resource allocation left until late in the process, if addressed at all. Benefits are often estimated in the broadest terms and assumptions made regarding their delivery. Integration teams can frequently prove inadequate for the scale of the job and have limited experience. They may be made up of people who are not needed elsewhere, rather than those who are trained and experienced.

One rationale for a lack of integration preparation and planning is that most deals fail in the initial stages and so there is a temptation to think 'we will consider the actual integration once the deal is done.' This only serves to draw out the integration process which is a time of great uncertainty for so many. The longer the period of uncertainty, the greater the risks.

In the case of the banks, a complete merger could result in substantial savings. Functional, regional management would not be needed, and one set of systems would cover both businesses, although this may require a protracted period of implementation.

Clearly there are sizeable risks, in that major cultural differences and a general lack of experience could result in a period of chaos for both banks.

Strategic Options

Research identifies that most businesses over 500 employees grow by acquisition. Unless they are in a very rapid growth industry, then for most larger businesses, organic growth will not normally be adequate for shareholders. Moving the dial sufficiently on growth will require acquisitions. As markets mature and growth slows, desperation starts to set in, and with it, the pressure to buy.

The temptation is to go big and attempt to satisfy the stakeholders in one transaction, before spending the next two or three years on the structural process of integration. This is rarely a good option as the overall multiple of a relatively large acquisition is likely to result in share price dilution (target pricing requires a higher multiple than the bidder attracts). The integration may also require extensive resources that simply are not made available either in terms of numbers, skills and capabilities. The organisation may not have them available, and consultants have their limitations—they are there for a finite period and any decisions made are likely to persist well beyond the consultants' presence ends.

So, what *are* the strategic options when it comes to growth? and how do they relate to the appropriate integration approach? (Fig. 2.2).

Strategy 1: 'Bulking Up'

Many firms buy competitors who operate in the same markets, which Christensen refers to as 'bulking up' (Christensen et al., 2011). Acquiring such businesses has the benefit of simultaneously removing a competitor and offering significant cost savings whilst increasing market share and power.

In terms of savings, the benefits can be substantial as head offices, regional and functional management, systems, processes and supply chains can all be rationalised. Increased distribution can be achieved for the products of both firms, and product ranges too can be reviewed. In fact, savings can be as much as 30% of the costs of the business acquired. Not only will market power and presence be developed, but supply chain benefits will likely be obtained from greater volumes of purchases.

The 2016 example of AB InBev (the world's largest brewer) buying SABMiller (the world's second largest brewer) for $106bn was an excellent

Fig. 2.2 Six strategic options for growing a business by M&A

example: the savings would be enormous, and AB InBev would gain access to previously inaccessible growth markets such as Africa. Somewhat predictably, however, they paid too much and competition authorities also had their say, resulting in the sale of all the purchased businesses in North America, Europe and China as a direct consequence. These rapid forced sales produced significant losses.

In horizontal acquisitions, most theory suggests that rapid and complete integration is the best way forward (Bower, 2001; Christensen et al., 2011; Haspeslagh & Jemison, 1991). AB InBev created a new executive committee to run the much bigger business following the acquisition but retained only one SABMiller employee on the 20-person board. Whilst this approach clears uncertainty rapidly and produces savings quickly, the acquisition overall was still a disaster, leaving too much debt due to the high price paid. That debt forced a cut in dividends and disposal of good businesses to improve the balance sheet.

Strategy 2: 'Reinventing the Business Model'

This approach occurs when an acquisition is needed in order to procure new technology, knowledge, capabilities or access to extended markets. Christensen's view here is *do not integrate*, retain the acquired management and give them the resources to develop the new business model (Christensen et al., 2011). Any subsequent integration would be slow and 'light touch.'

Some recent examples include Cisco's 2023 $28bn acquisition of Splunk, a developing cybersecurity firm. This price was around 15 times the revenue of the business and reflects the need for these currently in-demand capabilities. Cisco's main business is routers and associated bits of hardware plus software. This is a particularly high price for a position in a rapidly developing market.

Similarly in 2023, BAE—a UK-based defence business—acquired Ball Aerospace for £4.3bn for their space defence capabilities in satellites and missiles. There are unlikely to be synergies although most of Ball's customer base is US defence interests. It may be that BAE anticipate selling the technology to their own major customers which includes the UK Ministry of Defence and Saudi Arabia.

There are two major decisions to be made when considering the mode of integration. How fast to go and how deep. How to integrate a business depends on the extent of available synergistic benefits available and the need to retain management.

In short, if you want to keep existing management for their knowledge and expertise in an area that you don't have, then don't rush the integration and limit the depth of approach at least initially. Keep the existing management in charge and give them the relevant necessary resources to advance the business.

On the other hand, if there are major available benefits to be had from integration then rapid deep integration is usually necessary which is likely to risk or accelerate the loss of management.

The real problem arises when there are both significant benefits available and you also need to retain the management team. In those circumstances, slower and progressive integration may be the key, whilst keeping existing management 'in charge.'

Both Cisco and BAE are unlikely to integrate these acquisitions into their existing operations. Why? Integration is an excellent way of destroying what you have acquired. You need the people, know-how and market access which a bad integration strategy can wipe out with surprising ease.

Another example is Kingfisher's acquisition of Screwfix in the 1990s. Kingfisher ran 'big box' DIY stores predominantly in the UK and France. Screwfix was an online seller of building products such as screws, plumbing, fixings, etc. The business was developed separately and is now far bigger and more highly valued than the 'bricks and mortar' divisions.

Strategy 3: Product and Market Extensions

The key question here is whether integration destroys the very benefits one has sought to acquire. In the case of the brewery merger then AB InBev wanted brands, breweries, distribution and markets. The rest was surplus to requirements, so in terms of retaining a workforce, integration was relatively low risk. Provided the relationship with distribution could be retained—and that was always likely due to the scale of advertising—then the integration would be lower risk.

Integration is a compromise between the risk of destruction and what the buyer brings to the new business. If they bring nothing more than money, then integration can be very limited. If they bring technology, product range, know-how, branding and clarity of strategy, then integration must proceed in a manner which exploits those benefits and ensures the new business can directly benefit. Clearly, speed can vary and when there are clear capabilities which can be augmented then slower may be better. 'Light touch' allows time to introduce new approaches without destabilising the business. If the acquired business has been struggling, then speed is of the essence.

The golden rule is only integrate to the extent needed to generate the proposed benefits. Integrating for the sake of policy risks losing customers and key staff as well as running up significant costs without there necessarily being a payback.

In the instance of acquiring new markets for current products (typically internationalisation) then local management and their contacts become paramount and must be retained, incentivised and made to feel part of the new organisation.

Strategy 4: Unrelated Diversification

For corporates with plenty of cash or access to lines of credit, and an appetite for growth, unrelated acquisitions can seem attractive, and on occasions be successful. The objective is to buy a business large enough to already have a well-established management and the technology and knowledge to thrive in their market. The buyer acquires the business before providing it with the cash resources to accelerate growth. Aside from this, the new owner has little to offer, bar any political connections, which are more valuable in some countries than others. There are no other synergies as the business will not be merged with any other relevant entity.

Unlike the private equity model, there probably isn't a business improvement plan in place, but there will be a strategy and investment. The problem with this approach is that it is more portfolio management in picking the right business in the right industry than anything else. Having said that, long-term investments with major funds can be successful such as Warren Buffett and his investment vehicle Berkshire Hathaway. They are industry and business pickers who hold investments for the long term.

Another common problem is that the premium on unrelated acquisitions tends to weigh heavily without the synergies from integration or major improvements that private equity would make to justify it. Tata, the Indian conglomerate bought into the UK steel industry in 2007, in what turned out to be a disastrous investment in a market being destroyed by Chinese steel at low prices. They also invested in Jaguar Land Rover the following year which was initially very successful. However, the move to Electric Vehicles required enormous investment which Tata was less willing to find. Tata had focused on developing diesel engines and so the major industry change to electric meant finding enormous investment in order to stay in the game. Tata turned to the UK government to help fund the battery factory and related research and development.

Case Study 1: Hewlett Packard's M&A Travails

Printer and hardware company Hewlett Packard (HP) is a good example of a company in which stalling market growth forced them into hasty, high-risk acquisitions.

Since 1986 HP, have made a total of 129 acquisitions, becoming a global giant in their market. Growth in the industry, however, has rapidly slowed in the last decade and, although they have an existing successful business model throwing off lots of cash, HP have increasingly struggled for ideas on how and where to spend to create effective growth. Pressure from shareholders has driven investment in various, largely unrelated technologies that have not proved that successful.

In 2008, they acquired EDS, a technology services firm, for $14bn, and in 2012 wrote $6bn off the value (FT Aug 8th, 2012, HP in $8bn write down in services firm).

In 2011, flush with the success of EDS, they acquired a London-based big data firm Autonomy for $11.1bn. Comments by HP CEO Leo Apotheker stated that:

Autonomy presents an opportunity to accelerate our strategic vision to decisively and profitably lead a large (IT) space [...]Autonomy has an attractive business model [...] this bold action will [...] create significant value for our shareholders.

HP paid a 64% premium when acquiring the UK software company for $11.1bn in August 2011, but the next year were forced to write off $8.8bn due to significant 'accounting irregularities' (Hirst and Danbolt, 2008).

UBS Chairman, Raymond Lane (advisor) to HP CEO Leo Apotheker had recommended they pull out of the deal if they could as, in his view, they were overpaying. In his letter stating as much he is trying to determine how much HP stock buyback is needed to offset the dilution caused by the excessive premium on Autonomy as reported in *The Financial Times* ('HP internal mails provide new details on the crisis after the Autonomy deal' 28 Sept. 2015). He also suggests that Autonomy's growth was a result of roll-up deals and not the organic growth that was implied. In effect, they didn't know what they were buying.

They subsequently sued the seller, Mike Lynch, for misrepresenting the business. After a protracted legal battle, he was extradited to the USA to face fraud charges in 2023. Will HP get their money back? In 2024 Mike Lynch was found not guilty of all charges and returned to the UK, although the civil action was allowed to proceed. Sadly, in August 2024 Mike Lynch died with 6 others in a boating accident off Sicily. During the 'discovery' part of the extradition hearings it emerged that their 12 previous acquisitions had all failed to hit revenue targets, and most failed to achieve profit targets either.

Large companies rarely expect to achieve all the proposed benefits. Getting a proposal approved by shareholders and the board is one thing, subsequent performance is another. In short, corporates don't publicise their mistakes. 'Caveat Emptor' or 'let the buyer beware' presides over transactions. It is the buyer's responsibility to assure themselves they know what they are buying. If they don't, then the consequences are theirs, and of course, their shareholders too.

Strategy 5: Mergers of Equals

If a so-called 'merger of equals' does not fail, then it is very likely that it wasn't a merger of equals. Acquisitions are often badged as such to protect the ego and reputation of the acquired management and employees. This is sometimes necessary or appropriate in acquisitions in which the management of one country is to preside over another. In the case of Stellantis—a merger between PSA, a French-based car manufacturer and the Italian-based Fiat—national sentiments and protection were at stake. Governments had to be placated about investment and employment, but the French management were to run it.

Genuine 'mergers of equals' result in the duplication of management and a lack of overall control. Decisions to cut costs in operations are not made, and little collaboration occurs across the business, with management intent on protecting their own empires. In short, there are no benefits from the merger and often a lack of cooperation; someone needs to be in charge and responsible for driving the synergies before management cliques have the potential to damage the entire business.

Case Study 2: Daimler Chrysler, a 'Merger of Equals'?

Perhaps the best-known and well-reported example is that of German motor manufacturer Daimler who bought US-based Chrysler for $36bn in 1998. The resultant conglomerate had sales of over $150bn and was the fifth largest motor manufacturer globally. Daimler shareholders held 57% of the combined companies whilst Chrysler shareholders held the rest. Bob Eaton of Chrysler became joint CEO with Jergen Schremp of Daimler, but they reputedly spoke little.

Daimler wanted Chrysler to access North American markets, a territory in which they had previously struggled to make progress. However, Daimler was renowned for high-quality German engineering and produced premium quality vehicles. Chrysler vehicles were well marketed, very competitive in price and built to appeal more broadly. In effect, this was US marketing expertise meets high-quality German engineering expertise. Cultural differences were a significant hindrance to integration. It was decided to retain the US Chrysler management in view of their industry knowledge, however, there were major disparities with the Chrysler CEO, Bob Eaton, reputedly earning around 20 times more than Daimler co-CEO, Jergen Schremp.

Some of the proposed operational benefits included manufacturing Daimler vehicles using Chrysler production lines, something which was never going to happen in view of the vastly differing quality requirements. The perceived benefits were to have common platforms, engines and shared expertise. In the nine years of Daimler ownership none of this was to happen. After the first two years of inactivity, the lack of focus and compatibility significantly damaged the results of both Daimler and Chrysler. The subsequent collapse of the merger became a Daimler takeover—a common outcome in failed 'mergers of equals.' Eaton left in 2000 following many of his key executives. Chrysler haemorrhaged market share down to 14% of the US market and results plummeted to a loss of $2.2bn in 2001.

Jergen Schremp retired in 2005 and his successor sold Chrysler to Cerberus Capital for $6bn in 2007.

Case Study 3: Aberdeen Asset Management and Standard Life 'Merger of Equals'

A more recent example is the 2017 £11bn merger of two Scottish fund managers: Aberdeen Asset Management merged with Standard Life to become Standard Life Aberdeen. This billed 'merger of equals' effectively destroyed both businesses and immense shareholder value. By 2023 the value had more than halved to £4.5bn and the outlook remains bleak to date.

The overall intentions were to reduce costs and increase market presence. The two CEOs hoped to merge administrations and some investment teams. The idea was created by the two CEOs, Martin Gilbert of Aberdeen Asset Management and Keith Skeoch of Standard Life who regularly went fishing together, and at some stage between catches decided to become co-CEOs. Some major customers left, opposing the new combined business due to perceived competition through vertical integration. This included losing the major £25bn account of Scottish Widows who were averse to the merger.

Costs were never cut and the co-CEOs defended their own empires. Eventually the Chairman and both co-CEOs stepped down, but too late to stop the haemorrhage of customer value. In an attempt to create a new image and leave the merger fiasco behind, the business was renamed Abrdn Plc. Unfortunately, it will require substantially more than a few dropped vowels to repair the damage.

Comment

The strategic rationale behind the merger was strong, in that trade of both firms was then being squeezed by so-called 'passive funds' which sold index tracker products. The costs of these computer-traded funds were a fraction of those for managed funds. A computer simply traded stocks and shares to align with any chosen index, whilst managed funds had expensive teams of researchers monitoring and investigating stocks before selecting those they believed would do well in the future. Research is increasingly suggesting that, after expenses, only the top 20% of the managed funds has been outperforming the trackers, resulting in the migration of clients to trackers. The merger was intended to combine back offices and fund management teams to cut costs and better compete with the growing trackers.

There were two failures in implementation. Firstly, a review should have taken place that assessed customer requirements and gauged their likely reaction to the proposals. Some large customers that were also vertically integrated opposed the merger as it brought them into competition with the other partner. By 2024, Abrdn is still losing customers and shareholders are pressurising the Chairman and CEO to split the business. One suspects that the risks were known and considered but the determination to get the deal done resulted in taking the risks.

The second failure was that both CEOs wanted jobs and control of their individual empires. In effect they retained these, but with constant political battles regarding turf. Little integration or cost savings resulted. This does raise questions concerning the role of the chairman and how or why he allowed this conflicted situation to persist for so long.

Strategy 6: Vertical Integration

Over the last 30 years there has been a major move towards vertical disintegration. Businesses have increased the extent of activities which they choose to acquire from outside providers. Vertical integration in terms of owning suppliers to the business or downstream customers has come under pressure and internal justifications for vertical integration are constantly under review. Activities performed internally have become questioned as to whether they are better undertaken by someone else. That someone might offer more focus on the area, perhaps greater scale economies, developed technology and know-how, a supplier who competes with others in competitive markets.

At one time car manufacturers such as Ford owned steel, tyre and virtually all component manufacture. They also designed, assembled, distributed, marketed and retailed all their own vehicles. Now, whilst they make some components such as the body shell and engine/drive trains, which they assemble, and then market, the other activities are undertaken by others who bring focus, technology development and scale economies to the process, as they may supply several car manufacturers. Their margins are often higher than the car manufacturers as they develop the technology.

The presumption that all services would be provided 'in-house' is now moribund. Initially, it was security, catering, building maintenance and property provision which were outsourced followed by legal activities, accounting services, many marketing activities, components, maintenance and so on. The rationale is that a business should focus on its sources of competitive advantage rather than engaging in activities which may not add value and become a distraction.

At one time for many firms, there was not only a presumption that virtually all activities would be performed internally, but growth often came by acquiring suppliers and customers. There was a view that being a supplier or customer somehow provided a deep understanding of how the industry was run and the many activities required for competitive advantage. Research has identified that these are relatively unrelated technologies, products and markets which usually end up destroying value. Vertical integration has reduced in popularity. A strong rationale has been improved coordination through integration and mutual ownership. This is debateable although there are examples which may bear out the coordination argument. A counter-example is the car industry in which component supply and availability means the manufacturing line is surrounded by component supplier people ensuring that magazines are full.

Would exposure to competitive markets drive greater innovation and cost control? Internal providers have captive customers who must buy from components that are constantly available for the assembly crews. The level of integration and coordination is high despite the outsourced nature of the activity.

The following provides some questions to consider when deciding whether to outsource or undertake an activity.

1. Do you have competitive scale economies in the production of the service/product?
2. Are there lower cost suppliers available in the market of adequate quality and service?
3. Vertical integration compounds risk—if demand falls for the product/service then each element of the integrated supply chain suffers increased inefficiency through lower demand. The reverse may occur during periods of higher demand. Do you want increased risk?
4. Is the product/service a source of competitive advantage? If so, then do not outsource. Sources of competitive advantage need to be nurtured, developed and grown.
5. Is there a competitive market for the product/service allowing a competitive process when an outsourcing contract ends?
6. Will integration allow greater levels of coordination where these matter?
7. Can important private information leak which will help competitors?

Deal Size Does Matter

If we consider the global top ten biggest deals over the last 25 years, from internet supplier AOL acquiring Time Warner the content producer in 1999 for $202bn to telecoms and broadband supplier AT&T buying the same Time Warner in 2018, then we find little but value destruction. Of the ten major deals listed all but two destroyed significant amounts of shareholder value. The acquirer's value has never recovered from the destructive events of the deal over protracted periods up to 2024. A simple arithmetic mean of value destruction across the ten deals averages shareholder value losses of a third. None of the largest ten deals ever created shareholder value and nearly all destroyed large swathes of it. No wonder shareholders start selling when major deals are announced. In most cases, the price paid was far too high and could never be justified by any synergies generated by the integration process. These are nearly all a case of the 'winner's curse' and result in 'buyer's remorse.' One wonders at the cases presented to the respective boards and shareholders justifying the acquisitions. Even the two cases of the pharmaceutical tie-up of Glaxo Welcome and Smithkline Beecham and the defence merger of Raytheon with United Technologies failed to create value. The rest destroyed varying amounts of value. Are these big mistakes or did someone benefit? The only obvious beneficiaries are the shareholders of the target and, of course, the advisors (Fig. 2.3).

The Synergy Trap

In his book 'The Synergy Trap,' Mark Sirower contends that proposed synergies are often mirages which simply don't exist (Sirower, 1997). He argues that they merely serve to justify an 'acquisition enthusiasm' which simply can't deliver expectations and was never a realistic proposition.

Sirower identifies that, in many acquisition cases, the proposed savings are often based on highly optimistic assumptions. Revenue benefits gained from cross-selling are typically elusive and, as Christensen et al.'s (2011) paper concludes, rarely achievable. Sales forces are often narrow in their focus and adding far more products and services simply confuses the customer and the salespeople. Indeed, customers may simply not accept the new products or services being proffered as being better than those from their current supplier. Cross-selling assumptions are rarely borne out by ultimate reality, but frequently used to justify acquisitions.

An example is the 1970s trend for UK building societies to acquire estate agents, to sell insurance and mortgages related to housing. Many of the

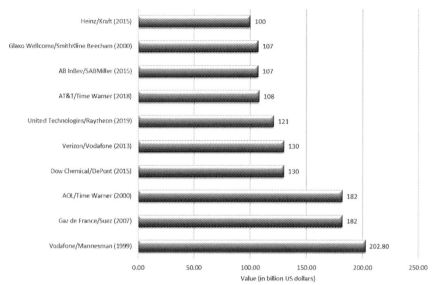

Fig. 2.3 Biggest global M&A transactions worldwide as of December 2022

building societies who grant mortgages felt they could benefit from this 'one stop' strategy. Virtually all failed and were subsequently disposed. The bureaucratically sluggish and conservative building societies were the wrong owners for nimble, sales-oriented estate agents. They did not understand the nature of the business and the very different incentive models. Customers did not choose to buy their financial products from the same estate agent selling houses. Estate agents are not top of the league when it comes to customer trust.

Cost savings are often overestimated and more difficult to achieve than proposals would suggest. At the time of the acquisition the focus is on gaining board and shareholder approval. Generous estimates are helpful in this process, however, the teams having to deliver these benefits are rarely involved in the development of the proposal assumptions.

Integration teams often first become involved once the acquisition is completed, when they are presented with savings estimates that may well be difficult, or even impossible to deliver. The rationale for not including them earlier is often the need for confidentiality to prevent potential suitors from becoming involved. Deals often fail so many people reason that there is little point in involving the integration team until the deal is done. In this case planning starts late and resource availability might be strained.

Another problem is that the people doing the deal are typically lawyers, bankers, consultants, deal specialists and accountants, none of whom will be involved in the integration and realisation of the benefits. Top management usually want the deal to run so 'helpful' estimates of benefits are very useful.

> **Lessons**
> 1. Growth is important to both investors and to increase competitive dynamics such as economies of scale, operational efficiencies and market power relative to competitors.
> 2. Maturing existing markets usually leads to attempts to grow through related products and markets.
> 3. Horizontal acquisitions of close competitors usually make good strategic sense provided competition authorities do not intervene. Overpaying is the main risk in this type of acquisition.
> 4. Vertical integration is best avoided unless there are very strong reasons for the strategy, such as securing raw material supplies or creating access to downstream markets which otherwise would be under stress. Vertical industries are very different to manage and require skill sets that management often lacks.
> 5. It is rare to find instances of successful unrelated diversification. Lack of real knowledge and experience of markets, products and technology in acquisitions usually proves a major handicap.
> 6. Related diversification in which growth is achieved through developing product markets, expanding sales to existing markets or exploiting technology capabilities has much better prospects.

References and Recommended Readings

Baaij, M., & Reinmoeller, P. (2018). *Mapping a Winning Strategy: Developing and Executing a Successful Strategy in Turbulent Markets* (1st ed.). Emerald Publishing Limited.

Barker, V. L., & Duhaime, I. M. (1997). Strategic Change in the Turnaround Process: Theory and Empirical Evidence. *Strategic Management Journal, 18*(1), 13–38.

Bower, J. L. (2001). Not All M&As Are Alike—And That Matters. *Harvard Business Review, 79*(3), 92–101.

Capron, L. (2016). Strategies for M&As: When Is Acquisition the Right Mode to Grow? *Accounting and Business Research, 46*(5), 453–462.

Capron, L., & Mitchell, W. (2012). *Build, Borrow or Buy: Solving the Growth Dilemma*. Harvard Business Press.

Christensen, C. M., Alton, R., Rising, C., & Waldeck, A. (2011). The Big Idea: The New M&A Playbook. *Harvard Business Review, 89*(3), 48–57.

DePamphilis, D. M. (2022). *Mergers, Acquisitions, and Other Restructuring Activities: An Integrated Approach to Process, Tools, Cases and Solutions* (11th ed.). Academic Press.

Early, S. (2004). New McKinsey Research Challenges Conventional M&A Wisdom. *Strategy & Leadership, 32*(2), 4–11.

Financial Times Limited. (n.d.). *Financial Times*. Financial Times.

Gadiesh, O., & Ormiston, C. (2002). Six Rationales to Guide Merger Success. *Strategy & Leadership, 30*(4), 38.

Giersberg, J., Krause, J., Rudnicki, J. and West, A. (2020). The Power of Through Cycle M & A. McKinsey Insights 4/30/2020, 1–7.

Grant, R. M. (2022). *Contemporary Strategy Analysis* (11th ed.). Wiley.

Greenwald, B. C. N., & Kahn J. (2005). *Competition Demystified: A Radically Simplified Approach to Business Strategy*. Portfolio.

Haspeslagh, P. C., & Jemison, D. B. (1991). *Managing Acquisitions: Creating Value Through Corporate Renewal*. Free Press.

Hirst, Ian & Danbolt, Jo & Jones, Edward. (2008). Required Rates of Return for Corporate Investment Appraisal in the Presence of Growth Opportunities. European Financial Management. 14. 989–1006.

Moraitis, T., & Keener, C. (2019). *Leading the Deal: The Secret to Successful Acquisition & Integration*. Urbane Publications.

Rovit, S., Harding, D., & Lemire, C. (2004). A Simple M&A Model for All Seasons. *Strategy & Leadership, 32*(5), 18–24.

Sirower, M. L. (1997). *The Synergy Trap: How Companies Lose the Acquisition Game*. Free Press.

Vinogradova, V. (2015). Value Creation in Strategic M&A: How to Make Your Growth Strategy Value-Creating? *Journal of Finance and Investment Analysis, 4*(1), 1–5.

3

Improving Integration Performance and Synergy Extraction

Introduction

This section reevaluates the frequently encountered attitude to M&A as a technical subject, to be handled by specialist advisors, either internal or external. This is often the root cause of any number of problems. The role of management should be to make the major decisions and manage the process for overall success. They also need to proactively manage the specialists to ensure that what they inherit, after the deal is done, can be a success story. It considers the necessary role of advisors and the key decisions which, along with their subsequent implementation, remain within management's responsibility.

This area is one in which the high integration failure rate can be vastly reduced and this chapter makes a number of practical suggestions intended to improve integration performance. It looks at the research and theories behind selecting the most appropriate mode of integration to support the overall strategic objectives.

The integration process is an exercise in major change management, and its success or failure usually hangs on whether its performance meets with expectations. The stakes are high as there are always tensions between the acquirers and the acquired in terms of who is to be retained and who will not be part of the new organisation. There is also much jockeying between management to ensure they are well-placed for the major roles. Uncertainty prevails amongst not just employees and management but also customers and suppliers and other stakeholders. We consider the advice John Kotter provides in his well-known change leadership framework and how this is relevant to integration processes.

We also explore the benefits of integration learning and building experience and deep knowledge of the process by making a number of acquisitions and developing specialist teams well versed in the process. A policy of not biting off too big an acquisition also helps. The bigger the acquired organisation then the more complexity, the stronger the culture and the greater the resistance to imposed change. In this context, we examine the consumer products acquisition of Gillette by Procter and Gamble in 2005.

Why Does Integration Often Fail?

There are many ways in which the integration process fails to meet the targets agreed, which form the very basis for the acquisition. In the following sections we explore through case studies the main challenges which must be met and offer advice as to how these may be avoided (Fig. 3.1).

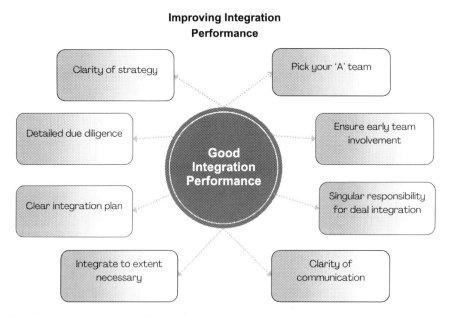

Fig. 3.1 Improving integration performance

The Deal Team

Contradictory as it might sound, the golden rule of integration is do not rely on the deal team. Their chief concern is to get the deal done, which, in itself, is a major achievement. To them, what happens afterwards is of limited importance. That is for others to worry about.

In this way, many organisations effectively operate two separate parts to the process—deal and integration, and rarely do they meet. Some may question if, considering how many deals collapse during negotiation, it is actually worth planning integration. If you are serious players then the answer to this is yes, it certainly is. Not doing so lays the foundation for bad integration in which Giersberg et al. suggest at least 65% fail to deliver the promised benefits (Giersberg et al., 2020). The cardinal rule for good integration, therefore, is to plan early, involve the integration team and accept the risk that the deal might fail to cross the line.

In the Dark

In business, there are few things more adrenalin-fuelled and all-consuming than deals. The negotiating team is largely made up of legal, financial and investment advisors, along with the consultants involved in due diligence. Meanwhile, integration teams are predominantly operational and commercial. For reasons of confidentiality, the integration team often has little awareness of the nature and scale of the deal until it is finalised, on the grounds that the fewer who know about it, the better. The risk is that some other party might become aware the target is 'in play' and pinch the deal themselves with a better offer. In addition, knowledge of impending change is likely to unnerve employees, suppliers and customers, so the negotiation is best kept quiet.

The result of this, however, can be that integration teams know little of the deal until completion. They may not have been consulted on the proposed benefits presented to the board, yet they are expected to deliver them. They will understandably feel that integration is being dumped on them at short notice and with an outline plan consisting of little more than the acquisition proposal that may vary in realistic expectations. Worse still, the board may have already employed external consultants to assist with the integration—a move almost guaranteed to undermine others within the business who can do little other than stand back and let the consultants get on with it. Indeed, consultants may be willing to buy into and support the original proposed strategy despite limited prospects of success. The one thing everyone knows is that the consultants will eventually leave and for management the hard work will begin.

Both the evidence and advice of experienced practitioners make clear—a plan for integration that crystallises the proposed benefits is ideally created *before* the deal concludes and informed by the due diligence findings and insight.

Integration by Consultants

The £4bn acquisition of BPB by St Gobain in 2006 discussed in Chapter 9 was largely integrated by consultants. The plan was to integrate the acquired business into a very different industry which relied on different technology and supply chains which had a limited cross-over in customers. The integration strategy was on a horizontal basis as if the companies were competitors and the task a merger of equals. The minute the consultants left, the integration had to be unwound in a dynamic of much confusion and bad feeling.

The only savings and benefits to be gained by the deal were the merging of head office functions such as finance, HR and company secretarial departments. This can usually be the case but does not alone provide a justification for acquisition. In this particular scenario, the buyer had overpaid with a 52% price premium and had no valid or feasible plan for integration. Instead, they hoped the well-known firm of consultants would come up with something. In practice the proposed plan had little to do with the strategy. The acquisition was in reality, entirely unrelated diversification for the buyer.

That is not to say that consultants are not useful during integrations, however, they should be used sparingly. In some major acquisitions, the host may not have the manpower or resources for the integration, in which case consulting can be used to augment local resources. This should ultimately be under the control of the senior manager and follow the integration plan of the host.

Consultants can create a block between local and acquired management as they come between the two. They may create an unfavourable impression for the acquired people. Ultimately, the two sets of managers must create working relationships, which can be difficult when consultants are in the way. For businesses new to the acquisition game, however, consultants bring useful expertise.

The clear lesson here is that a named person should be appointed to take overall responsibility for the deal and subsequent integration right from the beginning. They should determine the resource level required, develop the integration plan and be the point of contact and report for consultants. Consultants may well not welcome this, as they prefer to liaise with the CEO or Chairman.

Dimensions of Integration

Speed and Depth

There are many theoretical models of integration available, two of which are worth summarising as their fundamental principles remain at the heart of strategic thinking. They are Haspeslagh and Jemison's matrix—an early model developed in 1991 but still used extensively—and Joseph Bower's equally relevant 'five categories of strategy' (Bower, 2001).

Integration approaches hinge around the two dimensions of speed and depth. Should integration be 'light touch' or complete absorption? Should we go as fast as possible in order to resolve uncertainty and gain rapid benefits, or slowly so that we can learn as we go and assess staff carefully before we make decisions? It is wise to remember that advance assumptions before acquiring are usually incorrect by varying degrees.

Available Synergies and Management Autonomy

Haspeslagh and Jemison's (1991) model is a broad theoretical matrix of factors to consider when deciding the most appropriate integration strategy. This, they advise is achieved by evaluating the extent of synergies in relation to the need for autonomy of the acquired management (Fig. 3.2).

Where available benefits are high and the need for management autonomy low, then complete absorption is the logical answer; horizontal mergers within an industry are good examples. Conversely, if there are few synergies and a management that requires more, if not complete autonomy, then the best decision will either be to avoid integration or adopt a 'light touch' approach. In these latter acquisitions, the objective is to retain the management.

The other two options are more complex. High synergy availability in correspondence with a high need for autonomy means making some difficult decisions which are likely to result in the loss of some highly competent management. 'Symbiosis' may be a promising term, but it is also one that presages a difficult integration to come.

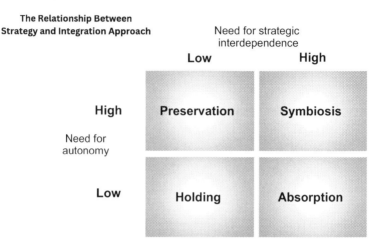

Fig. 3.2 The relationship between strategy and integration approach (adapted from Haspeslagh & Jemison, 1991)

Low synergy availability and management with little need for autonomy suggest an unwise acquisition. If there are few integration benefits available, then what can the acquirer bring to the business other than money?

A Typology of Strategy and Consequences for Integration

Joseph Bower's research (2001) attempts to apply more detailed strategies to specific modes of integration. Unlike Haspeslagh and Jemison, he starts by categorising strategies into a number of classifications:

1. **Overcapacity M&A** (horizontal integration). This refers to the acquisition of competitors which should, in theory, provide major cost savings, increased market presence and greater coordination and control when integrated. The risks are overpaying and taking on a target which is too big and which you may not have the requisite resources or capabilities to support. Rapid and deep integration is proposed here.
2. **Geographic Roll-Up M&A** This typically relates to internationalising and acquiring businesses in similar overseas markets. The key is to determine what you are buying, which in some countries and cases may be difficult to ascertain. Each market will differ and local management will need to be retained, as they own important customers and connections. Light touch integration of back office and procedures is appropriate, but

any integration attempts are best pursued slowly to prevent the loss of such contacts.
3. **Product or Market Extension M&A** This may be either domestic or international. If it is the latter, a similar approach to that applied in point 2 above is advisable. If domestic, then determine to what extent you need the management. This may well influence decisions regarding the speed and depth of integration.
4. **M&A as R&D** This is typical of technology companies who are acquiring potential competitors for their technology capability and development. Holding onto the talent is critical. If they don't like the new management or culture of the acquirer, you may lose the one asset you are acquiring. Careful handling is a must.
5. **Industry Convergence M&A** This is most applicable in the telecoms infrastructure business in which those purveying/selling content want to start producing it to provide exclusive content. For example, Netflix, Comcast and Sky, AT&T and Time Warner (2018) and before that, AOL and Time Warner (1998). This is a bet on the emergence of new industry, and an attempt to gain an optimal position before the industry matures and becomes dominated by a few strong players. In these circumstances integration and over involvement in management are best avoided. The loss of key people with the bulk of knowledge in an industry you don't really understand is highly problematic. AT&T and AOL learnt this the hard way.

Bower is concerned with relative size, concluding that acquiring relatively large businesses is always going to be problematic. Different cultures may not see eye to eye and will fall into competitive behaviours. Having the scale of resources to integrate will be difficult. In many ways integration is more a matter of change management under pressure. Various benefits will have been promised at the time of the project approval and the delivery timetable is often unrealistic. In addition, it is more than likely that many people will be anxious concerning their job security, as there may be significant cost savings planned. Further tensions may arise from cultural differences and means that eyes are often 'off the ball' during internal processing. Large integrations need a programme office and the detailed monitoring of progress that correlates with the overall plan.

Integrating Management: To Change or Not to Change?

The integration of two businesses is essentially a matter of change management: jobs will almost invariably be lost, and systems and approaches will be altered substantially, and unlikely to everyone's satisfaction. Furthermore, there may be cultural disparities which will always present obstacles to progress. In this respect, John Kotter's (2012) change management framework proves helpful in determining the steps which need to be prioritised during a major integration (Fig. 3.3).

1. Determine a clear vision of what the final integration will look like and the various benefits which are to be achieved.
2. Communicate the vision throughout the workforce so people know where they are going and why. This is a continuing activity as people rapidly forget why they are doing this and need constant reminding, particularly as it may be an unpopular activity.
3. Create a sense of urgency amongst the people concerned to progress the project. Driving change at speed requires real leadership and significant input from the top. In many ways this is the most difficult part as understanding why the project is necessary is one part, developing commitment can be more difficult.
4. Set up a guiding coalition to drive the project. It should include all senior interested parties, particularly those that might obstruct the project and team morale. It needs to be seen that senior management support the project. This coalition should have executive power to act.

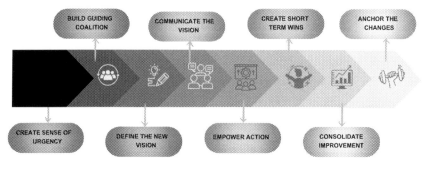

Fig. 3.3 John Kotter's 8-step change management model

5. Identify clear milestones so the project can be split into achievable chunks and individual stages celebrated. Frequently projects are so large and extend over protracted periods, to the point that this destroys motivation as progress is difficult to identify.
6. Remove obstacles to change. These are often people or lack of appropriate resources which need to be addressed and made available. This can be difficult in practice as it is rare that dissenters oppose a project directly. A more subtle unwillingness to cooperate is more common.
7. Build on the change. Maintain momentum as, once it is allowed to fall, it may be difficult to recover.
8. Consolidate change and ensure it becomes a routine procedure. Much change can be lost over time as support and consultancy services are withdrawn.

Integration Learning

As this book often reiterates, research such as that of McKinsey estimate that around 65% of integrations materially fail to meet expectations. We are equally aware that larger acquisitions, compared to the size of the buyer, are less likely to be effective, owing to both the sheer extent of the task and the lack of necessary resources for the integration. Cultural differences between large businesses can be enormous and persistent, even twenty years down the line, Giersberg et al. (2020) identify that sporadic large—where 'large' is defined as more than 30% of the value of the acquirer—acquisition policies destroy value. Higher prices and the sheer extent of the integration process are partly to blame. In many ways integration is change management under stress, as we know that the consequences of mistakes can be significant and many of the newly acquired employees are not sure they want to work for the new owner.

Integration capabilities rely on organisational learning and retained experience. These capabilities are built by frequent 'manageable' smaller acquisitions; this means that there is dedicated resource in the organisation to integrate a continuing stream of businesses. The process tends to be shorter, and it is accepted from the outset that the larger business will be dominant, and with it, their way of doing things instated. In larger businesses the acceptance of major change is likely to be much reduced. Through internal centres of experience (Dow Chemicals) advice and support can be lent to those carrying out the acquisition. This relies on a strategy of growth by frequent smaller acquisitions. This has a number of advantages including the expertise to integrate which can be documented in a manual and shared with others in the organisation, since there is usually a company way of approaching these complex and difficult tasks. There are also additional price benefits to be gained through multiple arbitrage which improves the likely returns on such a strategy. Again, Giersberg et al. identifies that these strategies overall create value.

> **Case Study: Feat or Flop? Procter and Gamble's Acquisition of Gillette**
> Uncertainty still prevails as to whether household products business P&G's 2005 acquisition of Gillette for $57bn was a success or not. Although a share swap this represented an 18% price premium to the previous undisturbed share price. P&G had a long list of household names, including Head and Shoulders, and Crest Toothpaste together with 300 other brands. Gillette had razors, Duracell, Braun and Oral-B.
>
> Very large acquisitions such as this are rarely successful either in the short or long term. Mankins et al. (2017) contend that such major horizontal deals are usually successful in terms of cost removal but fail to provide growth. That appears to be the case here, with cost savings in the region of $16bn, but revenue and earnings growth over the next 9 years lagged significantly behind their immediate competitors. Indeed, the 30% share price improvement over the next 9 years was only half that of arch-rivals Unilever and Colgate-Palmolive. This irritated shareholders immensely and started to attract the attention of activists. A. G. Lafley retired in 2009; he was replaced by Robert MacDonald, only for Lafley to be brought back in 2013 after MacDonald's retirement to recoup investor confidence.
>
> The integration exercise was enormous, merging the supply chain of the two businesses over several years. There were over 500 distribution centres across 180 countries with a plan to retain the largest best located centres and close the rest. In effect, this was an intense all-consuming internal exercise that caused such indigestion that much resource was directed towards making it work.
>
> One negative impact was that the top Gillette management team lost power in the enlarged business, and taking the opportunity to exit with money, subsequently left. This exodus was no doubt compounded by major cultural difficulties in the way each side operated. Ultimately, investors felt the overhead situation had become bloated and that management were not capable of addressing the problem. Whilst on paper the deal made sense and the price was reasonable, the sheer scale of integration left P&G with reduced growth, few new products or ideas and a complex and burdensome cost structure for many years after.

1. The complexity of the two supply chains was significant which made the integration protracted as supply chains had to move on to one set of systems. Would a more rapid process have helped?
2. Did the acquisition make sense in view of the size and complexity of the respective businesses?
3. Why did P&G fail to retain the Gillette management? Could they have done anything differently?

Comment

When an acquired business exceeds 30% of the valuation of the acquirer then the odds are already stacked against its chance of success. One of the key issues in this case was that, whilst many customers would take large amounts of both suppliers' products, P&G were experts in marketing their products to women, whilst Gillette's main advertising target was men. Gillette's razor blade model had already suffered during the banking crisis that had brought about a move to lower cost alternatives, one example being the 'Dollar Shave Club' which sold online. There was also stronger competition from more focused quality entrants such as Harry's and their vast array of shaving-associated products. Expensive Gillette razors, even backed by enormous advertising, had seen their best days.

In fact, male grooming itself has become a burgeoning market, with over 3500 barber shops opening across the country in the past five years alone. This social trend is not one that either of the above organisations can easily compete with.

Furthermore, the channel cross selling did not appear to work and there were limited revenue benefits. Pressure on suppliers may have yielded some benefits but this is also difficult to establish. Once size increases above a certain level then benefits offer diminishing returns.

The Gillette example shares much in common with the 2016 'Megabrew' case in which AB InBev acquired SABMiller for $106bn. Like Gillette, they were the top two global players in the market and would be entering into a horizontal acquisition of major competitors. Both instances were sold to shareholders on the basis of growth into new territories and channel cross-selling. Neither achieved these objectives. Both did make substantial cost and supply chain savings with rationalisation of manufacturing (beer) and distribution (P&G). They were effective in making savings, but these were, and usually are, short-lived.

The acquisition process in cases such as these is immense and a major distraction from the fundamental aim—to develop the business. Instead, the next few years become a relentless battle to remove cost. The strategy itself can be sensible when making smaller, more manageable acquisitions where multiple arbitrage on price is available. However, when premiums exceeding 50% are being paid on top of high valuations, then all value is lost before the process even begins. In the case of Gillette, the premium was a more reasonable 18% (although debt levels would also be relevant), yet even this resulted in considerable earnings dilution of the shares which weighed heavily on share price performance over the next nine years.

Silver Linings?

If nothing else this exercise in integration leadership can be used by organisations as a testing ground for future senior management. The uniquely difficult circumstances and the need to liaise with and manage many people, functions and stakeholders across the organisation will always be an excellent learning experience. If asked whether he would do the deal again, A.G. Lafley might well be less positive.

Risk Assessment and Monitoring

In advance of any acquisition an assessment of the key risks to the project is needed. If this had been effectively undertaken in the major acquisitions described earlier in the book such as AB InBev and SABMiller, Bayer and Monsanto, AT&T and Time Warner or RBS and ABN-AMRO then none of these deals would have been done. In the RBS case, very little due diligence was done to determine the risks. In the other three cases, it is more than likely that the enthusiasm to do the deal overwhelmed the objectivity when confronted by the due diligence findings.

Monitoring and managing key risks to both businesses during the integration phase is critical. Distraction, low productivity, loss of key staff, declining health and safety performance, higher staff churn rates and loss of market share are some of the major risks to both businesses. These should all be tightly monitored and controlled. Allocate responsible names to each risk which will vastly improve accountability and engagement with the process.

Culture

Cultural change and compatibility are never a quick or easy feat. It is likely to demand considerable time, sensitivity and workforce attrition. Indeed, in some cases, the effort may be pointless and energies better oriented towards making changes elsewhere.

An excellent example of this can be observed in the changes brought about by a new MD at British Gypsum when new competition opened in the UK. British Gypsum had monopolised the plasterboard market for some decades, during which it had grown into a bureaucratic, multi-layered culture with highly decentralised operations which were difficult to coordinate and control. The business had been in existence since before the First World War and had a culture to match. When competition offering better quality products at lower prices opened it plunged into losses and a new external MD was recruited.

His first move was to replace the board entirely, largely by promoting 'young blood' from within the business. Operations were centralised, the organisation delayered, old inefficient plants were closed and most contracts were put out to tender. In a short space of time, employee numbers were reduced from 3,500 to 1,300, all whilst overall output was increased. Various operations such as the vehicle fleet, security, catering and estate maintenance were all outsourced, the Head Office was closed entirely and staff relocated to a manufacturing site. In short, all trappings of status and seniority were removed.

Management felt empowered to make these major changes, which ultimately clarified and refocused the business. Whilst it would be a stretch to say the culture had changed entirely, the business was performing better and soon started to make significant returns.

Experiencing Integration

As an employee, being acquired and integrated is not a great experience. It is unsettling to feel that one's place within an organisation has altered and may be in question. The top management may well have left, resulting in a workforce that lacks direction. Whilst the new people may be perfectly amenable, it will take a considerable amount of time before you have faith in them. You feel they will probably favour their own people, interact largely with those they know and less easily accept the direction of acquired employees/ managers/executives. Motivation also flags and murmurings begin about termination payments; the culture of the workplace is not one of productivity.

Some of the immediate concerns of the acquired workforce were referred to in the previous Chapter 2 (Strategic Growth Options and Respective Risk Profiles, Fig. 1). Until employees are given some assurance regarding job security, track records, development and prospects, they will focus on little else.

Furthermore, these insecurities are likely to prompt an exodus of highly capable people, whilst those that remain will pay little attention to doing their jobs. Those who are to leave should know as soon as possible and be given accurate time scales for their employment. Bonus arrangements are one means of ensuring their continued cooperation and performance until that time. Those who are staying will need their questions answered and concerns addressed before they can refocus on the task. In offering support and attention, the new management must be prepared to put the time in.

People need a clear vision of where they are going and a map of how they are going to get there. Perhaps the most important way to develop confidence in the new management is through high levels of communication and being honest and transparent about the future.

Essentials for Effective Integration

A Detailed Plan

I have seen countless integrations in which there is no detailed plan for integration and no management team selected at the time of purchase. A strategy may well exist along with vague ideas as to how value might be created—developing presence in a particular growth area, cost reduction and increased market power, or even acquiring new technology or capabilities—however, there is seldom much detail established. With such a high failure rate acquirers often think 'we will get the deal over the line first, then worry about the integration itself.'

Another rationale behind such scant planning is the attempt to avoid leaks that might interest competing bidders, or rouse uncertainty amongst staff, customers and suppliers. With so much energy devoted to secrecy, the deal team may end up having little to do with the integration. Another view is that 'we don't quite know what we are buying in terms of organisational structure and who we want to keep. We will assess the business more thoroughly once acquired.' Both leave the task of integration itself to the operational people and with minimal notice.

The upshot of a poorly planned integration is lost time, confusion and reliance on consultants who ultimately have no real loyalty to the businesses concerned. They, after all, will be passing responsibility back sooner rather than later. Therefore, every opportunity should be taken during the deal to understand who and what is being acquired. This is the time for gathering intelligence, using the senior management presentations, available data and due diligence to inform the integration plan. The more detailed the plan the better the chance of success. A plan should not only specify how additional value will be created but include detailed plans for employees, suppliers and customers.

Communication

As in the case of British Gypsum, communication and clarity of procedure are key. On the day of deal completion team members should show up at the acquired business with prepared statements. These should be open and honest about what will happen; the more uncertainty which can be removed the better. If specific key staff are to be retained, then they should be told who they are and what future role they are to be offered. Those who will leave need terms and conditions of departure and retention bonuses to keep them whilst they are still needed. It is more than likely that rumours will already have been circulating; now is the time when people should be told as much as possible in order to build trust.

This is an issue that should not be underestimated. Staff productivity before and during an acquisition invariably declines, but it will hit an all-time low if you are not transparent about the organisation's future prospects.

Team

In order to manage this transitional stage, the integration team should have been selected sometime prior to the deal and fully briefed to move in rapidly. They should be the 'A team,' the most experienced and capable individuals to oversee a job that is invariably fraught with difficulty. It should not, therefore, be people who are surplus to requirements, or those still without an identified role in the future company structure. Lack of quality integration resources and preparedness are the most significant contributing factors in failed integrations.

Consequences for Strategy

What we now know is that integration of large acquisitions takes enormous resource levels, that are depleted further by the employment of consultants. In addition, such mediatory parties will ultimately be leaving the implementation of the deal to management. The degree of complexity and sheer scale of the overall integration often outweigh the potential benefits of synergies. Furthermore, larger organisations are likely to have more durable cultures which do not readily succumb to a new regime. In short, these integrations are major challenges with a limited chance of success. Add to this the likely price premium necessary to acquire a major organisation and you will likely see share price dilution rather than any multiple arbitrage benefits; the prospects of success are substantially hindered at each step of this process.

In contrast, a steady flow of smaller acquisitions will likely generate multiple arbitrage benefits. Allocating learning and resources to a flow of smaller integrations makes for a progressively more experienced integration team, with a clear approach and knowledge of how to reduce risks. Data from Giersberg et al. (2020) clearly shows that such strategies outperform organic growth, yet avoid the notorious underperformance brought about by major yet sporadic acquisitions.

Many of the points discussed here can be seen in the following 'real' case in which a major French multinational acquired a much smaller UK-based multinational in a hostile takeover approach. The case considers the strategy, pricing and integration in this context and identifies lessons which can be learnt from this approach.

Case Study: BPB Plc—Anatomy of a Hostile Takeover Bid

A Personal Recollection: The bid landed on the first day of the Lord's cricket test in July 2005, almost certainly due to BPB's CEO, Richard Cousins having an enthusiasm for cricket. St Gobain and their advisors knew he would be there enjoying himself. As Richard later recalled, the morning cricket was excellent, but the afternoon deteriorated in more ways than one. Richard had to leave the match to see BPB's investment bankers to start the defence discussion. The timing clearly meant war for two reasons, not just the cricket, but France would be disappearing on holiday for August. Cities were soon to become annual ghost towns with shops and restaurants closed and tumbleweed blowing down main streets. But the St Gobain team would be at work running the bid, demonstrating their commitment and forcing BPB's top team to cancel their holidays. The defence team of investment bankers

> and advisors, PR agencies and lawyers would all have to cancel their holidays too. The bid was definitely intended to catch them away and maximise inconvenience. Hostile means just that, no love lost.

BPB Plc was an FTSE 100 business and the world's largest plasterboard manufacturer with a global market share of 20% and a significant presence in 50 countries. It had sales of £2.3bn and profits of £272mn. St Gobain is a large French multinational with sales of around €40bn in a wide variety of building products. It can trace its heritage as far back as 1665 and producing the mirrors in Versailles. Headquartered in Paris and listed on the Paris bourse, St Gobain was a cornerstone of French industrialism.

The bid had come as a surprise to BPB and its shareholders as the share price was near its peak value anyway. As a bidder would have to find a price premium of 40%+ to win any bid then the price would be colossal for a building materials firm. After the defence, the actual premium ended up being 52%, an astonishing figure. St Gobain did not have plasterboard interests and so there would be few synergies. They would have little idea of how to run the business without retaining the management. Performance in these circumstances was more likely to deteriorate, rather than increase to justify the price.

Hostile Bids

A hostile takeover means the bidder appeals directly to the target's shareholders in the belief that the board is unlikely to agree on a bid. In terms of defence the target board attempts to force the bid price as high as possible by producing improved forecasts and promising to return more cash to shareholders. There are two reasons for this. Firstly, to drive the best deal for their own shareholders. Secondly to force the price to a point whereby the bidder loses interest as they will be paying too much, and then pull out. They, after all, have to justify the price paid to their own shareholders who vote on the deal.

Research suggests that hostile bids are unwise for several reasons:

1. The price paid is almost invariably higher than for an agreed bid.
2. Management teams are more likely to leave so retaining people is more difficult after such a public scrap.

3. Management remain in charge until the final day of ownership and can charge what they wish into the accounts. The bidder has received no undertakings to the contrary as would be the case with a negotiated bid.
4. There is no due diligence process which requires the agreement of the target management. The business is effectively bought as seen which means there are no warranties or indemnities, and the risks are that much higher. The acquirer has much less idea of what they are buying or how they may improve the business. It is also difficult for them to plan integration and determine synergies which might arise.

Defence and Attack

A hostile bid is much like a political election in which both sides make promises to persuade the shareholders to vote for their respective promises. The target management keep increasing forecast profits and proposed payments to shareholders whilst the bidders increase the bid to counter these promises.

The stock market rules give the bidder 60 days to either persuade the target shareholders/board to accept the offer or withdraw. This was extended by a further 42 days due to a legal determination as to whether there would be any competition issues. There weren't in this case due to the unrelated nature of the business being acquired.

The first bid was £6.70 rapidly increased to £7.20 which is a 41% premium to the undisturbed price. BPB then emptied out all their lockers to declare immense interim results up 30% and forecast full year profits of £350mn, which meant growth of 30% on the previous year. To further the defence a special dividend was announced of 120p per share or £600mn, funded by the sale of two small businesses and some land. The regular dividend would also be progressively doubled over the next three years. The rationale for the 120p special dividend was that if the bid failed then the share price would fall back to £6.00, 120p below its current share price (the special dividend would have been funded from borrowings and reduced investment. The proposed property and business disposals would not have made £100mn).

St Gobain clearly felt two could play that game, raising the bid to £7.75 or £3.9bn. The justifying rationale was that they had unearthed £100mn of savings, although it was never clear where from. St Gobain did not have similar interests and so they would be unable to realise synergies except for generic head office functions. The BPB shareholders really did not care as they were being offered 52% above an already high share price. It started to become clear they would be accepting this final knock-out offer.

At the very end of the bid period, some of the shareholders suggested that they were likely to accept the latest bid. However, much they liked the BPB management, the shareholders always have their price. Acceptance of the bid started to look inevitable and so at last the two companies met. BPB made major cash transfers to reduce funding deficits in the various pension schemes. St Gobain, to buy favour with a dispersed and substantial management team, agreed to pay out all share option schemes, whether vested or not, which was an enormous sum. They would also be stuck with the enormous costs of the bid on both sides. In effect they had acquired some large bills to add to their own. In total these additional costs added more than £500mn to the bid price.

The First Dinner

French business matters are usually conducted over top quality meals, and so it was for BPB after the final curtain on the bid. It felt like being a paraded 'Prisoner of War' turning up in Paris in the 'dead zone' period between Christmas and the New Year when the streets are bare. The Michelin-starred restaurant was up a tower and whilst the food was fine the dinner conversation felt strained. There was some crowing about the empire we were joining, and we were expected to say how delighted we were to be joining this marvellous business. This was difficult in view of the mud thrown during the defence. It all felt very uncomfortable. The president pointed out to me that the extra £100mn they had to up the bid by had been described as additional discovered synergies. He explained that I would need to discover them and then make them. Any ideas?

Integration

Integration was a sorry affair designed to convince the world that St Gobain's claims about synergies had some merit. An attempt was made to merge BPB with St Gobain's insulation division which was a very different business. Technology and products were completely different whilst there was some limited overlap in customers. The integration was chaotic and run by management consultants. Petty political wars abounded between management resulting in many of the BPB management leaving. The overwhelming feeling was that 'We have bought you and so we are in charge.' This might be true but felt rather unpalatable and certainly grated. Add to this the management consultants who brought much ego into every room and frequently not much else. People like to be masters of their own destiny and the things which previously motivated them such as their leaders, colleagues and to some extent, teams had largely disappeared. So why stay? The share options payout had made many managers very rich and so why put up with this new regime and why not seek your luck elsewhere?

There were few real synergies except the closure of the BPB head office. The integration was subsequently unwound slowly but not until after the damage had been done. Virtually all of the BPB board left, most to go on to greater things. The CEO Richard Cousins became CEO of Compass, a large catering company which he turned into an FTSE top 30 performer. The Compass share price multiplied around 6 times before Richard and his entire family died in a seaplane accident in 2017 near Sydney.

Postscript

Both the St Gobain CEO and Divisional Director were subsequently awarded the Legion d'Honeur for their part in the expansion of French corporate interests. The St Gobain shareholders paid for the expensive acquisition by seeing their stock fall in value and failing to recapture the value immediately prior to the bid until over 15 years later. Indeed, at the time of going to press 19 years later the share price was still below the undisturbed share price prior to the deal. It seems the shareholders have had to fund management expansionist ambitions. St Gobain has been a poorly performing stock ever since. As one senior St Gobain Director intimated to me 'We can buy them, but we can't run them.'

10 Lessons for Better Integration

1. 67% of integrations fail to achieve the forecasted benefits.÷ Loss of key employees and customers, collapsed productivity and poor market performance are all risks. The host can also be similarly affected by the immense distraction and resource requirement. Integration is a process to be respected.
2. The pace and depth of integration should be dictated by the chosen strategy. Horizontal acquisitions (in the same industry) usually need to be rapid and the integration deep to rapidly produce cost savings and

restrict the period of uncertainty affecting both organisations. In circumstances where retaining management is critical due to their knowledge, then integration needs to be light touch. The essence of integration is to do the minimum possible to achieve the projected synergistic benefits.
3. The integration team should be formed *prior* to the deal conclusion with the mutual agreement of target achievements and plan. One person should have overall responsibility for both the deal and realising the projected benefits through integration. The likelihood of a successful integration is directly related to the quality of the plan drawn up before the deal concludes.
4. Due diligence is an opportunity to develop a more detailed integration plan and test out the many synergy assumptions by including 'deep' commercial and operational due diligence. There are often benefits from using external consultants as, whilst lacking specific industry knowledge, they do bring an objective and independent view of both risks and opportunities. The strategic drive to do a deal can, on occasion, overwhelm the due diligence findings which may be ignored despite raising major concerns.
5. Whilst most of the planned cost savings are usually achieved during the integration phase, revenue gains can be far more elusive. Independent financial analysts usually disregard announced revenue gains when used to justify an acquisition. Cross-selling only occasionally proves effective (Christensen et al., 2011).
6. Project objectives are often constructed to ensure the deal is approved at the board level and, if necessary, by shareholders. They may well be unrealistic, particularly regarding the timetable for achieving targets. Most integration plans are not achieved by timetable. Even the better-implemented integrations take longer and cost more than expected. Planning is often too optimistic and results in few acquisitions achieving their stated goals.
7. The moment the deal concludes then a team should arrive at the acquired business to announce new ownership and communicate as much as is feasible about the new strategy and organisational structure. Senior management who will be leaving should be informed as soon as possible. It must be clear who is in charge and attempts should be made to resolve as much uncertainty as possible.
8. Uncertainty destroys performance and so prompt and frequent communication becomes critical. New management should be honest and transparent as to who is going and who will be staying. Acquired people should understand their position in the new organisation structure.

Retention bonuses may be appropriate for those temporarily needed otherwise they are likely to leave as soon as they can find other suitable employment. Productivity is usually a casualty of the acquisition unless strong leadership can be introduced rapidly.
9. Serial acquirers have the advantage of being able to develop knowledge and process for integrations. They may have integration manuals, centres of excellence offering advice, 'tacit' knowledge acquired over years and adequate and experienced resources available for integrations. They are more likely to have experienced integration teams who know what to do and when.
10. Consultants may be a valuable resource in integrations, but they can also undermine management. As always, they will have their own agenda which may not be entirely aligned with that of the client. In due course, they will leave and responsibility for what they have done becomes that of management. They should, therefore, report directly to the integration leader rather than the CEO to ensure they support the project leadership who is accountable for outcomes. Otherwise, management can become disenfranchised and blame any issues on the consultants.

Activity—A Case

A major US paper manufacturing company considers a deal proposed by its investment bank to merge with a major customer of similar size in China. The bank considers that there will be a significant back-office saving and the acquisition will secure a channel to the Chinese market. Currently the distributor is responsible for 25% of the paper companies' sales, which make up half of its sales in China.

What are the risks which may be associated with this proposed acquisition?

Comment

Downstream Acquisitions Such as This Often Fail for Several Reasons:

1. Manufacturing and distribution are very different 'unrelated' industries which in itself immediately limits the prospects of success. The ability to run businesses in one industry does not always transfer to businesses in another.

2. Acquiring downstream distributors often leads to a loss of other third-party distributors who do not like buying from a competitor. They take the view that vertically integrated suppliers/competitors are offering preferential terms to their own downstream distributors. In these circumstances it is likely some trade will be lost.
3. There are unlikely to be any back-office savings between a US manufacturer and a Chinese distributor. They are two completely different businesses operating in different environments and doing very different jobs.
4. The role of investment banks is to facilitate deals so that fees can be charged to clients. These deals may not necessarily be in the best interests of their clients. What happens after the deal is done is of little interest to the intermediary.

References and Recommended Readings

Angwin, D. N. (2000). Implementing Successful Post-acquisition Management. *Financial Times*. Prentice Hall.

Azan, W., & Huber Sutter, I. (2017). Knowledge Transfer in Post-merger Integration Management: Case Study of a Multinational Healthcare Company in Greece. *Knowledge Management Research & Practice, 8*(4), 307–321.

Bower, J. L. (2001). Not All M&As Are Alike—And That Matters. *Harvard Business Review, 79*(3), 92–164.

Burgelman, R. A., & Doz, Y. L. (2001). The Power of Strategic Integration. *MIT Sloan Management Review, 42*(3), 28.

Capron, L., & Mitchell, W. (2012). *Build, Borrow or Buy: Solving the Growth Dilemma*. Harvard Business Press.

Christensen, C. M., Alton, R., Rising, C., & Waldeck, A. (2011). The Big Idea: The New M&A Playbook. *Harvard Business Review, 89*(3), 48–57.

Duvall-Dickson, S. (2016). Blending Tribes: Leadership Challenges in Mergers and Acquisitions. S.A.M. *Advanced Management Journal (1984), 81*(4), 16.

Giersberg, J., Krause, J., Rudnicki, J., & West, A. (2020). The Power of Through-Cycle M&A. *McKinsey Insights, 4*(30/2020), 1–7.

Graebner, M. E., Heimeriks, K. H., Huy, Q. N., & Vaara, E. (2017). The Process of Postmerger Integration: A Review and Agenda for Future Research. *Academy of Management Annals, 11*(1), 1–32.

Haspeslagh, P. C., & Jemison, D. B. (1991). *Managing Acquisitions: Creating Value Through Corporate Renewal*. Free Press.

Heimeriks, K. H., Schijven, M., & Gates, S. (2012). Manifestations of Higher Order Routines: The Underlying Mechanisms of Deliberate Learning in the

Context of Postacquisition Integration. *Academy of Management Journal., 55*(3), 703–726.

Kotter, J. P. (2012). *Leading Change*. Harvard Business Review Press.

Mankins, M., Harris, K., & Harding, D. (2017). Strategy in the age of superabundant capital. Harvard Business Review, 95(2), 66-75.

Moraitis, T., & Keener, C. (2018). *Leading the Deal: The Secret to Successful Acquisition and Integration.* Urbane Publications Ltd.

Sirower, M. L. (1997). *The Synergy Trap: How Companies Lose the Acquisition Game.* Free Press.

Weber, Y., Shenkar, O., & Raveh, A. (1996). National and Corporate Cultural Fit in Mergers/Acquisitions: An Exploratory Study. *Management Science, 42*(8), 1215–1227. https://doi.org/10.2753/IMO0020-8825410305

Part III

M&A: The Private Equity Way—What Is There to Be Learnt?

4

Private Equity: A Rising Power

Introduction—Why Study Private Equity?

From the perspective of investors, there is little doubt that the PE (private equity) model is successful. Most data from the last 35 years suggests that the buy–improve–sell model outperforms major public company indices over almost any long-term period selected (Harris et al., 2014). Consequently, we are seeing a continuing expansion of PE and a simultaneous shrinkage in the number of public companies both in the USA and the UK. In 2021, PE was involved in 34% of global deal-making with $1tn of company sales and $1.2tn of acquisitions (Bain & Co. Global Private Equity Report, 2022). This raises an obvious question—why do public companies continually destroy so much value through their M&A activity whilst PE achieves such consistently high returns?

Clearly, not everyone is a fan of the PE approach or approves of the perceived excesses that some PE houses exhibit in terms of cost-cutting, high debt levels and sales price increases. However, there is much that can be learned by others from the PE approach; public companies and other privately owned businesses may well benefit from the philosophy, governance and incentives applied by PE. This chapter focuses on why long-term investors continue to move money into PE funds, and the mechanisms which PE employs to drive performance in acquired businesses.

Philosophy and Strategy

Private equity raises funds from investors such as pension and insurance schemes plus high net worth individuals. These are placed in funds and invested in buying businesses which are improved and sold within a 10-year window. After the PE partners have taken their 20% share of the profits the rest is returned to investors. According to Pitchbook data, the average Internal Rate of Return (IRR) across all PE investments over the 40-year period to 2021 is 15.9%, which makes them one of the highest yielding asset classes. They simply buy–improve–sell businesses which means they have to be very good at these three operations to generate such high returns. From an investors perspective, the downside is illiquidity which means money is tied up for a number of years. They outperform major stock exchange indices although stock market investments are liquid.

PE differs from other types of ownership in that the entire strategy is focused on one specific event—the exit or sale of the business. This is the only source of significant shareholder returns. Valuations are transitory and unrealised, whilst the eventual sale of the business crystallises added value in cash terms for the management immediately after the deal is done and the investors when it pays out, albeit through the PE investment fund.

Compared to public company ownership, PE bonuses to management are limited during the period of ownership. Similarly, dividends to shareholders are rarely paid. The exit event is generally planned for 3–5 years following acquisition, allowing for significant business change to be made. Subsequently, activity levels are directed towards implementing these changes. Through this singular focus on the exit event, the aim is to maximise shareholder proceeds at exit, at which point investor management working in the business stand to make strong returns, but not before.

Other forms of ownership such as the public model, frequently pride themselves on their 'strategic' long-term focus when investing and building the business. However, these objectives are often vague and reduce management accountability in the knowledge that other management is likely to be in post when the 'long term' eventually arrives.

This is assuming 'long term' ever arrives. There is an old joke that a bad investment is frequently described as a 'strategic' investment. It might pay back eventually, but it just as easily might not. Certainly, it is the case that strategic investors will make much longer-term investments to build a business than PE. PE takes the view that unless the investment will be making a major contribution by the point of exit then they will not entertain it. Indeed, the proposed investment needs to be delivered at a rate consistent with the planned exit criterion before PE will approve the investment.

> **An Example: Long and Short Payback Periods**
> Typically, a restaurant chain roll out will pay back almost immediately; people like to try somewhere new, accounting for high sales in the first year. In contrast, the construction of new capacity in the manufacturing industry can be hugely expensive and typically takes over two years to establish. Moreover, it is likely that it will only make money once an adequate plant loading is achieved, which may take a number of years and remains dependent on a growing market. If the market should fail to grow, then the money is wasted. In fact, payback periods in major capacity additions are often between 8 and 10 years. PE would typically not invest in this type of project, preferring to lose market share and potentially push prices upwards, rather than to risk investment in long-term projects that require added capacity.

As has been outlined, PE philosophy is focused entirely on shareholder returns. Other stakeholders are satisfied only to the extent that they support this. Employees, management, customers, suppliers and authorities must be satisfied, or else shareholder returns may suffer. They are not pursued as an end in themselves.

PE is usually highly compliant with the law as they have institutional shareholders who would not wish to be associated with wrongdoing. That said, ethics can on occasion be questionable.

Do KPIs Improve EBITDA?

There are other differences in emphasis apparent in PE. They pursue Key Performance Indices (KPI) in almost every area to drive performance, as illustrated in the 'Balanced Scorecard' approach (Kaplan & Norton, 1992). The view here is that appropriate training and development of staff leads to improved customer retention, which in turn improves ultimate financial performance. Similarly, learning and development training is viewed as a means of improving the capability of the workforce to benefit efficiencies, which may be measured through KPIs. In turn this is expected to improve financial performance.

Private equity introduces KPIs extensively to gain control of processes and provide insight into improving performance. They also require far more extensive reporting more generally to better capture control. Targets for improvement are set and monitoring of progress ensues. So-called 'operating partners' may also be introduced to assist management in making progress. These are likely to have some equity but are employed to ensure that progress is achieved in line with the plan. They are not always popular with management who see their 'helicopter' presence as having little responsibility but claiming credit when success is achieved.

Private equity are also enthusiastic customers for specialist consultancy services to improve efficiency in supply chain, manufacturing and market/sales effectiveness.

The fundamental basis is measurement, feedback from which is delivered to the relevant parties who then take action to improve the indices. The main drawback with this approach is that whatever is not measured and incentivised is likely to be ignored, or worse abused in the process of improving those focal KPIs. On occasion, the relationship between the selected KPI, the methods elected to improve them and subsequent performance may be questionable. Management can be adept at technical means and approaches to increasing KPIs in such a way that destroys rather than enhances shareholder value.

> **An Example: KPIs or Smoke Screens?**
> I recall a major public company which owned around 100 manufacturing plants worldwide. Performance excellence initiatives focused on plant yield and availability, almost to the exclusion of anything else. Plants were ranked and shamed for poor performance to the extent that local management spent vast sums on labour, training, maintenance and investment in capital equipment to improve these specific KPIs. Meanwhile, escalating costs were scarcely monitored—a fine example of KPIs being pursued at the expense of cost and efficiencies.

Governance and the Problem of Agency

A key difference between the public ownership model and PE is that, for the latter, there is no separation between the owners and the management. PE-owned business boards consist of top managers who, together, typically own 15–30% of the shares, and PE partners who own the rest of the equity. All are involved in operating the business and implementing the plan to add value, although only the management who know the business and industry are fully engaged in its running.

By contrast, in a public company, board members own on average just 3% of the total shares through options and equity, and the owners and board are effectively quite separate (Jensen & Meckling, 1976). Agency theory contends that in principal–agent relationships both parties pursue their own interests unless mechanisms are in place to align these. These mechanisms normally involve greater transparency, achieved through high levels of reporting and appointment of Non-Executive Directors and Chairpersons tasked with the specific remit of looking after and maintaining shareholder interests at board level. They are also concerned with ensuring high levels of governance are implemented and operational. These mechanisms involve independent committees at board level to ensure that remuneration, nominations and accounting standards are appropriately observed and in the interests of shareholders. All these measures are intended to combat the belief that the management will, as agents, pursue their own interests at the expense of their shareholder principals.

Nevertheless, public company management are often motivated by personal status, pay and power above maximising shareholder value. High-risk major acquisitions are an example of this approach. If the prospects of success for major acquisitions are minimal, why do boards approve them?

There are many who believe that the public company governance model has considerable limitations. It is expensive, bureaucratic and can distract attention away from the effective running of the business. Indeed, many question how far the Non-Executive Directors (NEDs) who frequently have limited knowledge of the business and industry itself, can be effective in their roles. The statistics regarding this are revealing: public listed businesses in the USA have reduced from around 10,000 to just 4000 over the last 10 years alone. In the UK, the number of listed companies have halved over the last 25 years. Many have disappeared into private ownership which does not have the extensive requirements of the US Sarbanes–Oxley listing requirements or any other rigid standards of listing to comply with. They may be happier and more efficient without the reporting requirements, governance and scrutiny of the public eye.

As the same problem of agency does not exist with PE, these measures are largely viewed as unnecessary which is evidenced in the board's more productive division of time. From my extensive experience with PE boards, they typically spend around 80% of their time on boosting performance and 20% on other matters. Public boards are the reverse, allocating the majority of board time to governance, reporting and other stakeholder matters. Usually, the Finance Director will be asked to report on performance and offer forecasts for the year. In addition, public boards focus far more on stock market announcements and governance than they do investigating, discussing and, most importantly, improving performance.

This is rendered all the more inefficient when public companies operate two-tier boards, wherein an executive committee runs the business, whilst the board, with its NEDs, reviews any major executive committee decisions, such as substantial investments, acquisitions and various other matters related to governance.

Satisficing: A Decision-Making Strategy?

In most major public businesses, there is an annual budget negotiation between the Head Office (HO) and individual divisions. Most employees are blissfully unaware that this negotiation even takes place. Divisional management are usually heavily bonused on annual profit performance measured against budget. This provides a major incentive for divisional management to propose low profit budgets for the coming year. Clearly, this needs to be agreed by HO and, as a means of making their proposal look more credible, they may suppress the current year's performance in order for the comparative forecast figure to demonstrate progression. In short, they satisfice. Indeed, the data supplied by each function and plant within a division might be similarly mediated in an attempt to maximise the following year's bonus.

Finance Directors (FDs) have plenty of similar opportunities to 'manage' results in terms of creating provisions, one example being asset write-offs. These tactics can lead to perpetual suppression of results, which ultimately removes any significant incentive to improve performance. This is at play to some extent in many major companies as a means of obtaining maximum bonuses with minimal effort. After all, outperformance simply makes the following year's bonus harder to achieve. Any incentives to cut overheads or increase prices are continually limited by counterproductive attempts to suppress performance. Before too long the annual budget setting becomes more of a negotiation than a collaborative attempt to maximise performance and fully utilise assets.

Further still, such budget 'negotiations' more closely resemble a straight discussion of the following year's bonus. Head Office management may be sympathetic towards higher bonuses, considering it is the shareholders who will be paying. This entire process can and often does result in fundamental corporate underperformance in which high bonuses are paid for average performance. Following this line, even the CEO will be proposing bonus plans based on corporate underperformance in an attempt to maximise their pay-out. Having been in similar situations previously, the NEDs may well be sympathetic to this tactic, and as the CEO has a clandestine hand in their selection, they may not want to provide too much opposition.

In contrast, PE tends not to offer significant profit-orientated bonuses, and if they do, they will likely be modest. The real payout, which is often enormous, only occurs on exit. Annual budgets are more closely aligned with their real purpose; they are simply stages in implementing the plan with sights set on the eventual exit.

The Exit

Before exploring incentives and the various means PE employs to add value, it is worth briefly discussing the exit. Whilst assessing the opportunity the key issue is how will an exit be achieved. If there are few interested in acquiring the 'improved' business, then there is little point in taking on the project. The first question is how will an exit be contrived in 3–5 years? Are there interested corporates who would see the business as part of their strategy? Could the business be floated on the stock market? A sale to another PE business is largely viewed as a last resort and would normally fetch lower proceeds. Whatever the proposed exit route, it is the first question to be addressed.

PE Incentives

Having multiple business objectives creates confusion as to which should be priorities. This almost invariably results in mediocre performance. Instead, focusing on a single event or measure provides clarity within an organisation and naturally aligns other actions towards that objective. Organisations attempting to pursue several objectives easily lose direction. This is often the case with charities and public sector organisations in which conflicts arise between staff welfare, service levels, cost effectiveness and the stakeholders that are being served.

In short, PE incentives are highly focused and relate specifically to the singular event of exit. Many in PE will corroborate the basic equation shown in Fig. 4.1.

To break this down further, the specific measures derived from this equation are made up of a number of constituent parts. The three key incentivised measures ('focused incentives') each intent on maximising exit sale proceeds (or 'Clarity of Objectives') are:

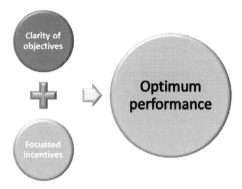

Fig. 4.1 Private equity's simplicity of focus

1. **Exit EBITDA**
2. **Exit Multiple**
3. **Cash Efficiency**

Again, this can be clarified using a simple equation (Fig. 4.2).

Earnings before interest, tax, depreciation and amortisation are a form of proxy for cash generated by a business prior to any working capital requirements and capital expenditure. It also omits funding costs, tax and accounting adjustments that reflect the use of assets, plus any previous payments made over and above asset value. These are the non-cash accounting adjustments that most closely reflect the consumption of other assets purchased in previous accounting periods.

PE is particularly focused on EBITDA as it can be used as a measure of how much debt the business will support. The EBITDA multiple is taken as common currency in the PE world and is used to value a business. It has the advantage of simplicity and often indicates where bidding is likely to open. Adjustments are normally needed for a number of factors which will be covered later in this chapter.

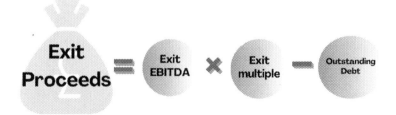

Fig. 4.2 Simplifying the key elements determining the exit proceeds

In essence, the funding costs are a consequence of whether the owner chooses to fund the business through debt or equity. The accounting adjustments for depreciation and amortisation reflect previous asset purchase prices, which are irrelevant to PE or indeed any other buyer. Tax can depend again on chosen tax structures and levels of tax-deductible interest. In short none of these are of great interest to the new owner who will make their own decisions regarding funding and tax.

The key points to remember:

- To optimise exit value then the higher the EBITDA, the better. Exit proceeds are usually assessed from recent comparative transactions in similar industries and are computed as an EBITDA multiple.
- The predominant means of improving EBITDA are through cost reduction, increased prices (provided much trade is not lost) and volume growth, often through finding new markets.
- It comes as a surprise to many how much cost can be removed from a business with a clear focus.

How Does Private Equity Create Value?

There is extensive research available which provides some insight into how private equity creates value. In broad terms, it can be split into three categories, the first being financial engineering (leverage) in which expensive equity is replaced by debt which is lower cost and tax deductible (Guo et al., 2011). Secondly, there is operational improvement which means reducing costs, increasing efficiency and creating growth (Acharya et al., 2013). Thirdly there is the timing of buying and selling, ability to negotiate effectively the deal process and multiple arbitrage (Guo et al., 2011). Multiple arbitrage is explained further later in this chapter, however, its basic rationale involves increasing the size of the business through 'roll-ups,' often known as 'buy and build.' Arbitrage can also be developed through stock market listings.

Broadly speaking, research has determined that each of these approaches contribute around a third to the created value.

1. Cost and Efficiency

Cost is the easiest lever to pull to rapidly increase the EBITDA. Nearly all businesses carry more cost than is strictly necessary. This may have been

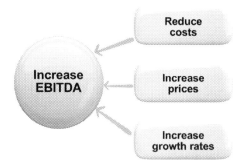

Fig. 4.3 Common measures taken to improve EBITDA

accrued over a protracted period and is often only addressed when the business experiences difficulties in trading, such as during recessions or outbreaks of severe competition. Often a more demanding criterion is needed to assess cost levels which consultants can provide (Fig. 4.3).

> **An Example:**
> Take a business likely to sell on an EBITDA multiple of 10. If we can reduce overheads by £1mn increasing EBITDA by a similar amount, then this is worth an extra £10mn to shareholders in a sale. Looking further we might well find an underperforming management position paid £100K a year. If we can manage without that job, it is worth £1mn to shareholders on exit. In effect, all annual cost savings are leveraged by the exit multiple. This gives rise to a highly incentivised low-cost structure. In public companies, few in management are concerned with staff savings to the same extent, viewing cost savings as a source of bad feeling, upheaval and a slump in morale. Overhead costs may only truly be addressed when the business is in trouble or results take a serious dive.

In addition, there are plant or process efficiencies that, when implemented, may benefit service industries significantly. Manufacturing consultants can be recruited to speed cycle times, reduce manning and cut waste in all plant areas, thereby creating multiple annual savings. Although local management may feel undermined by their presence and demanding regimes, these consultants can be very effective. Hostilities, however, cannot always be overcome; it is not unusual for plant managers who are concerned with pride, rather than plant efficiency to be obstructive and non-compliant. Ultimately, difficult decisions may have to be made.

Similar savings can be generated in supply chains and also service industries, although it should be noted that the areas of waste are quite different and usually reflect fluctuating demand and service levels.

Savings may arise from better controls through improved information systems and technology.

> **An Example: Why High Profits Aren't Always a Sign of Efficiency**
> A major FTSE 250 public company chairman was extolling the virtues of the business and how efficient it was. He failed to realise it was effectively a monopoly and that position was about to be lost as entrants arrived. The main business had 3,500 employees. It plunged into losses with the arrival of competition and a new CEO reduced the workforce to 1,300. Ten years later it was making greater profits than pre-competition times with increased manufactured volumes and a total staff of 1,400 employees. It was not alone in believing its own public relations regarding efficiency.
>
> High profits are often a barrier to efficiency as there is little incentive to review costs. Low profits or losses drive efficiency. Indeed, businesses in industries with lower entry barriers are often far more efficient than those in industries with higher entry barriers which act to protect the business from competition.

2. **Price Increases**

In industries that are not highly commoditised, there is often some scope for pushing prices up without significant loss of trade. Sometimes this can be substantial, for example, in the case of drug companies for which there are limited alternatives. In one scenario, PE has run a 'buy and build' strategy for vets. This allows for the combining of drug buying volumes which should then drive down bulk prices. In terms of selling drugs to pet owners needing pet medication, they can increase prices significantly. Indeed, insurance is now offered to pet owners to cover the vast increase in costs.

Another example is TransDigm, a business which buys up suppliers of parts to Boeing and Airbus, then vastly increases prices. The costs of testing and certifying proprietary parts and respective suppliers are so great that the plane manufacturers do not normally have a dual source or alternative; they simply have to pay. To develop alternative sources would take years and significant expense, but luckily these part cost increases are relatively insignificant to manufacturers on the scale of Boeing and Airbus.

> If you can increase prices without losing trade you have a very good business. If you have to have a prayer session before raising prices by a tenth of a cent, then you have a terrible business. (Warren Buffett, 2010)

Some industries are more price sensitive than others. The determining feature is usually the scale of the industry entry barriers, or the need to copy a product. When copying is difficult due to regulatory restrictions, certification issues or patents, then there may be scope for price increases. Often management do not push prices when they might. There can also be periods of high price inflation when consumers lose track of market prices. These are the times to push prices up. Times of strong resistance are usually those characterised by long-term price stability.

3. **Growth**

If new markets can be found, or the industry is growing rapidly then clearly EBITDA will benefit. This may be a straightforward roll out of a format which has previously proved successful. Typically, a restaurant format can be duplicated geographically, in fact, any sort of chain store formats such as coffee, food, fashion, jewellery or any mainstream retailers that simply require outlets, can be rolled out in areas with appropriate demographics and levels of affluence. In these cases, location is critical. Advertising costs benefit from scope economies, as does central procurement and administration. Indeed, these can be franchised, which limits the risk and investment needed, but can limit the returns.

Alternatively, new markets might be found through exporting or targeting other types of users who might be interested. As will be examined, increased growth rates can also increase the exit multiple.

Exit Multiple

The key element to maximising the exit multiple is timing—waiting for the point when relevant multiples are high, which usually sits alongside high deal volumes. Deal volumes are driven by liquidity and confidence, which means it is relatively easy for companies to borrow money at reasonably low cost. Cheap money drives the pursuit of growth through mergers and acquisitions. It is at this time that public companies are often flush with

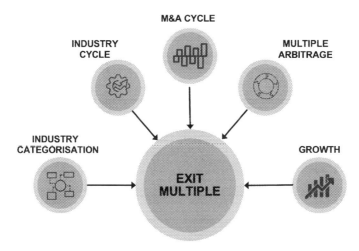

Fig. 4.4 Key factors determining the exit multiple

money and looking for targets. They may well be far less price sensitive than private buyers, again, ideal for the seller of a business. Furthermore, they are frequently less onerous in their negotiation demands.

In this way, public companies are rarely 'good' sellers. They tend to make strategic choices which are governed by speed; they want to see rapid implementation in order to announce their new strategic direction to shareholders. Divestments rapidly follow, regardless of market conditions. If these are poor, then it is the time for PE to buy at low prices. In effect much of the PE model is driven by this process of judiciously timed purchasing: buying cheap during slumps in price and activity cycles and selling high. One slightly different situation is when businesses are bought at the top of the cycle, these often have weaker returns and need to be held longer.

The exit multiple is driven by a number of factors all of which can be harnessed. The foremost of these are playing the relevant M&A and industry cycles, multiple arbitrage, growth and industry categorisation (Fig. 4.4).

M&A Cycle

Deal volumes and values are measured annually, and 2021 alone recorded $5.8tn of deals. This reflected a market in which:

1. There was high liquidity as interest rates remained low.
2. The impact of quantitative easing programmes resulted in commercial bonds being issued at low interest rates.

3. There was a backlog of deals following Covid.

Deal volumes and values do follow cyclical paths which reflect liquidity and confidence in the future. Typically, they are related to inflation, resultant interest rates and economic confidence. High inflation usually increases interest rates and costs, reduces demand and, therefore, lowers deal volumes.

Critically, multiples rise and fall with deal volumes. So those buying in 2021 will have paid high prices compared to other years. For example, US multiples increased by 60% from 2009 (immediately following the banking industry crisis) to 2021 (Pitchbook data, 2022). Those in Europe saw around a 30% rise over the same period. Predictions suggest, however, that both deal volumes and multiples will fall following the inflation of 2022/23, the consequence being higher interest rates and monetary tightening (Fig. 4.5).

As has been established, PE attempts to play the cycles by buying low and selling high wherever they can. In 2021 they sold over $1tn of businesses, but in the same year, flush with money from investors, they also invested in over $1.1tn of businesses (Bain & Co PE Report, 2022). In view of higher multiples, these deals may have to wait for a long time before an adequate return can be made from them.

A classic case in this regard is the purchase of the UK grocery supermarket chain Morrisons by a US PE firm, Clayton Dubilier & Rice, for an enterprise value of £10.1bn, 65% of which it intended to fund by bonds. As bond

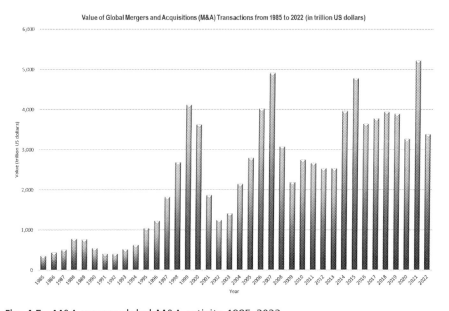

Fig. 4.5 M&A waves: global M&A activity 1985–2022

interest rates increased, the underwriting banks have found themselves in a difficult situation, especially given the amount paid was a massive 40% above the undisturbed share price and around 14 times EBITDA—a high price for an unexciting grocer in slow growth markets. Now CD&R needs to make a significant improvement in value at a very high purchase price. This case study is given a more detailed examination in Chapter 9.

Industry Cycle

Industries have their own cycles independent of M&A. For example, governments attempting to stimulate economies out of recession often invest in infrastructure early in the cycle. They may also choose to subsidise insulation for houses in an attempt to limit carbon production from the heating of homes. This typically stimulates growth within the industry, increasing profits and multiples.

PE will see industry cycles as an effective method of buying and selling at the right times when multiples allow their objectives to be achieved. In recent years, the move by investors to Environment, Social and Governance (ESG) stocks has been reflected in the increased multiples of certain industries, a key example being paper recycling. Broadly, ESG stocks measure their own performance and have targets, policies and procedures in place that are subsequently published. Technology stocks also tend to follow their own cycle. Since a peak in 2021, the fear of recession has seen investors switching from growth stocks to dividend stocks, typically in more mature industries, and technology stocks have been in steep decline although there will no doubt be some recovery in due course.

Commodities too have their own cycles, influencing multiples by fluctuations in their supply and demand. Recent years have seen heavy demand for commodities such as copper and lithium, partly due to heavy investment in the development of electric vehicles, thereby increasing the multiples of mining companies. No doubt in time supply will increase sufficiently to meet demand and prices will then decline, in reality though, it takes some years to open new mining capacity. On the other hand, recessions may reduce demand for what remain relatively expensive products, which would in turn reduce lithium prices. Projections and forecasts are always shifting, but ultimately the market is determined by any number of factors and overconfidence can be disastrous.

Multiple Arbitrage—Size and Public/Private

Multiple arbitrage has a major impact on M&A policy and forms the basis for much value augmentation by PE. Broadly speaking, how this drives strategy is through two basic rules:

1. **Larger Businesses in the Same Industry Command Higher Multiples than Smaller Businesses.**

The rationale is that larger businesses have broader influence, larger market share and greater buying power; when acquired they offer a more significant industry position to the acquirer. So, for example, manufacturing businesses in a particular industry with revenue of, say, £40mn might have an EBITDA multiple of 6, whilst similar but larger businesses of £200mn might have multiples of 8 or 9. This means that PE can buy a number of smaller businesses at a low multiple and then merge them into a larger business which can be sold at a higher multiple. This 'buy and build' strategy is a common means of generating value even, with limited integration.

Typically, there may be coordination of sales policies, procurement and limited back-office integration, but only as a means of driving economies of scope. This is currently a common policy in both the veterinary industry and builders' merchants where independent merchants are acquired in a chain that covers an increasingly larger geographic area. The hope is that buying power will be increased and competition between owned merchants reduced. Eventually, a higher multiple exit is anticipated based on the logic of multiple arbitrage.

2. **Public Companies Have Higher Multiples than Private Businesses for a Similar Size.**

This difference in valuation is a consequence of a number of factors, such as the ability to trade shares in a liquid market, high levels of reporting required by the listing stock market and specified levels of governance involving Non-Executive Directors, Committees and Board Meetings.

In terms of equity liquidity, reporting and governance there are few basic legal requirements for private business. As a result, investors often have less confidence in these businesses and more in public companies which have a higher valuation multiple. This has two PE effects in terms of adding value: the first is that an Initial Public Offering as an exit is likely to be at a higher multiple, assuming there is market appetite for the shares. An exit sale to a public company is also likely to command a higher multiple. The public company multiple will apply to profits of any related business they buy, allowing much more scope to pay a higher price. Indeed, PE views public companies as ideal buyers for this reason. In most sale situations then, the best proceeds are normally obtained from public companies. PE buyers pay far less. Indeed, Bargeron et al. (2007) found that, on average, public companies pay 55% more than PE when acquiring a business.

With higher multiples accorded to public companies compared to private, the latter can usually enhance their valuation simply by listing. This also results in greater ease of raising funds. It does also mean much higher costs of governance, audit, extensive reporting and controls on the flow of information due to price sensitivity.

Growth

In effect, the exit multiple is determined by the industry and the specific growth rate of the business. Industries such as technology may have high growth rates and are likely to see high multiples. If a business has been growing rapidly—either organically or through numerous acquisitions—then it may be accorded a higher multiple than the industry average. In short, growth matters both for industries and businesses; a good growth record should result in a higher valuation.

Industry Categorisation

Some industries simply have much higher multiples than others. For example, large consumer brands or pharmaceuticals usually command high multiples; this reflects their growth potential and the perceived difficulties others might have in copying the product or service. Technology shares exhibit similarly high multiples, both because copying their market position is seen as difficult and because shares are viewed as having substantial growth potential. A consequence is that Venture Capital (VC) or PE will try and reposition the business in a higher-valued industry, ideally in a sector which is seen as having high growth rates and/or positions which are difficult to copy.

In contrast, taxi firms would have low multiples due to low long-term margins, and subsequently, VC has tried to reposition them as technology firms. We see this with takeaway food delivery and short-term office space rental (such as WeWork)—indeed, it seems almost any company with an app can be treated as a technology firm. In fact, having an app has become almost standard for all firms and across many industries, although with varying quality and capability.

Through historic diversification or vertical integration, it can be the case that a business operates in more than one industry. This always leads to confusion in the valuation and discounting of the multiple. Disposal of such divisions usually enhances the remaining multiple, for example, a business with a small plastic packaging arm which is viewed as being in a declining market might receive a multiple of 4, whilst the main business in building materials has a multiple of 7. The market would, therefore, discount the entire business to say 5. In such a case selling off the smaller division would help realise the full potential of the building materials multiple.

Conglomerates which occupy positions in a number of industries are usually accorded low valuations. This is partly due to the difficulties in valuing the business but investors also dislike conglomerates; lack of transparency in reporting, cross-funding and a belief that management do not have the capabilities to manage across very different industries, are all contributing factors (Fig. 4.6).

Managing Cash Efficiency

In a business sale, the contract normally states that the business is sold both debt and cash free. This means that any debt must be deducted from the proceeds and any free cash added back. Therefore, minimising debt through good cash management practices increases the sale proceeds which are shared by management and PE, providing a major incentive for efficient cash management. Such incentives are rare in public companies and often insignificant, except when the business is faced with a major crash squeeze and there is a desperation to find cash.

Leverage

PE relies on borrowed funds for generating higher levels of return to equity. Debt is tax deductible and usually available at much lower cost than equity. It allows equity to generate much higher levels of return with much lower risk to the equity suppliers who are providing less investment whilst debt providers are carrying more risk. Clearly, the business as a whole is more at risk if circumstances result in an inability to pay debts as they become due. We examine the consequences of debt funding in more depth in the next chapter 'Process and Valuation.'

Fig. 4.6 How private equity reduce high-cost debt levels

Motivation Provided by Expensive Debt Funding

It is likely that a proportion of PE funding for a business is provided in the form of convertible debt finance, at an annual interest rate of around 10% or more. The arrangement is that management should pay this off over a specified period, normally around 3–5 years. Beyond this specified period, it converts to equity owned by PE, which vastly reduces the returns that management are likely to make. This provides a huge incentive to management to clear the PE debt as soon as possible.

Clearly, there are ways of reducing this expensive PE debt, the key means being:

1. **Minimise working capital** by extending trade creditors, reducing trade debtors and reducing stocks. In many ways, these are not difficult to do

but are often ignored due to lack of incentives. If shareholders are to keep any cash gains, that serves as a major incentive to do something. Longer credit terms can often be negotiated with suppliers, and there are processes which can result in trade debtors paying more promptly. Similarly, stock management can be enhanced through better focus and attention.
2. **Sell off unnecessary assets or auxiliary businesses**. A business may have property which can be sold and leased back. There may be saleable business streams which are independent of the main core business and can be sold by raising cash. All help with clearing the high-cost PE debt.
3. **Finance assets using commercial debt** which, having security, is usually a fraction of the interest cost of the PE debt. An alternative to the sale and leaseback of property is to borrow using the property as security which will have much lower interest rates and contribute to paying down PE debt.
4. **Use retained profits to pay down PE debt** rather than reinvesting in marginal capital investments and R&D projects, unless they have a strong chance of making good returns. Retained profits in many corporations are reinvested in high-risk projects which have a limited chance of making acceptable returns rather than being returned to shareholders.

Summary

As we have seen, PE has a variety of techniques at their disposal to increase exit proceeds. Through focused management of EBITDA, the exit multiple and cash, the incentives to shareholders can be enormous and direct. There is generally little in the way of pay-outs to management and shareholders until exit. My experience and analysis suggest PE provides a clear road map of how value can be added, and a basic blueprint of elements which are applicable to other forms of ownership, including public companies. Clearly, highly focused incentives are needed to help management concentrate on the right elements.

When it comes to buying and selling businesses, timing is all: buy at low points in the cycle and sell at higher points. Prepare businesses for sale by reducing costs and finding growth markets to improve performance and offer a growth-based future. Arbitrage works for public companies as well as any other. Safer strategies, such as buying smaller businesses at lower multiples, are consistently shown to be more effective than buying large businesses (public or private) at high multiples which risks value dilution. If the integration is then ineffective, the acquisition is very likely to destroy significant shareholder value.

Most, if not all, of the typical PE approaches and philosophies can be applied to businesses in other ownership forms to good effect. Cash efficiency is available to all—it is simply a matter of identifying the most appropriate and motivating incentives.

Key Questions PE Investors Ask When Identifying Targets

1. Can the target business be bought at a price which will allow the scope for making the necessary returns investors are anticipating?
2. Who will buy the business in 3 to 5 years time? What will be the exit route?
3. What is the opportunity? Can we reduce costs, increase prices or find growth markets?
4. Is the management team appropriate for the challenge of major change and improving the business to the extent planned?
5. Are there assets or parts of the business which are unnecessary to sustain the core business and could be sold off to reduce the debt?
6. Are there assets which can be used as collateral against debt to allow access to low-cost borrowing?
7. Can we increase the exit multiple through timing the various cycles, increasing the growth rate or improving the industry categorisation?
8. Can we build a bigger business by acquiring similar businesses and merging them to increase the exit multiple? Can we list the business as an exit option to increase the exit multiple?

References and Recommended Readings

Acharya, A., Gottschalg, O., Hahn, M., & Kehoe, C. (2013). Corporate Governance and Value Creation: Evidence from Private Equity. *The Review of Financial Studies, 26*(2), 368–402.

Aramonte, S., & Avalos, F. (2021). The Rise of Private Markets. *BIS Quarterly Review*, 21-12.

Bain and Co. (2022). *Private Equity Global Report 2022*.

Bargeron, L., Schlingeman, F. P., Stulz, R., & Zutter, C. J. (2007). Why Do Private Acquirers Pay so Little Compared to Public Acquirers? *Monetary Economics*.

Barber, F. & Gould, (2007). The Strategic Secret of Private Equity. *Harvard Business Review, vol. 85* (9). 53–62.

Buffett, W. (2010, May 28). *Transcript of Interview with Warren Buffett*. United States of America Financial Crisis Inquiry Commission.

Burrough, B., & Helyar, J. (1990). *Barbarians at the Gate: The Fall of RJR Nabisco*. Arrow Books.

Fraser-Sampson, G. (2010). *Private Equity as an Asset Class* (2nd ed.). Wiley.

Gadiesh, O., & MacArthur, H. (2008). *Lessons From Private Equity Any Company Can Use*. Harvard Business Review Press.

Gompers, P. A., & Kaplan, S. N. (2022). *Advanced Introduction to Private Equity*. Elgar Advanced Introductions.

Guo, S., Hotchkiss, E. S., & Song, W. (2011). Do Buyouts (Still) Create Value? *Journal of Finance, 66*(2), 479–517.

Harris, R., Jenkinson, T., & Kaplan, S. (2014). Performance of Private Equity Funds: What Do We Know? *Journal of Finance, 69*(5), 1851–1882.

Jensen, M. & Meckling, W. (1976). Theory of the firm: Managerial behavior, agency costs and capital structure. *Journal of Financial Economics*, 3, 305–360.

Kaplan, R.S., & Norton, D. (1992). The Balanced Scorecard: Measures that Drive Performance. *Harvard Business Review, 70*(1), 71.

Pozen, R. C. (2007). If Private Equity Sized Up Your Business. *Harvard Business Review, 85*(11), 78–152.

5

Comparing Private Equity and Corporate Approaches to M&A

Introduction

This chapter compares the approach to mergers and acquisitions (M&A) of private equity (PE) with that of corporates. Its advice makes certain, necessary generalisations, for example, that PE investors are reasonably consistent in their approach, whilst corporates vary dramatically in their professionalism and attitudes towards generating value. The objective of this comparison is to tease out guidance regarding best practice which can be adopted by those who are involved in strategy, negotiations or integration at all levels of management seniority.

The PE model has many enemies, attracting criticism for the active pursuit of cost reduction and high leverage. However, there is much to be learnt from PE's thorough and consistent disciplines when it comes to buying, managing and selling businesses. It is possible to select and implement certain value-adding practices without necessarily adopting the elements of PE that are singularly oriented towards an exit point.

Chapter 6 considers possible scenarios for the future of PE. It has been growing rapidly and at the expense of public listed corporations which in the USA and UK have roughly halved in number over the last 25 years. PE's success has allowed them to raise enormous sums of dry powder which can subsequently be invested, recently estimated at $3.7tn globally (see Fig. 5.1). PE has access to a pool of investors' money which needs investing in new schemes. This increasing pressure to invest is something to be cautious of,

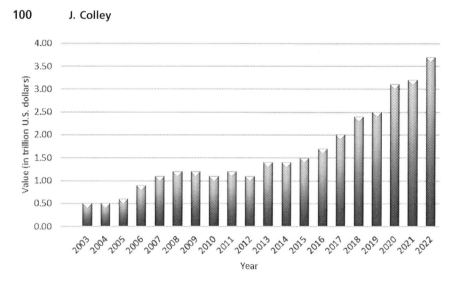

Fig. 5.1 Value of private equity dry powder globally 2003–2022

given that it is likely to result in higher-risk investments as a means of maintaining previous return levels. Targets are only likely to be made available if higher prices are paid.

From 2022 onwards, liquidity has tightened, and the cost of debt has drastically increased. The era of cheap borrowing is over for now, which means not only more difficulty in borrowing, but lower returns on projects as the costs of debt take their toll. PE investors are struggling to sell businesses as buyers have disappeared, which means selling them to other PE funds, a transaction fraught with conflicts of interest. This chapter considers some of the likely consequences of these complex dynamics, and what mechanisms are in place to support their implementation.

How Corporates and PE Differ in Approach to M&A

Philosophy and Objectives

Before we can really explore what can be learnt from the highly disciplined approach of private equity, it is useful to examine the differences in philosophy and objectives between PE and corporates. Some consultants hold the view that the difference is fundamentally one of 'professionals' and 'amateurs' when it comes to deals. Undoubtedly there are many professional corporates when it comes to M&A but equally there are many which are not.

The opinion is based on the premise that much of PE's skill set is first and foremost that of undertaking transactions, which for some is a full-time job.

Meanwhile, corporates view deal-making as a 'means to an end,' and not a source of value in itself. Periodically they make decisions to dispose of businesses, which amounts to just that—a rapid transaction with limited determination as to extracting the best possible value. Limited attention is given to preparing the business for sale or timing, such as where in the pricing and M&A activity cycle the disposal will occur. In short, little effort is made to maximise proceeds other than running a competitive tender process. For corporates, the strategy is the dominant feature rather than worrying about extracting value from the M&A process itself.

1. Improvement Versus Integration Synergies

PE's approach is that transactions such as buying and selling businesses are important elements of value creation, as is the improvement process. Their job is to buy low and sell high. This contrasts with that of the corporates which have a long-term strategic plan in which the acquisition is presumed to fit. Subsequently, the negotiation is far less about value and more about ensuring the target is acquired. This difference in motivation means a failed negotiation is viewed more as a strategic failure rather than a dispute over value. One result of this is that prices paid for businesses are higher and less demands are made in terms of warranties and indemnities. Bargeron et al. found that in bids for US public companies between 1996 and 2005, the difference between the successful bid and the undisturbed share price was 44.6% for public bidders and 27.6% for PE (Bargeron et al., 2007).

Corporates generate value from acquisitions that create synergies with the rest of their business, so the integration process is the main source of creating strategic value. In contrast, PE only occasionally integrates and typically seeks to improve their businesses through efficiency measures and means of growth.

What then can corporates learn from PE in terms of value creation? This question is addressed through different stages of the M&A process.

2. Negotiation

PE investors have their own specialist negotiators who are renowned for giving little away. They know exactly where the value lies in a negotiation, what risks they will accept and which they will leave with the other party. They also have very clear 'red lines' which they will not cross when it comes to value. If you are negotiating with PE investors, then expect a hard time and to be lumbered with plenty of warranties and indemnities. They are also constantly attempting to pull value onto their side of the line, despite the agreed heads of terms which document the initial agreement (which are not legally binding). In short, they are tough, highly skilled negotiators who will 'chip' value at every opportunity. Consider how interested in transacting with them you may be before approaching the negotiation. Some PE houses will bid high, then constantly 'chip' the price once other bidders have dropped out of the running. Research finds that 36.2% of PE negotiations fail, predominantly over price disputes, whilst the comparative figure for public companies is just 13.8%. Most of the PE withdrawals are a result of disputes following due diligence.

In a recent deal in which I was involved, a corporate was so determined to buy a business that they were willing to pay 14 × EBITDA, when PE would have valued the business at around just 6 × EBITDA and, such was the haste to complete the deal, virtually no indemnities or warranties required. The benefits to that corporate were that they made their money upstream and so could supply raw materials downstream to the acquired business at a substantial profit. They envisaged long-term strategic benefits from the transaction and so were willing to pay whatever price was necessary. It was also a relatively small deal in the context of that business, which meant they were less concerned with the amount agreed on. Some of their deal team members were experienced in the process of deals and some were not; this again contrasts with PE investors who are exclusively experienced in the deal process.

Corporates often use external advisory parties and may be occasional in their approach to deals. Consequently, some are less experienced in transactions and negotiations. Large corporates who grow through acquisition often do many deals and are highly professional in their approach, developing their own centres of excellence, manuals, training and a house approach for relevant employees. In short, they have dedicated professionals perpetually occupied in deals and integrations. It is the occasional dealers who are more exposed. Typically, corporates exceeding 5 smaller deals every year are far more successful than those which undertake a large transformative deal every few years (Giersberg et al., 2020).

3. Time Frames, Benefits and Pricing

PE investors have a very clear medium-term focus of approximately 3 to 5 years between buying and selling a given business. This invariably creates the expectation that major focused change needs to occur in a short space of time. As we have seen, this specific focus is on adding value through increasing the EBITDA, the multiple and the cash flow in a bid to minimise debt. This drives an almost manic pace of change in the business to find growth markets in which they can compete.

This change dynamism can be more difficult to identify and harness in large corporates, who become easily bogged down with a variety of internal initiatives. This often results in difficulties prioritising, and the same level and type of value-adding change may receive a lower priority and take much longer. PE investors, therefore, adopt a more single-minded focus, consistently pursuing initiatives which will improve exit proceeds.

Corporates actively look to create benefits through integration synergies by merging new acquisitions into their current businesses. The benefits of this might include lower costs, increased revenue, a greater resource of expertise or technology and the ability to capture upstream supply or downstream demand. These same benefits can also be achieved by entering new markets, both related and unrelated. Time scales in such circumstances may be significantly longer, but the belief in extending and expanding reach and revenue is more important than specific efficiency measures. Consequently, the latter of these are often sidelined unless depressed results demand action.

4. Fear of Missing Out (FOMO) and Relative Competitor Advantage

Corporates buy a business on the basis that they will keep it. In a bidding war, this easily pushes the price upwards, driven by a real fear of a missed opportunity. If they fail to acquire and it goes to a competitor, then it may never become available again. They may then have to suffer a permanent strategic disadvantage against a competitor who won the deal. Should the target go to PE, then it will become available again in time but at a much higher price.

PE takes a different view; their philosophy dictates that unless they can make a return for their investors in a finite time, they will not initiate the deal. It is usually the case that they will be looking at many potential deals consecutively and can quite easily move on to one that is more likely to deliver the significant economic benefits they require. Evidence consistently finds that PE investors pay less than corporates (Bargeron et al., 2007).

PE investors apply consultants to any part of the business they believe can be made more efficient. This includes supply chains, manufacturing, stock fulfilment, selling and overheads. Similarly, they will use consultants to explore new markets and assess any as yet unharnessed benefits in the future. They do not believe they are the oracle as far as industry or business knowledge is concerned, but they will certainly make an objective assessment that evaluates the most effective source of improvement for the business. Many of these efficiencies could be achieved by corporates if they were inclined to both adopt a more rigorous outlook and consider sources of revenue beyond their own resources.

An example of this would be the exclusion of manufacturing consultants simply to avoid the injured pride of the current manufacturing management. Even when consultants are used to drive efficiency, any benefits and new approaches introduced are often lost once the consultants leave. Permanent change can be difficult to maintain. PE partners are much less forgiving of management and use Key Performance Indicators (KPIs) extensively to monitor change and maintain target conditions.

5. Performance

PE investors are driven by a cycle of fundraising every 2–3 years which requires their previous performance to be disclosed and marketed as a means of raising new funds. Their ability to raise new funds depends on past performance, they too need to perform in the deals they take on.

Corporates may perform well but with modest-sized deals they do not have to declare subsequent performance. This lessens the degree of pressure and also means failures can be 'buried,' provided they are not too big. Very few corporates promote deal performance in any detail, and transparency is not a given part of the reporting of acquisition outcomes and performance. In major deals listing requirements may necessitate some indication of subsequent performance to be disclosed, but this may be both limited and short term. It can also be manipulated to present a more favourable picture.

In 2022 Unilever were accused by a fund manager, Terry Smith, of having made a number of acquisitions without disclosing any indication of subsequent performance (*FT*, Jan 11, 2023). Unilever responded that the acquisitions in question had shown growth in the mid-teens percentage but steadfastly refused to provide any further detail. Large deals are much harder to obscure and there will be a greater expectation that performance is disclosed. They are also much more likely to influence the share price. Terry Smith of 'Fundsmith' is known for his mantra 'Buy good companies, do not overpay, do nothing.'

6. Due Diligence

Due diligence is the process by which a potential buyer can conduct a thorough examination of the affairs of the business it wishes to acquire. The process normally involves third parties performing in-depth investigations and delivering a report on their findings to the client. It is not a cheap process, so buyers need to be serious before commissioning such work. Sellers may attempt to limit the scope of the due diligence citing time or commercial secrecy (particularly if the buyer is a competitor). This is in addition to the data room made available by the seller to potential acquirers. Due diligence takes different forms depending on whether the buyer is a corporate or PE and reflects the different philosophies underlying their approach.

Corporates want to be reassured that there are no major hidden risks in a target acquisition. Typically, they use external parties to perform legal and financial due diligence but use their own people to undertake the operational and commercial due diligence, the rationale being that they have specific industry knowledge of these areas. The in-house due diligence may not be that deep but may serve to increase understanding and determine whether what they believe already is correct. If there is a strong drive from the senior team to make the acquisition, then this is likely to influence the depth of the internal due diligence. In effect, internal commercial and operational due diligence is more about familiarisation than looking for deal breakers or price chips. In-house due diligence teams are often as enthusiastic as senior management about achieving the acquisition, so their investigation is not intended to identify deal breakers.

For PE, due diligence serves several rather different objectives. Commercial and operational due diligence is normally externally sourced and very deep, intended to not only identify risks but to inform any subsequent transformation plan. It may assess the quality of people and whether and where efficiencies can be achieved, usually by engaging consultants or investment. Similarly, market reviews may be about whether there are underexploited markets or segments that can be realistically accessed alongside the more typical areas, such as customer concentration and customer margins. Clearly high customer concentration can be a major risk post-acquisition. Competitors will be assessed for relative strength and threats posed by developments. Margins will be assessed to see whether there is scope for better prices without losing too much business. There is also usually an evaluation of the quality of information available for management to control the business.

PE investors are much more likely to use the due diligence to chip away at the price, and they are far more likely to walk away from a deal if they believe the price should be lower, due to investment requirements or having uncovered other disadvantages. If adverse factors or risks place the hurdle rate of return in jeopardy, then they will ask for a lower price or walk away (Bargeron et al., 2007).

7. Consideration

PE always pays with cash. There may be management earnouts if their forecast performance (upon which the price may be based) is demanding. However, these are becoming less popular as they restrict the new owners from taking full control and making changes during the earn out period. The management would claim that PE intervention had destroyed their chances of hitting forecasts.

Corporates often offer a mix of their own shares and cash. This has the advantage of conserving cash and requires less external access to capital. To the seller it means some tax can be deferred until they sell their new shares. It also means that they must accept the risks and benefits of owning the new shares. If they have a large number, then they may be required to 'lock in' for a period of a year or more during when they cannot sell their shares, so as to prevent collapsing the share price through large volumes of shares being pushed onto the market.

8. Culture

There are very different attitudes to culture between corporates and PE. For the most part, PE investors ignore culture as the management are often retained post-acquisition, and there is unlikely to be an integration with another business. There will, however, be other stresses on management as the pace of change will need to be increased under PE and this will likely be met with some cultural and managerial opposition. PE investors largely take the view that they will change the people, if necessary, to achieve their objectives. For 'buy and build' strategies, integration is normally limited to the areas which will produce benefits such as buying in bulk or coordinating sales efforts, limiting the problems associated with conflicting cultures.

For corporates, different and incompatible cultures can be a major problem during and after integration. Cultural issues will slow the integration progress and, therefore, any derivable benefits. Large, well-established businesses will only change culture slowly whatever the intervention. I have worked in a number of businesses which have existed for over 200 years and entrenched cultures usually win the battle over new management. Many consultants offer 'culture change' training, but I am sceptical as to their long-term effectiveness. Learning to work with different cultures is more likely to be helpful.

9. **Disposals**

Attitudes towards disposals between PE and corporates are very different. Corporates typically redefine their core industries periodically to focus on growth. Businesses sitting outside the newly defined core or those considered perennial under-performers are presented for disposal almost immediately. The corporation wants to demonstrate the new strategy immediately to shareholders, media and other stakeholders. The board are keen to demonstrate a strategic shift is being promptly implemented.

A second reason for 'dumping' the business without ceremony is internal opposition. There will be significant constituencies within the corporate who want to retain these units, including the senior executives who have responsibility for them. All see their empires diminishing and conceivably a round of cost-cutting for those supplying functional, product or geographic services. Mounting opposition can defer or hinder implementation whilst internal lobbying is rife. A rapid sale circumvents much of this.

The consequence of a hasty disposal is usually a poor price. Lack of preparation and timing, coupled with little real determination around disposal price means proceeds are likely to be poor. A UK FTSE 100 business I previously worked for decided to refocus its core towards very specific markets, including a greater geographic reach. Seven businesses sat outside this core definition and so were immediately marketed by a very inexperienced central strategy team. The businesses concerned had limited market shares in their industries and were largely underinvested. The sale proceeds were significantly below expectations. One of the businesses was retained after much internal lobbying, which would have been better sold.

In contrast, PEs' entire rationale is to maximise disposal proceeds. From the moment the business is acquired, all efforts are directed towards the exit event. EBITDA is enhanced through cost-cutting and growth measures and the multiple increased by ascertaining growth markets and developing products which will transform the nature of the business. The timing of the marketing process for the business is critical. We know that M&A activity is cyclically governed by liquidity, interest rates and cash availability. It also relies on confidence in the future business environment. Transaction multiples do tend to shift with overall acquisition activity. They also move with industry business cyclicality and sentiment towards the industry. During periods of high liquidity, for example, between 2015 and 2021, growth stocks were in vogue and particularly technology stocks. Growth stock multiples ran at high levels, whilst more mature income stocks were undervalued. As inflation increased, government quantitative easing was withdrawn and interest rates increased, growth stocks collapsed in value, whilst perceived income stocks recovered value.

PE investors are adept at preparing businesses to be marketed at the right time to exploit both industry and overall M&A activity. In short, they play the cycles. In addition, they are professional negotiators who know where the value lies in a deal. They are highly disciplined and leave maximum risk and liability to the other parties in any negotiation. Their business is deals and practise builds a high skill set with which corporates doing occasional deals cannot compete.

10. CEOs

Research has found significant character differences between CEOs employed by PE and those of corporates (Kaplan et al., 2012). PE investors often change the CEO to someone who understands both their philosophy and their financial approach. This person must be capable of achieving rapid transformation and be willing to facilitate rapid change such as cutting costs and overheads, improving efficiencies and identifying new channels to market. Many CEOs dislike the process of cost reduction, which frequently involves redundancies and terminations. The sheer pace of PE change must be experienced to be understood, and the CEOs selected to run such businesses have often worked with PE before.

Corporates look for people with a track record that demonstrates excellent communication skills (Kaplan et al., 2012). They must convince shareholders and many other stakeholders of the chosen strategy and deal with public relations for important issues. Corporates must disclose large amounts of information, meaning they can be held accountable by governments, customers, employees and pressure groups. PE investors disclose very little which means, aside from their own investors, they are far less accountable. Governance requirements are also much reduced, and this subject is examined in relation to both corporates and PE in Chapter 8.

Lessons
1. PE investors are highly professional negotiators and approach the deal process as a source of value generation. If they can't buy at the right price, they know there will be other deals and will walk away.
2. Corporates view deals and negotiations as a means of achieving a strategy rather than a means of generating immediate value.

3. Evidence suggests that corporates who undertake a number of smaller deals each year have more successful strategies in place (Giersberg et al., 2020). A combination of practice and having dedicated teams for deals and integration improves the prospects of value creation.
4. Integration can be a fraught process and an easy way to destroy value if ineptly handled. It requires intense internal focus and can result in other efficiency and cost opportunities being sidelined.
5. PE investors generally avoid integration even in 'buy and build' strategies, and only integrate as part of certain value-creating activities, for example, the buying function in which combined volumes/services can leverage lower prices or market coordination.
6. Can consultants help with operational, commercial, supply chain and overhead efficiency? If you believe so then do not be deterred by internal opposition; it often reflects pride as opposed to an objective assessment of effectiveness.
7. Timings of acquisitions and disposals matter. Acquisitions at the top of the cycle and disposals at the bottom of the market both spell value destruction.
8. Corporates buy when their performance is strong and sell when performing badly. PE investors attempt to do the opposite.
9. Due diligence is viewed by PE as a critical part of the process and is usually undertaken by external advisors and consultants. It is a deep and thorough assessment which supports both the negotiation and subsequent improvement plan. For corporates, due diligence may focus on legal and financial enquiry only and is designed to ensure there are no major unknown liabilities. Even if risks are identified, corporates may sometimes remain keen to pursue the deal.
10. Due diligence is used to inform the improvement plan for PE. This should be created and ready to be implemented immediately after acquisition. Whilst the same should be true for corporates, it may often be less clear.
11. When disposing of a business, aim to find a corporate buyer rather than PE, simply because they are likely to pay more, reflect the synergies that can be extracted and engage in less onerous negotiations.

References and Recommended Readings

Acharya, V., Gottschalg, O., Hahn, M., & Kehoe, C. (2012). *Corporate Governance and Value Creation: Evidence from Private Equity; European Corporate Governance Institute Finance*. Working Paper.

Barber, F., & Gould, M. (2007, September). The Strategic Secret of PE. *Harvard Business Review*.

Bargeron, L. L., Schingeman, F. P., Stulz, R. M., & Zutter, C. J. (2007). Why Do Private Acquirers Pay so Little Compared to Public Acquirers? *Journal of Financial Economics, 89*(3), 375–390.

Giersberg, J., Krause, J., Rudnicki, J., & West, A. (2020, April 30). The Power of Through Cycle M&A. *McKinsey Quarterly*.

Gottschalg, O., & Phalippou, L. (2007). The Truth About Private Equity Performance. *Harvard Business Review, 85*(12).

Gompers, P. A., & Kaplan, S. N. (2022). *Advanced Introduction to Private Equity*. Elgar Advanced Introductions.

Kaplan, S. N., Klebanov, M. M., & Sorensen, M. (2012). Which CEO Characteristics and Abilities Matter? *The Journal of Finance, 67*(3), 973–1007.

Walsh, B., Morris, J., Pau, P., & Pais, L. (2023). How Private Equity Firms Create Value in Uncertain Times. *Harvard Business Review*.

6

The Future of Private Equity

Introduction

In many ways, PE can be viewed as standing at a developmental crossroads as to whether it can keep growing or has now reached a plateau. In terms of past success, the PE model outperforms most other forms of investment. As a direct consequence they have been able to raise large investment funds, which raises several questions:

- Will there still be suitable available targets which can be acquired at attractive prices?
- Will those involved in PE need to take greater risks to achieve targeted returns?
- Will adequate, appropriately priced exits continue to be available when disposing of businesses? The PE model relies on identifying buyers who are willing to pay a price which allows PE to make a substantial return.
- In what looks to be an era of higher interest rates, how will this affect the profitability of the PE model, which in part depends on low-cost finance?
- PE's rapid expansion has been, in part, at the expense of stock market-listed corporates for which numbers are continuing to fall rapidly. How will this influence investors, stock markets and the nature of industry?

Recent Developments

What we know about PE is that they are keen to follow the money and pursue demand trends which result in higher business valuations. So, whatever is in vogue from an investor perspective then PE will pursue for as long as it increases exit valuations. Investor trends do come and go over time, which means pursuing a particular investor market during a period when trends change can leave PE exposed. For example, early-stage technology stocks have suffered as investors position themselves for recession by moving into dividend stocks. Indeed, during 2022, technology stocks collapsed in value, partly due to the shift to more mature stocks but also due to the dawning realisation that previous expectations of growth were overly optimistic. More speculative early-stage businesses are struggling to find investors following a refocus on lower risk areas. Recent trends which have benefitted from higher valuations include:

1. Stocks with strong sustainability credentials
2. Software developers
3. Early-stage technology start-ups
4. Public to private companies

Performance

In the 10 years prior to 2022, global PE returns achieved an Internal Rate of Return (IRR) of 16.9% annualised (according to PitchBook data). In effect, the initial investment is generating an aggregate compound return of 16.9% each year. This includes the peak period of Covid commencing 2020 when few investments were made or sold. It also includes the third quarter of 2022 when deal transactions collapsed, falling 60% compared to the first half.

Fundraising by PE approached $800bn in 2021, but fell back to $655bn in 2022, which is closer to the average fundraising over the last five years. 10 years ago, average fundraising was around $200bn a year (McKinsey Global Markets Review, 2023). PE activity has effectively more than tripled over the last decade, whilst listed markets in North America and Europe have continued to decline rapidly. PE Assets Under (Fig. 6.1) Management (AUM) now total $11.7tn.

Future growth expectations are important in determining the sectors targeted for investment. It is never easy selling businesses in low growth

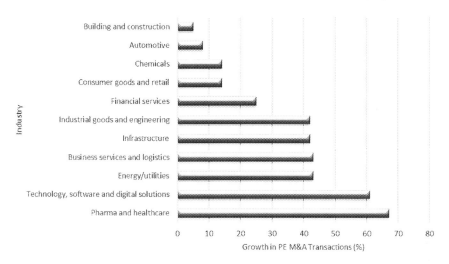

Fig. 6.1 Growth expectations of private equity M&A in Europe 2023 (by industry)

sectors. At the same time, high growth sectors typically attract high multiples for both buying and selling. As we can see from (Fig. 6.2), the higher growth sectors attract high multiples.

1. **Sustainability Credentials**

There is little doubt that PE is highly focused on shareholder rather than stakeholder returns. If improving other stakeholder benefits also further enhances shareholder returns, then that becomes an attractive course of action. Indeed, PE investors have few preconceived ideas about other stakeholders and, if benefitting their situation improves overall returns, then they will. If improving wages and employee relations, customer service and products and local and government relations may be advantageous for shareholder returns, then that too accords with PE aims. Similarly, sustainability, climate change and minimising wastage are all likely to be positive for shareholders, not least because this means they may be eligible for inclusion in 'sustainability funds.'.

In recent years, some organisations have required investment in 'green' funds that encourage the pursuit of activities viewed as beneficial to society. Funds with 'green' credentials have seen their value rise. Indeed, between 2019 and 2021, funds flowing into 'sustainable' stocks tripled from around $200bn to $600bn globally. The vast bulk of this increase came from within Europe and the UK. Subsequently, fund in-flows have slowed as performance has not satisfied expectations.

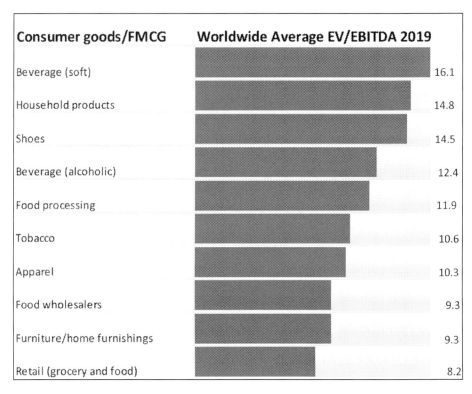

Fig. 6.2 Consumer goods/FMCG global average multiples by sector

Financial regulators are becoming more concerned with the proliferation of spurious claims made by fund managers to claim a share of this 'sustainable' funds flow. There are few generally agreed-upon criteria as to which businesses should qualify, hence why fund managers and consultants have taken to inventing their own. The highly flexible nature of the concept has allowed them to rebadge funds as 'sustainable' despite dubious credentials. 'Greenwashing' as it has been named, has become prevalent enough to damage the very concept for those businesses who are making genuine and material efforts towards sustainability.

For PE wishing to exit 'improved' businesses, qualifying for the sustainable funds' criterion is an opportune means of enhancing value. In practice, this means introducing suitable policies and targets, appropriate reporting of progress and frequent audits to ensure compliance. This approach and its documentation need to be transparent and made available to all stakeholders. Progress against measures and targets will likely require investment in both capital and higher levels of training throughout the organisation. The benefits are likely to go way beyond share valuation but only with markedly reduced energy usage and less waste. Clearly, the policy needs to extend beyond the confines of the business to include the supply chain and eventual disposal of products produced and sold.

PE investors are notoriously quick to seize on an opportunity. This one may be transitory, given the rise in 'greenwashing' and the scepticism now surrounding the concept. Financial regulators are doing little more than warning the most extreme transgressors, but until there are accepted standards (as there are with product performance claims) accompanied by regular audits and mandatory certification, then the situation will not improve.

2. Software

Software development businesses have done well in recent years and generally command higher valuations than many other industries. PE investors believe this trend is robust and long term. Around 60% of early-stage businesses are software development-based, which has attracted the interest of PE. Returns on exit (Multiples on Invested Capital) have been in the region of 2.4 × investment which compares to 2.2 more generally for PE (Bain and Co. Report, 2022). 2022 saw an investor shift to 'value' businesses from 'growth', which resulted in growth business valuations falling 25% compared to the 5% fall in the value sector (*Financial Times*, 7 Dec 2022). This fall will no doubt have affected software business valuations. PE growth investments have been the highest performing sector over the last 10 years, the bulk of which is software.

3. Early Stage

Historically, PE has been separated from Venture Capital (VC) due to major differences in the way that investments are managed and valued. The PE question is 'How can the business be improved to increase its value?' Whilst the VC question is 'Is there a viable business?' One deals with relatively mature businesses, whilst the other is concerned with the early-stage development of businesses for which there may not be a clear and valid business model. In recent years, most of the major PE houses have developed substantial VC operations.

Over the last 15 years valuations of early-stage businesses have rocketed, driven principally by technology and gig economies in which the right idea at the right time can generate enormous value. Facebook, Amazon and Google were all start-ups which have become worth many billions of dollars driving other valuations for Snap Inc, Twitter, Uber, Lyft, Airbnb and countless more.

The criterion for investment has also changed, such that technology and gig economy businesses regularly list despite little immediate prospect of profits. Uber, for example, is approaching 15 years since its inception but remains a long way from breaking even. It was listed in 2017 despite losing around $5bn a year, and continued growth in revenue has maintained its high market valuation ever since, regardless of limited mitigation of the losses.

In 2022, Elon Musk paid $44 Bn for Twitter, a social media business which had previously struggled to break even, despite claiming 450 million users since 2006. In 2023, there were signs that Twitter was worth less than half this figure as the markets for technology collapsed. For once, Elon Musk may have made a major mistake, proof that, as always with M&A, timing is everything.

This enormous demand for growth businesses has attracted the interest of PE. Different skills are needed, and start-ups typically require sound business advice on an ongoing basis. PE business management generally needs a combination of the right plan, timetable and monitoring, together with the right team. Once these components are securely in place, they can largely be left to get on with it. Subsequent monitoring is not necessarily that intensive in such circumstances provided progress is made with the plan.

4. Valuations

Valuations for PE businesses are ascertained by comparatives within the relevant industry for recent, similar transactions that can indicate an estimated value of a business. The estimated value of a business this gives can be quite different from the actual exit valuation, depending on market interest at the time of the sale. VC valuation of loss-making growth businesses is more complex, as the rate of growth and ability to scale are also relevant, plus the nature of the industry must be taken into account. VC initial investors have the scope in each round of fundraising to vary the valuation. These estimates also depend on investor interest and at what valuation they are willing to invest.

The basic rule is that valuations should keep rising to make room for a new wave of investors with the next round of equity issues. A 'down' valuation is problematic; it suggests that the venture has run into headwinds and may create doubt about its long-term viability. The willingness of public markets and their investors to list major loss-makers has meant that the demands of a viable business do not have to be met before listing. For venture capital backers this could not be better—they do not even have to prove the business model is viable now before listing and commencing their exit. As always it is when the music stops that the fun begins…

In the period running up to 2022 funds have chased growth, often at the exclusion of slow-growing, mature businesses. This is reminiscent of the dot-com era in which any internet-based business was accorded an enormous valuation and could readily raise funds. The term 'rate of cash burn' was viewed as a positive for businesses with its clear suggestion that progress was being made. Dot-coms had far greater valuations than highly profitable mature businesses despite often being little more than an idea and much spending. That all crashed in 2000 when the era suddenly imploded and most dot-coms could no longer raise funds and went bust. In their wake, valuations of mature dividend businesses rocketed as funds reverted to more traditional business investments.

2022 carried numerous similar cases. Tech valuations have fallen further, even for the more mature businesses such as Facebook, Google and Amazon. Investors have realised the exposure to advertising spend and how sensitive this is to recession. In the case of Amazon, their marketplace has seen contraction as suppliers have moved to selling fuller and more attractive ranges on their own website. Amazon's capturing of data and imitation of successful products is finally starting to haunt them. Start-ups are struggling to raise new finance and are unable to become cash neutral, on what they have previously raised; the result is them having to sell out. The world has become a much more difficult place for early-stage businesses.

5. **Public to Private**

Historically, PE investors have avoided buying public listed businesses. Valuations have been too high which means disposal at an even higher valuation can be hard to achieve. Public companies normally command higher valuations as investors have some reassurance regarding governance, reporting standards and liquidity of shares. Shares are tradeable, unlike those for private companies. This means that exit is likely to be at a higher price and Non-Executive Directors can ensure fairness in governance as a means of protecting shareholder interests. There is also a more efficient and transparent market for buying and selling shares, whilst disposals and acquisitions of stock are easier to transact. Private companies are not required to fulfil most of these requirements. In fact, they are required to do little more than file an annual set of statutory accounts for auditing. These, along with any required terms of governance or reporting can be limited in detail.

The difference in valuation between public and private businesses of a similar size and in the same industry can be substantial. Provided there is investor interest then a listing is likely to offer a higher value to shareholders and a means of exit for those no longer wishing to hold the shares. The reverse is rarely correct, but occasions do arise when public markets choose to reduce the value of a particular industry. In the UK, investors chose to reduce the value of supermarkets due to a mixed outlook occasioned by low-cost entrants. PE investors exercised the opportunity in 2021 to acquire two major UK supermarket chains. The high price paid after a bidding battle means that an eventual profit on the Morrisons transaction seems remote.

In 2021, PE investors bought a significant number of businesses from stock markets. Indeed, 40% by value were public to private (PitchBook data). Public companies are generally larger, hence why this amounts to fewer transactions. Some explanation for this is that, firstly, some sectors recovered slowly after Covid and presented buying opportunities. Secondly, PE had raised large amounts of 'dry powder' (believed to be around $3.7tn in 2023) which means they have had to widen the net in the search for targets (Bain & Co, 2023). The scope has increased to include public companies. The claim is that the traditional difference in valuation between private and public companies has narrowed. In part, this is due to rising valuations of private companies as 'war chests' built up during the period of Covid lockdowns and market closures are invested. Widening PE scope and higher 2021 valuations driven by demand may well mean much lower future exit profits.

PE investors are focusing on FTSE 250 companies in the UK, which have valuations up to £5bn, a 'sweet spot' for PE transactions. Due to predictions of an incoming recession, valuations were depressed in 2023, which makes certain industries targets. The strength of the US dollar against the pound also makes businesses cheaper in the UK. In many ways, this is a sign that investors prefer the PE model to the listed model when it comes to returns, despite the lack of liquidity of PE funds.

The extent of funds to be invested by PE has meant paying higher prices and taking greater risks. Future profits will be harder to come by and holding investments longer will only partially ameliorate the problem. It is likely that PE investors will find the future less kind than the past.

Inflation, Interest Rates, Recession and Closed Markets

Market conditions for the 12 years prior to 2022 have been almost ideal for PE to flourish. Low interest rates and high liquidity, occasioned by the government's widespread use of quantitative easing to stimulate economies following the banking crisis, have provided fertile ground. Funding costs have been low, and the banks are willing to lend up to half the cost of acquisitions. In the case of CD&R acquiring Morrisons in the UK, bonds and bank borrowing were expected to fund 65% of the £10.1bn purchase cost. In such cases, PE downside exposure is limited, even as the funding structure allows PE maximum exposure to the upside on any gain.

Public markets have also been keen on new offerings as potential investors enjoyed low funding costs. In many cases, this has provided a convenient exit route for PE. The sheer volume of money has driven the valuation of growth stocks much higher, leading to substantial profits on exit. According to Bain, the average European PE fund returned 18% per year in the 10 years to 2019, whilst US funds returned 15%. The M&A cycle improved during the decade to 2021 with ever-increasing volumes of trade and higher multiples. 2021 was a peak year, with transactions totalling $5.8tn.

Multiples were at record highs, and inevitably, could not be sustained. The second half of 2022 has therefore seen a collapse of markets now faced with high inflation and high interest rates. The disappearance of buyers and sellers means that PE investors will have to hold businesses much longer amidst increased funding costs. Securitised money borrowed from banks at 3/4% per annum has more than doubled at 6/7%. In the UK, base rates have reached 5.25% in 2023 which means, with risk, PE will be borrowing at 10/11% for unsecuritised borrowing within their businesses. Banks have tightened their borrowing sensing a higher level of risk and private equity are having to use their own funds instead. Funds on which they then need to make a high return. There is little appetite from investors for commercial bonds which further limits the ability of PE to raise cheaper funds. Potential buyers will be concentrating on weathering the recession storm rather than acquiring businesses.

Returns will be much harder to achieve for several years as there will be few buyers for disposals. The cost of holding investments will be that much higher. IPO markets will not be available and valuations that much lower. Many listed growth stocks have halved in value over the last two years.

The rationale of PE is to buy low and sell high. Companies bought at the top of the market during 2021 will prove difficult to show a profit on the original high purchase price, however long PE might hold them. The outlook for PE is certainly depressing, although the more optimistic investors will see it as a buying opportunity. If we consider how PE creates wealth, we may develop a feel for how they will be affected by the change in economies.

A further complication is that identifying exits is becoming increasingly difficult for PE. PE funds still need to close and payout even if not all businesses held by the fund have been sold. Enter the continuation fund, in which PE transfers the remaining investments at a valuation. Clearly, there are conflicts of interest in this manoeuvre and investors in the new fund may be less than impressed. Private equity will have to wait out the downturn before they can sell their investments. Returns are likely to be disappointing.

Sources of value to PE are estimated based on published returns and have three main components:

1. **Leverage**. Around a third of all value created is a product of much higher levels of borrowing, which allow 'sweet equity' to increase its returns (Guo et al., 2011). The extent of borrowing for the future will be limited and its cost will rise significantly, but still be well below the cost of equity; benefits will still ensue from high leverage, but to a more limited extent.
2. **Efficiency**. Another third of total benefits stem from a combination of cost-cutting and higher levels of efficiency (Acharya et al., 2012). This will remain a critical capability and focus. PE investors are much less hindered by integrated cultures or management's reluctance to address their cost base. Cutting costs is invariably unpleasant and can deter management from making major changes. In a recession, those who can rapidly adapt and address costs will be the victors. It is nearly always the case that business costings were developed for a much higher level of activity; a more demanding future means it becomes more important than ever to restore levels of efficiency.
3. **Multiples**. The remainder of value added is related to improving multiples through buying low and selling high. This may be unavailable for a while as PE investors will be waiting for deal activity and valuations to start improving before they choose to sell (Guo et al., 2011). Improving growth potential by finding new markets remains a viable option.

PE as Conglomerates?

Many have pointed out that there are some similarities between larger PE houses and the conglomerates of past decades such as GE, Hanson, Williams Holdings, BTR and many more. These conglomerates acquired many completely different businesses which they ran to in order to produce sufficient cash to buy more businesses. As they grew faster through unrelated diversification their valuation multiples increased, making further acquisitions comparatively cheap. The conglomerate Head Offices were capital allocators that provided little more than various generic corporate services such as insurance, legal and finance. Ultimately, these conglomerates lost favour with investors due to lack of real investor benefits and stalling growth.

They were then broken up by selling off and floating divisions which, ironically, released value as share prices had slumped.

Large PE houses such as KKR, TPG and Blackstone hold large numbers of businesses. Indeed, the latter of these held over 200 businesses in 2023. The major difference is that they are held temporarily until ready for sale. Some central services have also been provided, such as bulk purchasing that creates scale economies and better buying prices. There have been instances of supplying investment banking, legal and due diligence consultancy. Broadly this kind of corporate structure runs counter to the PE culture and their mode of working. PE investors are keen on personal responsibility for partners and management teams. The more one requires them to rely on internal services, the less autonomy and personal accountability they have.

PE's more usual approach is to be 'asset light' maintaining few or none of their own services and accessing the market instead where plenty of competition exists and quality matters. Investment banking, legal and consulting services are therefore usually sourced competitively from the market. This allows competitive tension and, more importantly, quality to be sustained. Once a firm builds overheads and service provision capability, then costs typically rise, quality becomes variable and there is capacity to be filled. In effect, internal services have captive customers who cannot go elsewhere to buy services. 'Asset light' also means that costs can be shared with others, as services are often priced based on success with little to be paid if the deal fails. The case study of 'Garrett Motion' set out in Chapter 9 focuses on the response to turbulent and transient markets and later consequences which often involve being 'asset light.'

Expertise and Focus

PE houses try and build expertise in specific areas so that they can monitor developments and identify potential targets and exit routes. Sectors with strong growth profiles such as healthcare attract particular attention. Their 'buy and build' strategies common in the UK involve buying many smaller businesses in a fragmented industry to create a far larger business for which they can harness buying and market power in terms of pricing. Builders' merchants and timber merchants are seeing much interest in the UK. These are low multiple, cyclical industries in which both buying benefits and marketing benefits might be extracted. Cyclical industries offer the opportunity to sell at higher valuations when the industry recovers. Alongside health care, veterinary services in the UK have been identified as subject to similar PE mechanisms. Inevitably, this 'buy and build' approach concentrates PE interests in certain industries and is starting to attract the interest of competition authorities.

Lessons
1. PE investors are willing to change their target policies rapidly depending on how and where markets see value. Software and healthcare are seen as offering good long-term markets.
2. Early-stage businesses have been successful for PE but, after a period of high inflation and reduced liquidity, valuations have declined.
3. Public markets can be very emotional, frequently over or undervaluing sectors which creates opportunities to buy and sell at the best time.
4. ESG does present opportunities with higher valuations to businesses who can demonstrate credible records in this area and robust policies, reporting and audits.
5. Recessions, high interest rates and depressed markets mean that PE investors must hold businesses longer and tighten margins as leverage becomes more expensive.
6. There are advantages to being 'asset light' in industries where competitive markets exist for services. It allows cost and quality tension to be maintained whilst sharing downsides with other providers.
7. Future PE performance may decline as the vast sums of money raised mean acquiring more high-risk, low-return businesses. Finding exits for these may prove increasingly difficult.

References and Recommended Readings

Acharya, V., Gottschalg, O., Hahn, M., & Kehoe, C. (2012). *Corporate Governance and Value Creation: Evidence from Private Equity; European Corporate Governance Institute Finance*. Working Paper.

Bain and Co. (2022). *Private Equity Global Report 2022*.

Bain and Co. (2023). *Private Equity Global Report 2023*.

Braun, R., & Stoff, I. (2016). The Cost of Private Equity Investing and the Impact of Dry Powder. *Journal of Private Equity, 19*(2), 22–33.

Cantrell, A. (2020). 'Private Equity Exits Have All But Stopped' McKinsey Says. In *The Institutional Investor* (U.S. ed.). Euromoney Trading Limited.

Guo, S., Hotchkiss, E. S., & Song, W. (2011). Do Buyouts (Still) Create Value? *Journal of Finance, 66*(2), 479–517.

Morris, P., & Phalippou, L. (2019). 30 Years After Jensen's Prediction—Is PE a Superior form of Ownership? *Oxford Review of Economic Policy, 36*(2), 291–313.

Teitelman, R. (2013). M&A: Where It's Been, Where It's Going. *Mergers and Acquisitions, 48*(1), 28.

Part IV

Valuation, Process, Governance and Case Studies

7

Business Valuation, Process and Negotiation

Introduction

I recall it was the day after Logan Roy died in *Succession*. I was halfway through my hake fish dinner in a London club when my host said, 'I was thinking around the £100mn mark (or eight times EBITDA) as an enterprise value.' 'Do not react, just concentrate on the fish' I thought, and asked 'What about the property?' He said they might be able to accommodate that but would want an adjustment for the pension. 'Paper or cash?' 'A mix' came the answer.

The offer came from a listed business who would be looking to pay an earnings multiple less than their own. We are a privately owned business. He would know that PE wouldn't have a competitive offer in comparison to his, probably offering a multiple of six at best. His main concern would be if we listed ourselves. 'I have been talking to a stockbroker about a direct listing ourselves,' I said. He looked worried. 'Are you big enough?' 'According to the broker we are. He was talking about a future earnings multiple of nearer 12.' Now my host knew he would have to go further. 'Let's keep talking.'

The trick with negotiation is to put yourself in the shoes of the other party. Where will their benefits come from? Your job is then to extract as many of their benefits from the negotiation as you possibly can. In this case, his benefit arises from multiple arbitrage and cost savings. We can make some of the savings ourselves providing management is up to it, which increases our EBITDA and valuation and erodes his benefit. We can also reduce his benefits from arbitrage by negotiating a better price multiple. Ultimately, we could list the business but that would be an expensive, risky and time-consuming process. Obtaining a better price from the would-be buyer would be the best option all round.

In a negotiation, never say 'yes,' or offer any suggestion that the price offered might be enough. In the above exchange, the other party made the approach, so it was already evident he was keen, and that the price could almost certainly be negotiated upwards, and the terms improved. When buying businesses, people rarely start with their best offer. On occasion, they might open with a good bid and then try and whittle it away once interest has been attracted. The trick in that instance is to nail down as many figures, warranties and indemnities as possible in the heads of terms agreement.

M&A, if done well, can be a rapid and effective means of growing a business and creating value. Many businesses have built experience and learnt, often the hard way, what works and what does not. This chapter considers the process of acquiring businesses from the perspective of risk and how to avoid the many pitfalls which most people learn from painful experiences. It really does not have to be that way.

In the HBO series *Succession*, Logan Roy is the ageing founder of global media and entertainment corporation Waystar Royco. The series' incisive plot is one that constantly pits Logan against his three children—Kendall, Shiv and Roman—who all expect to inherit the business from their father. Series 4, episode 1 finds Logan Roy bidding against his children for a much smaller business, Pierce Global Media. Driven by a potent mixture of hubris and a lifelong blood feud, the children bid the price up to a dizzy $10bn. Roman rings their investment bankers and asks what the business is really worth. 'It's worth whatever someone is willing to pay for it' replies the investment banker advisor. Somewhat sarcastically, Roman returns, 'I wish I'd been to Harvard Business School.' Logan Roy phones his children after the bidding closes to retort, 'Congratulations, on saying the biggest number, you f*****g morons!'.

The message is clear: bid too much and repent at leisure.

When discussing the investment bank advisors later in the episode, Roman says to Kendall, 'Which do you think they would prefer, $5mn for a funding raise or $35mn for an acquisition? Duh!'

Strategic Vs. Private Equity Buyers

If one is considering selling or, indeed buying a business, then how do you go about it? What advisors do you need and what is the procedure? What should you be wary of, and will your advisors warn you? For example, in most cases when selling a business, a strategic buyer will pay substantially more than PE and therefore be a preferable acquirer. PE investors are more difficult to negotiate with and less likely to compromise than strategic buyers. They are also much more likely to walk away on the basis of price or due diligence findings and will be far more demanding in terms of the contract terms, indemnities and warranties required.

In all the deals I have been involved with, advisors have not mentioned these points when it comes to marketing a business. Advisors have their own motives and incentives which will invariably narrow the range and extent of advice they present. Advisors will not mislead you but may choose to remain silent when you are faced with significant decisions. In terms of fees, it is usually in the best interests of advisors if the deal runs.

Buying or selling a business is a high-risk activity, fraught with conflicted advice and many charming people who are interested in making money for themselves. Maintaining a clear, rational and objective view in the midst of so many self-motivated individuals is almost impossible for the inexperienced and difficult for the experienced. The high money stakes bring with it seasoned, experienced, intelligent people, but remember their job is to maximise their own fees. Their technical advice is critical to the deal, but their commercial manoeuvring is not necessarily always in your best interests. To maximise their fees or position advisors need the deal to happen even if it is poor value to you and will constantly be trying to find compromises for both sides that will ensure this. Are these compromises in your best interests? Despite emanating from your own advisors, they may be otherwise.

Charming people (such as those buying or selling businesses) are charming for a reason; they see where value can be generated for themselves as much as for you. You need to head into transactions with your eyes open and try to be as objective as possible. This is not easy as they do this every day whilst for you this is an infrequent event. The advisors usually take charge of the process and you, as either management or a shareholder, are swept along. No one is giving you advice about your position and what you should do to look after your own interests. Management compensation during the process is often described by advisors as 'leakage,' that is, money lost from the main players in the deal.

Forecasts will be created by the selling bank/advisors and management will be asked to support them, however unrealistic they may be. Of course, the successful buyer may expect them to be delivered once the deal is completed and management belongs to new owners. It is at times like this that management starts regretting that their contracts were not more carefully negotiated to protect their interests.

During the sale process management may receive their own offer of employment from potential buyers to persuade them to stay, at least initially. These 'offers' are often vague and become diluted once the deal is done.

Shareholders and management should remember that many deals fail at some point in the negotiation. In which case then they will all have to cooperate with each other afterwards.

It is not only the buyer and the advisors that have a position but so too does management, which may differ again from that of the owners selling the business. They are also vulnerable to a buyer's charm offensives and may need large bonuses to maintain their motivation and focus whilst the process unfolds. Distraction, uncertainty and self-interest are all common consequences. After all, if the business is acquired by another corporate that operates in similar markets, they may well be out of a job. Indeed, it is everyone for themselves as the process slowly unfolds.

Which Advisors?

In most instances of buying or selling a business, you will need a corporate lawyer who specialises in transactions. They are essential and expensive. They do not normally work on a contingency basis and generally quote for the job, rather than hours worked. Although if the transaction fails then they will fall back on hours worked. A good lawyer can help with pitfalls and advice on what is worth fighting for in the negotiation and what is not. Like all advisors, they are trying to find a middle ground by way of compromises between both sides. As the principal, you need to consider carefully whether these are compromises you want or need to make, or, if the other side is evidently keen on the transaction, whether you need to offer compromises at all.

You are likely to need an investment bank or a chartered financial advisor to help with tactics, funding and framing offers. They act as middle parties and advise on what can be very legally complex transactions in terms of taxation and funding. They are usually active in the negotiation and may effectively conduct the negotiation with your lawyers; you may be little more than a bystander. In circumstances in which a sale is agreed and straightforward, then they may not be necessary. They often work on a contingency basis, which means they are only paid if the deal is completed. The drawback of this is the influence it may have on the nature of their advice. If the deal drags on over a long period, they may lose interest on the grounds that they see the likelihood of their fee becoming payable as remote.

Plenty of other professionals may be needed in terms of consultants to do the due diligence. Deep due diligence is expensive, and parties do not normally commission it without exclusivity being granted. Typically, PE investors will use separate consultancies for financial, legal, operational and commercial due diligence. Each will deliver separate and extensive reports which may have implications in terms of pricing or withdrawal. They lay out the extent of risks being acquired. However, the decision as to 'chipping' the price, withdrawing or accepting the risks is that of the principal. With strategic buyers, it is not uncommon to accept risks which are substantial. An example in 2016 was the decision of German conglomerate Bayer to buy the US agribusiness, Monsanto. The weedkiller 'Roundup' which Monsanto had made and sold for many years was later found to have severe carcinogenic health risks to humans. This resulted in several billion dollars of claims which Bayer ultimately had to settle. The due diligence would almost certainly have identified the legal risks involved in the acquisition. Clearly, Bayer's decision was still to go ahead, and even today lawsuits for compensation continue.

PE investors are far more thorough when it comes to due diligence. They take it very seriously and act on its findings. Strategic buyers do financial and legal due diligence but often do commercial and operational due diligence themselves. If the CEO is very keen on the transaction, it can be an exercise in 'going with the flow' or merely a formality. In the 2007 €71bn acquisition of Dutch bank ABN-AMRO by the UK bank RBS, the due diligence was superficial, and the findings were not acted upon. This was later admitted in a government enquiry by RBS's CEO Fred Goodwin. As ABN-AMRO had more than its fair share of sub-prime bonds and synthetics, its value collapsed in the banking crisis resulting in a government bailout to ensure RBS's survival.

Why Value a Business?

It is important to distinguish between valuing a business and expectations of what potential buyers might pay. The latter depends on numerous factors, not least whether there are several potential buyers. Many businesses are marketed after a valuation only to find there is almost no interest. Either it is the wrong time in terms of liquidity, or results are seen to be declining which usually defers interest until they level out. The industry may be depressed, in decline or the business simply viewed as unappealing at that time.

Two determined potential buyers can double the price paid. This was the case in 2018 when Sky sold its cable interests in Europe with 23mn customers and 31,000 employees. Three bidders, including 21st Century Fox, Disney and Comcast drove the price to almost a 100% premium over the previous undisturbed share price of £18bn.

What valuations do provide is some indication as to where bidding might open, as any wise potential bidder will be considering whether they can fund the acquisition. They are also useful in the context of private companies in which there is no real market for the shares. Private shareholders might want to exit or buy into a business. Valuations are a significant means of arriving at a fair price.

Valuation Methods

There are two main methods commonly used in valuing a business, although amended forms may form the basis of other valuation methods. Most potential acquirers would apply both methods.

The four main methods are Comparable Multiples, Discounted Cash Flows and Net Present Value, Asset-Based Approach and Net Book Values. The latter two are often used in breakup situations and taken as beyond the scope of this chapter.

1. **Comparative Multiples**

The first commonly used method of valuation involves comparative multiples. Typically, this will be EBITDA multiples or profit before tax and interest multiples. Comparative multiples are identified from previous transactions in similar industries. Some amendments must be made to take account of whether public or private and relative size. Similarly, amendments may be made to take account of property in the business which may be segregated and replaced with an economic rent charge. Businesses are sold cash and debt free so further appropriate adjustments will be needed. This method is almost universally used as part of a valuation. It does provide an indication of where the bidding will start.

The assumption is based on the equation:

$$\text{Valuation} = \text{EBITDA} \times \text{Comparative Multiple} - \text{Debt}$$

Or

$$\text{Valuation} = \text{Profit Before Interest and Tax} \times \text{Comparative Multiple} - \text{Debt}$$

EBITDA multiples are normally low (say, between 6 and 8) for low-growth industries facing difficult futures such as cyclical stocks in a downturn. For industries seen as high growth, for example health care or technology, multiples can be very high indeed.

Declining industries, such as those related to petrol or diesel engines, or print media, may be low as they are seen as a source of dividends but little real prospect of further growth.

2. **Discounted Cash Flow and Net Present Value Methods**

The second method is based on future Discounted Cash Flows (DCF) which leads to a Net Present Value (NPV) figure after discounting at the weighted average cost of capital for the business. All factors and timings can be included, and sensitivity analyses readily performed. Unfortunately, whilst highly flexible, this method can be easily misused to arrive at the required answer. Indeed, in some cases, projected benefits can be a work of fiction, and analysis from Mckinsey suggests that in 60–70% of projects, the projections are not realised. In part, this is due to overly optimistic forecasts and the confident presumption that everything will go well. It rarely does. The DCF can be adapted to produce sensitivity analyses of low, medium, and high future performance. In effect, it can be used to value estimates of future synergies on the assumption that they will be deliverable. We know that cross-selling benefits and revenue increases resulting from the deal are frequently not achieved. Cost-based synergies have a greater likelihood of being implemented.

Similar methods can incorporate funding means such as the amount of debt and its cost, taxation and cash generated to reduce debt, such that returns to equity can be produced. This is particularly useful to private equity who are using funding as well as business changes plus purchase price of the business and presumed sale price to calculate the ultimate returns to equity.

Timing

Timing is critical when selling a business, as markets and prices tend to rise and fall together during periods of tight liquidity and limited confidence in the future economy. Between 2008 and 2022, US multiples increased by over 60%, only to fall rapidly in the following year as liquidity tightened and confidence declined. In Europe, multiples did rise over a similar period but only by 20–30%.

Market timing for a sale may be crucial but if the time is not right then preparations can be made to improve results by cost reduction. In the case of a business disposal, a corporate may need to retain high-quality management by transferring their employment to other owned business divisions. It is also essential to sell a business with increasing or at least stable results. Declining results mean continual reductions in bids followed by a desperation to 'dump' a business; this almost invariably results in either very poor proceeds or a failed sale process.

Where will the interest come from? Are there interested competitors, suppliers or customers? PE investors are likely to be interested but often at a price well below expectations.

Process Stages

Broadly speaking, there are several stages in any deal process. These are referred to frequently throughout this book using the seven headings: Strategy, Intelligence, Valuation, Negotiation, Due Diligence, Deal and Integration, and are summarised below.

Strategy

Fundamentally, acquiring a business and integrating should create more value than the two businesses could have produced separately. Indeed, this is the essence of M&A which, sadly, is often not achieved. The strategy has growth as a central objective. A growth strategy will determine what key unique capabilities and resources a business controls and identifies where they are best placed in order to grow a business.

This growth ambition may involve exploiting current customers by expanding ranges and selling them more products/services, finding new markets for existing products or using existing technology to enter new markets. These approaches are known as related diversification.

In all these cases, there is an existing understanding and experience of certain key elements (markets, products, technology), so the risk is contained.

Entering new markets with new products and services and different technology is unlikely to be effective and research strongly supports these assertions. The best-performing businesses follow these related lines when diversifying (Paliach et al., 2000). Unrelated diversification is rarely successful. Beware CEO rhetoric which hides unrelated diversification in which there are few real synergies. For example, US telecoms infrastructure provider

AT&T's 2018 acquisition of content producer Time Warner for $100bn which destroyed the results of both businesses and ended with spinning off Time Warner in 2021 in a joint venture with Discovery. The *New York Times* estimates the losses on the deal to be around $43bn.

Cloud and PC software supplier Microsoft's 2016 acquisition of social media provider LinkedIn for $26bn had similar 'unrelated' elements. It is not clear whether this can yet be considered a success or otherwise, although it is telling that Microsoft has failed to add to their social media division since. Towards the end of 2022 and early 2023, valuations of social media businesses crashed as advertisers cut budgets. Elon Musk's $44bn acquisition of Twitter in 2022 is now thought to be worth a fraction of that price, despite its rebranding under the name 'X', possibly even less than the debt attached to the business. Following recent trends, it is likely that Microsoft will, at some point in the future, sell LinkedIn as the industry develops and diversifies with demand.

Intelligence

Once a list of potential targets that are consistent with the agreed strategy has been created, then intelligence needs to be collected on each target. Along with the abundance of publicly available channels, certain consultancies specialise in collecting data on targets. They will speak with competitors, suppliers, customers and ex-employees to collect insight into the business. Due to their independence, expertise and capability in extracting data, they are better positioned to aggregate and collate critical data. Many corporates rely entirely on their own intelligence collection which is rarely as effective. They are also unlikely to have access to the type of sources professional focused consultancies might use.

Negotiation

Critically with any negotiation or deal, being willing to walk away if the deal goes beyond what you can realistically accept is crucial. A judicious approach changes the dynamics of any negotiation and ensures that you do not accept a bad deal. On major points, it is not necessary to arrive at an agreement immediately and if the other side is not well-disposed towards some conditions, it may be wise to slow the negotiation whilst they 'acclimatise' to your requests.

Frequently the determination to complete a deal drives it way beyond what is sensible for one party. On the other hand, the longer the negotiation process takes, the less likely it is that the deal will ever be completed. Time does kill deals, so a motivation to see it through is required on both sides. Negotiation is therefore a difficult balance between time and achieving your objectives.

The main deal breakers are often any due diligence findings which are worrying for the buyer. These need to be significant to kill the deal entirely, although PE investors are more inclined to cut the price and walk away if their reduced bid is rejected. The other big factor jeopardising a deal is the declining results of the business being sold during the later stages of the negotiation. This creates uncertainty in the buyer who may then cut the bid significantly or walk away completely. Selling a business in a falling market is inadvisable for these reasons.

Due Diligence

Due diligence is the process whereby a potential buyer can make further enquiries of the seller beyond the data and any information already provided. It occurs once the most favourable bidder has been selected and granted a period of exclusivity. It also signifies the point at which the preferred bidder starts to incur significant costs in legal and due diligence fees. Prior to this point in the process, there may be any number of 'sightseers' who are only engaged in the process to obtain information. Some will be competitors unless they have been specifically excluded, although competitors are often the most likely buyers. At the point of due diligence an indicative price has usually been agreed, although other terms will need to be negotiated.

Typically, due diligence takes the form of further commercial, operational, financial and legal enquiries. Commercial information is usually limited in availability and delayed until late in the process as other parties, particularly competitors, can potentially benefit from the information. The due diligence may be undertaken by employees or third-party agencies who specialise in this work. Where possible it is in the sellers' interests to limit the time and scope of the work, as it is frequently used as a price chip or reason to pull out. Placing limits on the extent of commercial and operational due diligence and limiting the time available is therefore quite common. At this stage, valuation prices will only reduce, not increase.

PE investors usually employ third parties and are much more likely to walk away if they do find information which questions the value of the business, whilst corporates often use their own people as they believe that their industry knowledge allows better insight. They may have the necessary insight if they are already in that industry; however, one criticism is that, when determined to do the deal, they may be selective and focus on certain specific interests rather than undertaking a fuller, more objective investigation.

Distraction

Any significant business acquisition or sale provides an intense focus for management. The highly complex process requires many advisors, meetings and decisions and is all-consuming for the senior vendor management involved. Consequently, they may be distracted from running their own business, and market share is frequently lost during the process. Declining results then put pressure on the deal, particularly when the deal negotiation is protracted. The 2019 acquisition of UK supermarket Asda by Sainsbury failed due to a competition ruling. During the lengthy nine-month investigation Sainsbury's lost market share and ultimately their CEO as a direct consequence. The cost to Sainsbury of the failed bid was over £50mn in addition to the lost market share.

Management is also likely to be distracted by the possibility of losing their jobs with new ownership. They may also be exploring their own Management Buy Out with financial backers which could create significant conflicts of interest. Alignment with both a potential acquirer and the current employer is bound to create tensions.

The Pass

Which side makes the initial approach does matter as it can dictate the balance of power in the ensuing negotiation. It is rare that both parties are equally keen on the deal, and so the price, terms and conditions must balance the relative motivations. Many approaches follow a discussion between senior directors or chairmen at industry dinners or similar events. Whoever makes the first move is usually in a position of slight weakness throughout the negotiation. The other party may use this opportunity to 'play hard to get,' driving the terms, conditions and price paid. To avoid this, third parties are often engaged to act on their behalf, ensuring the approach remains anonymous, distant and seemingly disinterested.

Historically, PE investors have waited for potential acquisitions to be brought to them via intermediaries or ex-directors with a plan to add value.

Almost all potential buyers behave charmingly up to the point of negotiation, at which time attitudes change, and their real plans become evident. With PE in particular, the various shareholder agreements and the sale and purchase contract may be onerous on management. The devil really is in the detail. Consequences can be severe for missing the plan or failing to hit the various repayment targets with management's equity being diluted. Whatever the respective shareholdings power, overall the key decisions resides with PE. They may be unaware of how difficult their shareholder agreement will be until well into the negotiation process.

> **Two Examples**
> 1. In one example, a listed plc was so determined to buy a particular private business that they were willing to fix a price, irrespective of the forecast results for the year. In addition, they chose to forego due diligence and settle for minimal warranties. The deal was done in four months despite declining results and a depressed market outlook for the business. The resolve to push the deal through was such that any sense of value was lost. The sellers were ambivalent about parting company with the business and so would only sell for a top price and minimal conditions. The corporate paid almost twice the price PE would have paid. One driver of the deal was cash raised through a 'green' bond which needed to be spent on businesses producing sustainable products. This created a determination to invest the money rapidly despite disadvantageous terms.
> 2. In another case, a director of a family business sought an AIM-listed buyer to avoid inheritance tax issues for the shareholders. The proposed deal would be based around a share swap, plus a cash alternative for those not wanting the shares. The potential acquirer, like much of the industry, suffered from a dramatic decline in share price over the previous year, so the value offered would necessarily be low. This was a mistimed approach which resulted in a low bid and was rejected.

Management Buy Outs (MBOs) and Conflicts of Interest

Once a corporate decides to sell a division, then an option may arise for an MBO. This is when the divisional management asks to be allowed to make an offer for the business. The MBO team will try and raise funds from bank borrowing, usually against assets such as property or trade debtors in the business, plus a financial backer such as private equity.

Before they invest, PE investors will want to see a convincing plan from management as to how they will significantly add value over the next three to five years. The credibility of the MD, FD and team is important. The plan will normally need to make significant changes so that the PE investors can see multiples of their investments being returned. Typically, plans involve cost reduction, sale of unwanted parts of the business and reinvestment in new growth areas.

'Skin in the Game'

Management stands to own anything from 10 to 60% of the business in terms of equity, although there will be an extensive set of agreements that allow PE powers that go way beyond the normal voting power accorded to their equity holding. The management will be required to pay for the equity, although the maximum is likely to be around one times salary after tax. This is termed 'skin in the game' and is to prevent them from walking away if things do not go well. It is intended to be a meaningful figure to management but seldom represents the current economic value of their shareholding. If the business then performs and is sold at a significant profit, they will share pro rata to PE in the profits. This is likely to be a significant sum, often running into millions.

To the corporate making the sale, an MBO can be a convenient means of selling a division rapidly; however, major conflicts of interest may arise, to the extent that the seller refuses to entertain a bid from management. If an MBO is allowed to progress, then it is in the divisional management's interest to pull the price down as low as possible. As they are the team controlling the accounts of the business, there are many ways they can reduce its value. In addition, if other bidders are involved, they will want to meet the management and discuss a plan for the business. The management may not cooperate with the process, and limit knowledge to themselves and PE. It is in the management's interest to deter other potential buyers so as to clear the way for their own bid.

Incentivisation

In these circumstances, the seller may simply refuse an MBO and/or incentivise the team to help sell the business, usually in the form of a bonus—likely around a year's salary—that is only payable on cooperating with a successful sale.

An MBO is a major opportunity for management of the division to become rich and run the business without the tight corporate restrictions in terms of funding and bureaucracy that their ownership can bring. It is amazing how imaginative management can be once they become part owners of the business. The difference now is that the investment is their own money, and they have major equity incentives to cut costs, improve cash flow and invest wisely; it can make a major difference to business performance.

What is required is a three-way negotiation: management have to negotiate their own terms and conditions, amount of equity, etc., with PE, negotiate with the seller over price and terms and conditions to buy the business, whilst also needing to come to an agreement with lenders, such as banks, or property businesses for selling and leasing back property. Clearly, PE investors do assist with some elements of this process; however, the time and energy it demands can be a distraction that has a deleterious impact on the business.

Divestments: Exclusive Sale or Market the Business?

Once a business has made the decision to dispose of a division/company then there are further choices to be made. First, a valuation is needed to get a feel for what is an acceptable price. Next, an MBO might be considered if there is a management team that can run the business separately. It must be ascertained whether they have the skills to manage a buy-out, which requires a strong team and a very good Finance Director. Many management teams lack these qualities.

The key decision, however, is whether to market the business to a wide audience or approach a single interested buyer for exclusive negotiations which will be known about by a selective few people. This exclusivity has the benefit that few interested parties are distracted by the event, principally because they will not know about it until completion. Evidence suggests that both methods are applied approximately equally and are here reviewed in turn.

1. An exclusive sale

Clearly, for an exclusive sale, a previously identified interested party is necessary. Perhaps a competitor, supplier or customer might have previously enquired about any likelihood of divestment. A business is needed which has an appropriate growth strategy and can raise the funds to buy the equity and assume the debt. The ideal buyer would be able to generate significant benefits and synergies by combining with the disposal, creating value that would underpin a 'full' price. Assuming such an offer is forthcoming then an exclusive sale process is pursued. It might be asked how such a deal has adequate tension and commitment to complete in these circumstances. To counteract this, an agreed exclusivity period (say four months) can be put in place before it will then be marketed more generally. The threat of a marketing process should ensure that the deal remains competitive.

2. Open marketing

Many will argue that the competitive tension of several bidders is the best way of getting a high price; however, there are significant downsides with such an approach. An investment bank advisor will compile a list of potential interested parties. It will contain competitors, suppliers, customers and other parties in the industry who might be interested. They will be sent a 'teaser' which does not name the business being disposed of but highlights its various strengths. Clearly, anyone in the same industry will likely guess this for themselves. If there are interested parties, then a Non-Disclosure Agreement (NDA) is signed before receiving more information. These are widely flouted and subsequently proving the source of a leak is very difficult. As a consequence, management, employees, suppliers, competitors and customers soon know that the business is for sale.

Uncertainty is a major distraction which reduces productivity and affects all parties. Employees are concerned that a new owner may bring closures and redundancies. Management may be concerned that an integration may see them lose their jobs. Suppliers will be concerned that the supply chain may change, and some will lose out, plus it provides an opportune time for competitors to exploit customers' insecurities as to who they are really buying from. They may also approach key employees with a view to gaining more experienced workers. If the sale process then fails, much damage will have been done to no avail. If results deteriorate during a negotiation, then agreed prices start to fall or even withdrawn.

It is true to say that selling a business by open marketing does come with significant risks, not least that the outcome may satisfy no one. It is usually encouraged by investment banks but frequently fails unless the business on the market is very attractive.

If approaching corporates for potential interest does not look hopeful, then the next stage is to involve private equity. PE investors are seldom a first choice and generally pay much lower prices than corporates in the same industry, largely because they are unable to generate integration synergies. PE investors will drive a harder bargain not only on price but warranties and indemnities. If they are 'last in' bidders, then they will offer a 'low ball' price with the chance of picking up the business on the cheap.

Private Equity Tactics

These have been given more detailed consideration in the earlier chapter, but their involvement in M&As is often underestimated, and their tactics could be profitably applied elsewhere. There are some elements of PE that are generally (but not uniformly) true.

- Firstly, they normally pay significantly less for a business (Bargenon et al., 2007) and demand more warranties and indemnities than corporates. For this reason, it is usually wise to exhaust corporate options first before extending the bidding to PE.
- A tactic employed by some PE investors is to bid high in order to earn exclusivity and then use every conceivable excuse to cut the price, betting that the seller will not go back to the other PE bidders. Due diligence, if done thoroughly, often provides plenty of ammunition to chip the price.
- Another tactic is to be difficult over the working capital. When a business is sold, the assumption is that there will be adequate working capital to allow the business to run. Needless to say, that leaves plenty of scope for argument. There are several ways of computing what an adequate figure is, however, PE investors dig in to ensure they benefit from a low figure if selling and a high figure if buying. The difference can run to millions. How the value of working capital is to be determined should be agreed upon at the head of terms stage to avoid nasty surprises at the end of the negotiation.
- PE investors will only offer cash as they do not have shares to trade, whilst a corporate will try and issue shares to make up some of the consideration. The advantage of shares is that it allows deferral of any tax liability to a

time when the shares might be sold. The downside is that it exposes the buyer to the shares of a business which might just have paid too much for a large acquisition. A subsequent failed integration may be value-destroying.

PE Charm Offensive

A potential buyer may appear charming, highly flexible and willing to accommodate the wishes of management in the first stages of the bidding process; however, this bonhomie will not necessarily last. Management often finds themselves being invited out for dinner and promised certain positions, equity and investment in the new entity. Unless these promises are enshrined in legally valid documents or side letters, however, they should be treated as part of the notorious 'charm offensive' that lures management into favouring the deal. This is a normal approach of PE and many other buyers, but once the deal and associated agreements are signed then the world can be a very different place.

PE agreements with management can contain clauses which allow PE investors to change management and 'swamp' their shares. If there is a failure to repay some loans to the PE investors by the business in a certain time period, then the loans are at risk of being converted to equity, thereby 'swamping' management's equity and reducing its value. At the time the deal is signed, the general air of optimism may obscure certain risks by all parties, including management. Circumstances can change alarmingly. Management is wise to be tougher in negotiations with PE investors in order to 'water down' some of these terms and remain realistic about what might happen.

Bear in mind that PE investors generally need the management team and may well not buy the business without them. It is risky to recruit from outside a team when acquiring a business. Having said that, PE investors will often change the CEO to someone who is used to working the PE way and understands the focused nature of their demands and pursuit of rapid change. Many CEOs simply do not have the capability to make significant change or the stomach to make unpopular decisions. The CEOs of many public companies are often great communicators (which is a necessity of the job), but less capable of achieving the meaningful change that is consistent with their partners objectives (Kaplan et al., 1992).

Earnouts

This is a device to resolve major differences in price expectation between buyer and seller that is often employed in a PE acquisition when the management is being retained. Buyers typically value a business on historical performance, whilst sellers prefer to sell on performance forecasts. The difference can result in a major argument in terms of price expectations. One solution is for the management to stay, achieve the forecasts and be rewarded with a sizeable part of the consideration. The period of earnout is often three years but can be longer or shorter.

Earnouts are becoming less popular, as the conditions—management remaining in situ over the period—prevent the buyer from interfering in the running of the business for its course. If they do, management will claim they would have achieved the performance had it not been for interference. It is also more difficult to replace management if they fail to perform during the earnout period. Corporates rarely employ earnouts as they usually wish to develop synergies during the relevant period.

Conclusions

This chapter deals with many of the risks which await the inexperienced buyer or seller of businesses. 'Inexperience' can apply to any level of employment, even CEOs of large businesses may have a strategy that calls for the use of M&A but have had little direct involvement in previous transactions. Many rely on advisors which, whilst essential to the process, can often be narrow, for example, they may fail to warn of problems which could be avoided if only the principal had been made aware. Advisors generally want deals to run due to compensation issues and may limit information which might jeopardise that situation.

> **Lessons**
> 1. Do not rush negotiations, unless both parties are equally hasty (which is rare); speed results in giving away more than one would otherwise.
> 2. Try and understand what the benefits are for both parties. This will give you a good idea of what they might be willing to pay. In some cases, you might be able to extract some of those benefits yourself.
> 3. Valuing a business does not mean that is what it is worth. The real value depends on context—the benefits, synergies and improvements that might

be obtained. Private equity virtually always pays less than corporates, and of those, listed corporates are usually the best buyers to sell to.
4. Always consider whether there will be interest at the price you are willing to accept. The process of selling is hugely distracting for all stakeholders and a failed deal process can be costly.
5. Consider an exclusive sale process to whoever will have the most synergies, as they will be willing to pay the best price. An exclusive process will create less distraction without other stakeholders becoming aware.
6. If selling to PE investors, then be ready for price 'chips' once the invariably thorough due diligence has been done. They are also much more likely to walk if you do not concede to their demands.
7. Management Buy Outs (MBOs) result in management finding their own financial backers and producing a plan to add value. Significant conflicts of interest may arise between the selling corporate and the management who control the business and accounts as negotiations proceed. For this reason, many sellers will not entertain MBOs.

References and Recommended Readings

Bargeron, L., Schlingeman, F. P., Stulz, R., & Zutter, C. J. (2007). Why Do Private Acquirers Pay So Little Compared to Public Acquirers? *Monetary Economics*.

Fernandez-Aranzubía, C., Iqbal, S., & Ritter, J. (2015, April). Leadership Lessons from Great Family Businesses. *Harvard Business Review*.

Gale, S. F. (2003). Memo to AOL Time Warner: Why Mergers Fail (Case Studies). *Workforce, 82*(2), 60.

Jenkinson, T., Sousa, M., & Stucke, R. (2013). *How Fair Are the Valuations of Private Equity Funds?*

Kaplan, R. S., & Norton, D. (1992). The Balanced Scorecard: Measures that Drive Performance. *Harvard Business Review, 70*(1), 71.

Koller, T., Goedhart, M. H., & Wessels, D. (2020). *Valuation: Measuring and Managing the Value of Companies* (7th ed.). Wiley.

Malone, D., & Turner, J. (2010). The Merger of AOL and Time Warner: A Case Study. *Journal of the International Academy for Case Studies, 16*(8), 151.

Mellen, C. M., & Evans, F. C. (2018). *Valuation for M&A: Building and Measuring Private Company Value* (3rd ed.). Wiley.

Mercer, Z. C., & Harms, T. (2020). *Business Valuation: An Integrated Theory* (3rd ed.). Wiley.

Palepu, K. G., Healy, P. M., & Peek, E. (2022). *Business Analysis and Valuation: IFRS Edition* (6th ed.). Cengage.

Paliach, L. E., Cardinal, L. B., & Miller, C. C. (2000). Curvilinearity in the Diversification-Performance Linkage: An Examination of over Three Decades of Research. *Strategic Management Journal, 21*(2), 155–174.

Wade, J. (2010). The Failed Merger of AOL/Time Warner. *Risk Management, 57*, 22.

8

Effective Governance and M&A

Introduction

This section explores the effectiveness of governance arrangements. By examining several cases, it considers why governance proved ineffective in preventing unnecessary shareholder value destruction. It identifies the key issues that arise in the pursuit of effective governance and asks how far the requirements for listed businesses act to protect shareholders, or merely provide part-time employment for those who no longer want executive work. To what extent do governance requirements ensure shareholder interests are considered in the boardroom? Most fundamentally, it seeks to ascertain what key factors determine good governance.

The chapter goes on to compare the governance arrangements of listed businesses with those of both private equity and family businesses. In this, it considers some of the key elements of governance arrangements such as the impact of the 'agency' problem, board size and make-up, shareholder and stakeholder objectives, incentives and active business management.

In three well-known cases, it identifies points at which governance processes could or should have been reviewed, why public company governance didn't prevent the deals concerned happening, and what preventative actions could have been employed. These are all cases that can be used to inform future approaches to effective business governance.

Personal Interest

My own interest in governance has arisen over the last 28 years of chairing a wide variety of businesses. These have included public listed corporations, those owned by private equity, family businesses and divisions of large corporates. Governance structures are often associated with preventing fraud or management extracting excess funds without the agreement of shareholders, ensuring correct reporting to stakeholders and safeguarding a business's assets.

The key question of the chapter is how far some systems of governance act to drive better performance in a business than others. If so, what are the key elements of these systems? How are effective boards constituted, and what sort of people should be on the board? How big should a board be in number? How should the Non-Executive Directors be chosen and how can you ensure the board receives the necessary information to do its job properly?

Is this performance for shareholders or other stakeholders? At a business I joined as Chairman following Covid, there was a huge bounce in trade for the industry generally. The excess profits ended up with around a third paid out as management bonuses, another third was extracted by an elderly final salary pension scheme which had a funding deficit and the remainder was shared between the bank to reduce indebtedness, and the shareholders as dividend. Management, employees, pensioners and banks are also stakeholders. The question then becomes what is a fair distribution of profits? Who should benefit and in what proportion? Sometimes the shareholders can find themselves at the end of a long queue. The consequences are difficulties in raising new capital and a diminishing shareholder base. Shareholders may then want to sell out to interested parties.

In any publicly owned business, there is some tension between the demands of different stakeholder categories. There may also be some tension between short and long term objectives depending on shareholder pressure. Transparency in reporting creates a forum for stakeholder pressure.

For private equity, the priorities demonstrate a clear focus on shareholder returns, and the planning period is in the medium term range of 3 to 5 years until the exit. Transparency is deliberately limited to prevent pressure from other stakeholders.

In contrast, family businesses are long term in focus as they wish to provide future employment for further generations to come. Their focus is the family shareholders and employees.

Some may recall a case in 2024 heard by the Delaware commercial courts in which Elon Musk wanted to pay himself a bonus of $55bn from Tesla, the electric car business. The court denied the bonus on the grounds that Elon

Musk had loaded the board with 'connected people', in effect Elon Musk's stooges. Now Elon Musk had 22% of the voting rights in Tesla, so the other 78% of shareholders may have thought the bonus was less well earned. Musk's response was to move the incorporation of Tesla and some of his other businesses to Texas in the belief he could get his own way in their courts. Time will tell. Whatever happens, these events cast light on the inadequacies of public company governance.

Elon Musk may well be worth every cent of his $55bn but that is not the point. The loading of boards with friends and supporters to ensure that the CEO gets his own way is unfair to the other shareholders.

Case Study 1: GE
Until 2001, Jack Welch spent 20 years as CEO of the US conglomerate GE, developing it into a world leader, largely through buying and selling businesses. In fact, during this two-decade tenure, he bought more than 1,000 businesses, which averages out to almost 50 deals a year (Gryta & Mann, 2020). The more rapidly he grew GE, the higher the multiple of the stock market attributed to the shares. In turn, Welch could use his high-priced shares to buy targets at lower multiples, with each consecutive acquisition increasing the value of GE through a process known as 'Multiple Arbitrage.' (The MA process is described elsewhere in this book, but in brief, it proposes that larger businesses have higher multiples than smaller businesses and public-owned businesses have higher multiples than privately owned businesses). The more businesses he bought then the more GE's value increased and the higher the value of the shares. As a conglomerate, integration was no longer critical to GE's strategy. Having said that, there is evidence to suggest that Welch's performance-driven culture and governance methods yielded better performance in many of the businesses acquired (Welch, 2005).

The conglomerate was involved in many industries including manufacturing jet engines, lighting, health equipment and providing financial services and media. A new Non-Executive Director is reputed to have asked the Senior Independent Director what his role was. 'Applause' came the answer. The NEDs were given so little detailed information on the enormous conglomerate that there was little they could contribute and quarrelling with Welch was viewed as unwise. Welch selected Jeff Immelt as a successor of the CEO position when he eventually retired in 2001. In 2000, the stock market value of the business reached $600bn. Jack paid himself an enormous exit package which included lifelong use of a private jet, paid for by GE.

Jeff spent the next 16 years reducing GE to rubble through a policy of buying and selling businesses. Like Welch he was also prolific in his acquisitions, managing to buy over 700 businesses during his tenure. Unfortunately,

> the major deals he made, such as Alsthom, destroyed value through a combination of paying too much and subsequent poor operating performance. He also inherited some of his predecessor's excesses and dubious accounting devices, which did not serve him so well. It took 16 years for the Non-Executive Directors to wake up and fire Jeff. Shortly after leaving GE, Jeff authored a piece in the *Harvard Business Review* titled 'How I Remade GE' and extolling the strategic virtues of his tenure (Immelt, 2017). Sadly, it did not explain the value destruction nor the reasons for its decline, which resided principally in bad deals. NEDs must be made of stern stuff to oppose such delusion. By this stage, the stock market valuation had fallen to $98bn and GE is now a pale shadow of its former self. It is fair to say that Welch's legacy was not quite all it seemed. The good news for some at least is that investment banks pulled in $6bn of fees from GE, purely through advising on what were a progressive series of mistakes.

Analysis

This case poses the question as to clearly ineffective corporate governance at GE that ultimately allowed so much value to be destroyed. Were the NEDs powerless or did they simply not understand what was happening? The historical problems associated with conglomerates include a generalised lack of transparency in performance and funding between divisions. Cross-funding between divisions and a loss of clarity as to divisional performance can leave investors with limited information on which to invest. The consequence is usually discounted valuations (Fig. 8.1).

NEDs are unlikely to have much understanding of the many industries which are represented in the business, plus they may have been given limited information about each significant acquisition. Of course, what they would have received would have been very positive. In such circumstances, NEDs fall back on process rather than any deep knowledge of the business. The correct committees exist, meet and receive appropriate reports, but some may consider this approach to be 'skin deep' with a general reluctance to address any of the more significant decisions.

Clearly, the board was excessively tolerant of Jeff Immelt over his 16 years, despite his decisions being characterised by underperformance and value destruction. For some of those early years he may have blamed his misfortune on his predecessor, who it must be admitted, lumbered him with a very large financial division which was set to become problematic in the years following

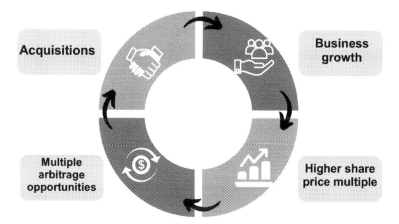

Fig. 8.1 The virtuous circle: higher multiples following acquisition-fuelled growth

the banking crisis. Jeff did big deals which resulted in share price dilution. There is limited justification for this, as a conglomerate such as GE would be unable to generate much in the way of synergies through integration.

> **Case Study 2: RBS**
> Meanwhile, in the UK, Fred Goodwin was busy transforming the Royal Bank of Scotland into the world's largest bank by buying and merging with other banks. In the case of the National Westminster Bank, merging, closing and extracting cost savings from the back office removed 18,000 jobs. Fred was so successful that the government of the day awarded him a knighthood. His downfall was a deal too far in his acquisition of the Dutch bank ABN-AMRO for €71bn in 2007. This, on the eve of the banking collapse in 2008, could not have been worse timing. Sir Fred paid too much and bought a bank full of high-risk sub-prime mortgages just as the market collapsed. Fred admitted at the subsequent enquiry that he had done little due diligence on ABN-AMRO before buying it. RBS effectively went bust and had to be bailed out by the government who then took a large stake in return. Sir Fred was fired and, with the removal of his knighthood in government retribution, became Fred again.

Analysis

Fred probably hoped that the substantial risks he took when overpaying and undertaking limited due diligence would all be lost in future market turbulence and less likely to be pinned on his acquisition decisions. Such was his determination to do the deal that due diligence was viewed as little more than an encumbrance and source of delay (this CEO approach to due diligence is not unusual). No doubt he was overconfident, some might say hubristic after a run of successful deals, although none had equalled the size of ABN-AMRO. All the signs suggested this enormous and highly dilutive deal would need a miracle to work out.

There is little doubt that Fred dominated his board and, through a combination of deal-making and cost-cutting, brought success to what was originally a sleepy bank. Why didn't the NEDs challenge Fred over the lack of due diligence and the price paid? What information were they given?

This touches on a wider question as to why NEDs feel so powerless. In this case, some of the NEDs were not from the banking industry, which does require specialised knowledge, and a lack of such understanding may well have hampered their appreciation of the risks being taken.

Case Study 3: AB InBev

Next up, AB InBev—the world's biggest brewer under the leadership of Carlos Brito. Through mergers Brito acquired many of the world's major brands in the beer market, allowing him to dispense with much of the management, systems, back offices and Head Offices (this was discussed in some depth in Chapter 1 of this book). In 2016, however, he set off on a deal too far when he acquired SABMiller for $106bn. Given that his attempt would mean claiming production and distribution of almost a third of the world's beer consumption, he should have anticipated running into the competition authorities in North America, Europe and China. They required immediate disposal of all the acquired assets in their jurisdiction. These were extensive, and the rapid disposal meant they fetched a much lower price than he had paid for them, forcing the cost of the retained businesses still higher. The remaining assets were acquired at an enormous earnings multiple of 23 which for a slow-growth beer business is excessive by any count. The deal was overpriced and the risks excessive, but even knowing this didn't deter Brito from continuing.

AB InBev's debt mountain of $106bn weighed heavily; the shareholders became concerned that Brito would ask them to pay for it further as the dividend was halved, and the share price similarly collapsed. Disposals became

> necessary to reduce debt and the management team was replaced. Advisors gained almost $3bn from this deal.

Analysis

Yet again, this case raises the question as to what the board was doing as they were presented with such a high-risk acquisition proposal. As a listed business on the London Stock Exchange, the bidding and negotiations for SABMiller started at a high price. Hedge funds forced the price higher, and the disposals required by the competition authorities pushed it higher still. Some of the planned cost savings would be difficult to achieve, for example, the South African competition authorities would only approve the deal if the business retained the Johannesburg SABMiller head office. In effect, value leaked out of the deal, yet no one at the board level prevented the deal despite having the opportunity to do so.

Legal due diligence would almost certainly have raised the competition risks with management, or they may have believed that the risks were acceptable. When the world's largest brewer buys the second largest to create over 30% of the global market share, competition authorities are bound to act. Yet again, previous success with deals may have compromised the objectivity of management. Despite its price and risks, this was an exciting venture, but all concerned failed to consider the very real possibility of failure. If they didn't do the deal, however, what would they have done instead with limited scale options available? Ultimately the board took unacceptable risks and, along with the shareholders, paid the price for their failure.

Risk and Due Diligence

In these examples, the CEOs' developing confidence in M&A activity resulted in progressively larger deals. Even though risk also escalates with size, the CEOs ignored the findings of due diligence in their haste to finalise the deals. The RBS imploded, rendering the equity worthless, whilst the share price more than halved at AB InBev. In both cases, the top team was eventually removed and replaced. As for GE, the shares became worth a fraction of their value under Welch and Jeff Immelt left, probably 10 years too late.

Large deals are always going to be expensive, and the debt will weigh heavily. GE ran a version of a Ponzi scheme, in which multiple arbitrage drove growth and stock valuation, but only whilst the business continued to grow through acquisition. Deals needed to be big to 'move the needle' on scale in relation to the size of GE. Once acquisitions diminished, growth rates declined, and the stock prices went into reverse. The pursuit of growth and share price through acquisitions was common to all three businesses and with unsustainable momentum. Ultimately, M&A transactions driven by overconfidence often end badly, the only issue is when. In addition, the timing of AB InBev and RBS's acquisitions could not have been worse. Significant share price dilution plus high levels of debt and bad timing instantly limited prospects of success.

In Chapter 3, we considered the top 10 largest global deals as of 2022. These occurred from 1999 to 2024. If we consider the valuation of the acquirer at the time of the deal, in eight instances these deals have destroyed significant shareholder value over the intervening period. Only two of the deals had even reached the original pre-bid valuation by the end of the period studied. A simple arithmetic mean would suggest that on average more than a third of the original shareholder value had been destroyed. Clearly, the deals had failed to create shareholder value, so who did they benefit? Was it the executives who ran these enterprises in terms of pay, status and power commensurate with running a much bigger business? What happened to governance?

Growth: Earnings or Size

The common theme of the case studies discussed is that of a horizontal merger followed by dramatic cost-reduction measures. Can this really be considered as growth? It does not increase any inherent industry growth, but a simple case of one business buying another out. What is apparent is that the integration process leaves the combined business without the capability to grow in the future. The intense internal process involved in major cost reductions, in addition to the day-to-day running of the business, is believed to be responsible for this. In their *Harvard Business Review* article, Mankins et al. (2017) conclude that this type of deal frequently suffers from overpaying, the extensive cost rationalisation over the following 2 to 3 years leaves a business incapable of further growth.

The cost-reduction integration efforts may drive earnings for a couple of years but afterwards there is often contraction. An example is the $45bn Kraft Heinz food merger of 2015 which ultimately followed this path. $12.5bn had to be written off the value of the acquisition and the remaining shares halved in value due to an inability to grow; product innovation was an additional casualty of resources being channelled elsewhere.

Is Previous Success a Liability?

In all three cases, the acquirers had a successful history of acquisitions driving both their rapid growth rate and their stock price. Success can all too easily breed arrogance amongst senior executives who, after a series of relative successes, believe they can 'walk on water.' The resulting hubris leads them to ignore some of the basic but unwritten rules of the M&A game: size and dilution *do* matter.

Eventually, the increased risks materialise and the 'gung-ho' pursuit of big deals goes sadly wrong. Ignoring due diligence findings or limiting due diligence seems to be uppermost in the list of mistakes. Paying far too much is a close contender. Jeff Immelt, Carlos Brito and Fred Goodwin all took enormous risks by ignoring the due diligence, or in the case of Fred Goodwin and the ABN-AMRO bank, simply not doing any at all. Carlos Brito ignored the legal due diligence of competition law when buying SABMiller.

Previous success does not necessarily translate to the future. What got you there will be likely to stop working at some point, particularly when in pursuit of ever bigger businesses and paying ever higher prices; in this case, adverse due diligence findings should have raised alarms.

Deal Success or Failure, and for Whom?

There is always a question, when considering the success or failure of a deal, as to whose perspective we are going to take. Instinctively we think shareholders as, ultimately, they own the business, despite there being many other stakeholders affected by a deal. However, the people controlling the deal process are the management who may well have other objectives in mind when making major decisions. Could there be self-interest involved? Shareholders always want growth for their business both in terms of sales and earnings. This creates the mandate for acquisitions as organic growth tends to be slow for larger businesses. The temptation is to opt for large acquisitions to move the dial adequately. As we have seen, large acquisitions can work for several years but the risks escalate with size.

Management also suffers from mixed incentives, as evidence suggests that pay tends to follow business size rather more than earnings growth (Zhou,

2000). Similarly, acquisitions of any substance increase the power and status of the senior management. Everyone prefers to run a bigger business than a smaller one. Meeks and Meeks comment that 'The acquirer's executives mostly gain from the deal and their advisers always do' (2022). Whilst some research suggests that these benefits drive behaviour, my feeling is that these factors are not necessarily the most significant influences. The major motivator is more likely to be that of excitement at what might be a chance to revolutionise the business through a significant purchase and go down in history as the leader who transformed its fortunes.

Meeks and Meeks go on to argue that, in any number of cases, the destruction of value stemming from M&A is such that it would be better if management desisted entirely. My feeling is that this disregards the pressures on management from investors to grow the business. Organic growth alone provides inadequate growth in most industries, most of which then resort to M&A.

Once a team of advisor professionals has been assembled around the CEO and FD, then they will all motivate each other in the chase to get the deal over the line. Serious consideration of pulling out when significant risks are uncovered is unappealing to all. No one wants to destroy the dream.

Large deals normally attract the attention of the media, particularly the business pages. They are seen as 'imaginative,' demonstrating 'real ambition' and a clear strategy. Profile, interviews and the prospects of a still bigger job may be a consequence, or indeed even a book. But remember, much of the financial media is written for consultants, advisors, lawyers, and accountants, all of whom are employed in deals. I am always astonished at the media positivity given to large deals that are almost certain to fail and almost invariably do. If the deal does go wrong, it may be years before it becomes apparent, and even then, it may be possible to obscure the root cause.

Dealing with the Fallout

So how do businesses deal with the fallout from large deals once value destruction becomes apparent? Even those which fail to deliver the positive forecasts that convinced the shareholders and the board require careful management.

Markets are emotional. They can veer from excessive optimism to excessive pessimism. Take the 'gig economy' and the many technology shares which, up until 2022, had high ratings. So what changed? Shares collapsed as investors switched to the 'dividend' stocks widely viewed as being safer during recessions.

Covid destroyed many shares of businesses which depended on people either going to work or taking holidays, such as sandwich and coffee shops like Pret a Manger. Many sectors were slow to recover, making them prime takeover targets. This market emotionality can be a friend when it comes to making bids for others; it creates both buying and selling opportunities.

At the time of the deal/bid the buyer's share price is normally high. Management is aware that this is helpful and so timing is related to performance. This is often a consequence of positive forecasts both before the deal and of the proposed benefits following it. In effect, acquirers may manage their share price to instil confidence in potential funders and investors. Large deals must be made from a position of strength and provide confidence in the markets that will have to fund the deal. This might be issuing share paper or bonds or borrowing from banks.

An alternative explanation is that, when businesses are performing well and liquidity plentiful, access to significant funds 'burns a hole in the pocket' of CEOs. Optimism, confidence and, in some cases, hubris send them out shopping for targets without being adequately selective. This is exactly when available liquidity and a positive economy have driven deal transactions and prices are high. The wise CEO would deduce that this is the time to sell, not to buy.

The Proverbial Hockey Stick

Performance forecasts following a deal are distinctive and frequently adopt some rendering of the 'proverbial hockey stick.' This is a graph of projected performance which declines over the following year or two, before making dramatic improvements. This usually reflects the costs of integration and some disruption before predicted improvements occur in the years to come. Valuations of some of the major deals this book considers, such as AB InBev at the time of acquiring SABMiller in 2016, Bayer when buying Monsanto, Dow and DuPont, Standard Life and Aberdeen Asset Management are all prime examples. All would have projected improving shareholder returns after an initial dip, but ultimately failed to deliver such projections on a major scale.

In the words of Lewis Carroll and *Through the Looking Glass,* this is encapsulated by the phrase 'jam tomorrow': 'jam yesterday, jam tomorrow, but never jam today.' In effect the benefits never arise nor shareholder value materialise, despite continuing promises. As management strives to justify the acquisition, the nature of the proposed benefits may change. Elon Musk, in his acquisition of Twitter (renamed 'X') first justified the acquisition on the grounds of improving business performance. As this improvement failed to materialise, the business model was reframed, as the less tangible, more idealised pursuit of 'freedom of speech.' Unfortunately, his advertisers had a different view of what extent this freedom should permit; many subsequently withdrew their support.

One response when the longer-term post-acquisition performance disappoints is for management to move the 'hockey stick' forward into the future, indicating to boards and shareholders that benefits are still expected but are merely delayed. This measure effectively stalls for time in the hope that some legitimate circumstantial factors arise which might be blamed: recession, Covid, banking or sectoral collapse and adverse regulations are all helpful in formulating an acceptable explanation for poor performance. In effect, management may seize on the opportunity to obscure the real reasons behind poor performance. In most of the examples given, top management was replaced once the consequences of the deal could no longer be hidden. In smaller deals, the investors may never become aware of the value destruction or reasons for a failed integration process.

Many businesses do not have a formal post-acquisition review process to assess the extent to which subsequent performance was in accordance with the approved proposal. Consequently, boards are excluded from potentially useful feedback on acquisition policy and performance; in any number of cases I have seen, this has been intentional.

Meeks and Meeks list the various devices used to cover up the fiasco and indeed get them approved in the first place (2022). These normally involve optimistic forecasts of deal benefits which are rarely realised.

Governance Failures

Where are the Non-Executive Directors whilst this is happening? The prospects of success for large deals are limited in statistical terms but can be catastrophic at their worst. Faced with a CEO who has a good track record of success with acquisitions, it becomes difficult for NEDs to quarrel or question a further major acquisition which may substantially dilute earnings by the time a price is struck. Needless to say, there will be forecasts of future synergies presented to the board which will be very positive.

Unless there have been previous disasters, then how do you oppose a deal simply on the grounds of research? Executives with a good track record often believe that they can beat the statistics. Even when proven wrong, they will still blame environmental factors. This unshakeable belief is not easily challenged. NEDs are generally given quite limited information and those who are not from the industry may have limited insight. NEDs generally do not want to 'make waves' unless there is a very strong case to do so. This raises major questions as to whether corporate governance in this sense really works. Only once a deal is done and value destroyed does it become easier for NEDs to act. CEOs and CFOs often pay the price, as the impact of a deal becomes apparent and impossible to hide. By then, however, shareholder value has been destroyed.

Why Don't the NEDs Do More to Stop These Deals?

In a nutshell:

- Boards are often presented with limited information which shows the deal in a positive light. Forecasts and assumptions may well be optimistic and unlikely to be achieved. These are difficult for NEDs to argue with.
- Businesses often do not have any formal review process to assess whether acquisitions have been performed to their prospectus and reported back to the board.
- NEDs are not typically from the industry and have limited insight into the proposal.
- The CEO presenting the case may have a good track record of acquisitions and so it becomes difficult to effectively argue with their record, even though this may be the highest-risk acquisition to date.
- Whilst NEDs are supposed to be selected by Nomination Committees chaired by a NED, the reality is that CEOs have a strong say. NEDs do not wish to offend a CEO.
- NEDs frequently have several jobs and limited time for each role. This results in too little time to get over-involved in any one business to the depth needed.
- In large boards, it becomes difficult for NEDs to create a challenge. The larger the board the less effective its operation. Indeed, large boards tend to provide an audience rather than insightful questioning.

- NEDs often form a network and may struggle to attract further positions if they prove too challenging. Other CEOs might not necessarily want someone who is overactive on their board.

Effective Models of Governance

Agency Theory

A well-known theory substantiated by research considers the relationship between the principal and employed agent; it contests that, despite the agent being employed to work in the best interests of the principal, they will still pursue their own objectives unless measures are in place to prevent it. Such measures or precautions might include increased levels of transparency through reporting, and monitoring controls to ensure the agent acts in the interests of the principal.

In the case of publicly listed companies, the principals are the shareholders, whilst the agents are the board. Transparency is achieved through extensive corporate reporting, whilst monitoring controls include stipulations such as the requisite NEDs, committees for audit, directors' remuneration, board appointments (by nomination) and a plethora of processes and reporting that includes the involvement of auditors. Some would argue that, in practice, NEDs are often chosen by the Chairman and CEO, rarely have the industry knowledge and may be given limited information—all points that constrain their ability to form incisive judgements. Without additional knowledge and information then NEDs are in a position whereby they can only arrive at the conclusion which the executive directors require.

NEDs are selected as individuals who already have prominent roles in their own organisations, and in theory, may bring experience to the table. However, they may also bring ego into the room as well, which potentially hinders the open discussions most needed. Listed business boards are often large (12 or more people) which makes open debate difficult, if not impossible. As a board member on one of my boards remarked, the more NEDs appointed then the more egos there are to be massaged and managed. Research into board size suggests that they are most effective when made up of closer to seven members in number. One school of thought is that large boards are created to avoid accountability and governance but provide an audience for the chairman and CEO.

Shareholders nearly always prefer board members to also own shares, as a guarantee that their interests will be better aligned. Typically, board members for listed businesses hold an average of around 3% of the equity which may not be substantial enough to create aligned incentives.

Family Businesses

It does appear that boards made up predominantly of shareholders do perform better than those that own little equity. One example of this is family businesses in which the family owners are both the board and the ones running the business. Evidence suggests that larger, long-standing family businesses outperform listed businesses across the economic cycle (Bloch et al., 2012). They invest less in research, development and major capital projects, but are more selective about chosen projects, which reduces risk to the business. They perform better through recessions but worse in boom times when they struggle to add rapid capacity. In short, they do better over the economic cycle but may grow more slowly.

Decision-making benefits from the 'own money' syndrome—the presumption being that, since you are spending your own money, then you are more careful than when spending someone else's money. Family businesses are reluctant to issue shares to raise cash for investment and rely predominantly on bank borrowing and internally generated funds for growth. As excessive borrowing would be seen as a risk to the family itself, then that too is usually restricted. A consequence is that there is less money available to invest, which limits funding to only high-yielding and low-risk investments.

Family businesses also tend to change leadership less frequently than public companies and spend a long time grooming the chosen successor. Previous incumbents remain to offer advice as the family shares a common interest in wanting the business to do well for the next generation to benefit. Growth, whilst desirable, is not as critical as for public companies or PE. The main objective is to provide the family with a good living and the next generation with employment.

> **Case Study: A Family Business**
> After existing for over a century, a lack of interest in the family meant this business has resorted to an entirely professional board. Despite this significantly altered dynamic, they retain the long-standing rule that only family members can hold shares, and these are fragmented between more than 100 separate shareholders. Whilst similar governance arrangements are operated as they would be for public listed companies, the family continue to harbour

doubts as to whether the board's interests are aligned with those of the family, especially given the board are not shareholders.

Historic events have created a further layer of suspicion amongst the shareholders after a previous non-family CEO attempted to mount his own PE-backed bid for the business. This would have created a major conflict of interest, given that the CEO would be both selling and buying the business. As a buyer, he would want the best deal he could get, yet as a seller, he was well-placed to manipulate the accounts and, consequently, the value of the business downwards. After a difficult period, he was invited to leave. Some shareholders described the CEO as trying to steal the business from the family, such was the feeling. This was no doubt exacerbated by family attitudes to 'non-blood' management.

More recently, many family shareholders have expressed the wish to sell the business to provide liquidity for the shares. The restrictive arrangements on ownership mean there is no effective internal market for the shares without an exit event. Although the number of family shareholders voting to sell is a majority, they wouldn't achieve the 75% needed under the articles to approve a sale. The concern is that the professional board has no incentive to sell the business, and so are no longer aligned. For them, a successful bid would mean the NEDs would lose their jobs, and the Executive Directors might also be in a perilous position. Will they discourage approaches or limit shareholder knowledge regarding buyer interest? Clearly, if the board owned significant numbers of shares, then they might have similar incentives to boost business performance towards an exit event.

In such cases, the alignment of interests between the board and shareholders is key; it mitigates the potential suspicions regarding personal interests and motivations that can arise.

Private Equity

How does all this affect PE? First, PE usually avoids very large deals without good reason. There are exceptions however; one instance of this was towards the end of the post-Covid M&A boom when some sizeable PE deals were undertaken. When such deals are done there are certainly risk factors. The infamous 'Barbarians at the Gate' RJB-Nabisco fiasco was a failure with a price tag of $25bn (Burrough & Helyar, 1990).

More recently, in 2021, PE firm Clayton, Dubilier & Rice acquired the listed UK supermarket chain Morrisons for £10.1bn after a bidding war. This looked to be doomed from the start due to several inadvisable factors:

paying too much, bad timing when transacting at the M&A market peak and temporary finance over a turbulent economic period that resulted in high costs. Moreover, there was no clear strategy, other than to break up if, or when, markets recovered. Following the Issey Brothers' £7.1bn acquisition of Asda from Walmart earlier in the year, supermarket valuations had increased. The combination of Morrisons' listed business status and the ensuing bidding war meant Clayton, Dubilier & Rice ended up paying a price too high to ever make much money (LLC MarketLine Company Profile, n.d.). These exceptions to the norm are relatively rare in PE.

The earlier private equity chapter established that PE boards are comprised of shareholders in the business, so the potential 'agency' problem does not arise. Management owns, say, 25% of the shares, whilst PE owns the remainder, with a board consisting of both PE owners and management. It has been found that the long-term PE fund performance is around 3% IRR (Internal Rate of Return) better each year than for public listed businesses. The PE board are spending their own money and are therefore more careful as to how they invest it. Mistakes may be made, but their M&A performance proves far better than listed businesses which tend to 'go shopping' when they generate surplus cash rather than give it to shareholders.

Eclipse of the Corporation?

Michael Jensen's *Harvard Business Review* article 'Eclipse of the Corporation' points out that listed companies only return around 10% of their generated cash to shareholders through dividends and share buybacks (Jensen, 1989). The rest is 'invested' in schemes that vary in success and advisability. In many ways, Jensen's article is perceptive in laying out the rationale for why PE exists. It extols the virtue of debt versus equity in driving managerial discipline. Jensen's belief is that equity funding is too flexible and easy to abuse, whilst debt funding is inflexible in terms of performance. The requirements regarding covenants and interest payments mean the business has to perform.

One illustration of this concept was voiced by the CEO of a board I recently chaired. During a budget review for the following year, he said, 'We'll just have to cut the dividend next year.' By this, he meant that the business would underperform, and the shareholders would suffer as a result. As Chairman, representing the views of shareholders, I felt he could do far more in terms of cost-cutting than he was willing. This, however, would involve redundancies and 'doing more with less people,' an approach I knew the CEO was uncomfortable with. Covenants surrounding the debt reduced the options available, as breaching these would incur substantial charges by the bank and inflict various costs on the business. The bottom line remained: the CEO should make the business perform better rather than cut the dividend. Debt offers fewer options.

Many would point out the obvious: too much debt endangers the business, management, employees and shareholders. The question is what *is* too much? Corporates like to minimise debt and stockpile unused bank facilities and cash. This provides a cushion against misfortune. Such a stockpile of cash provides a 'war chest' to acquire businesses and make attractive investments. Conversely, it can 'burn a hole' in the pocket of CEOs who spend it on unwise, high-risk and overpriced acquisitions. There are two sides to this argument. The more efficient capital structure suggested by Jensen is lower cost and, in his view, provides a greater incentive to run the business more effectively. This, however, comes with greater risk to the business and its stakeholders.

NEDs: How Effective Are They?

Jensen has plenty to say on public corporations and governance through the appointment of NEDs. 'The idea that outside directors with little or no equity stake in the company could effectively monitor and discipline managers who have selected them has proven hollow at best' (Jensen, 1989).

Institutional equity investors, who make up the bulk of corporate investors, are rarely involved in the management of the businesses in which they own shares. They are passive investors. Consequently, there are few effective motivations for management to run the business in the interests of investors rather than their own interests. The board has little equity, NEDs may only prove effective in the most extreme of circumstances, and the investors have little influence. Incentives are largely derived *by* management *for* management, with NEDs being little more than a rubber stamp.

Again there are two sides to this argument. There are some excellent NEDs who are willing to stand up and be counted, just as there are plenty who 'go with the flow' and do not challenge significant issues. Where there is a clear separation of ownership from management the NEDs might be the next best alternative.

Jensen on PE

Jensen's arguments are well aligned with my own insights, particularly in terms of the impact of private equity on acquired businesses and how this differs from corporates. Jensen says, '…. they can motivate the same people with the same resources to perform so much more effectively under private ownership than in the publicly held firm' (Jensen, 1989). Jensen refers here to the frequent scenarios in which a division is bought out of a corporate and the management team retained. They are then expected to implement a newly produced plan which significantly increases the value of the business through measures such as cost-cutting and entering new markets. This gives rise to the obvious question as to why they failed to perform in a similar manner when previously owned by the corporation. Lack of investment and endless battles with Head Office are often prominent in the list of reasons. One might also add that when it is their own money invested, motivation invariably increases, with the additional freedom from the chains of central control.

Jensen is an exponent of the view that the corporate governance model is not effective and that there are better models, namely private equity, that make for a more effective running of businesses. The major decline in Western-listed businesses suggests that he is not alone in his beliefs and that investors are voting with their feet. PE is increasing rapidly whilst the number of corporates listed in both the UK and the USA has almost halved in the last twenty years.

Incentives

Neither the PE partners nor the management running the acquired business earn serious incentive payments unless they can exit at a substantial profit to the buying price. As a result, there is less motivation towards creating business scale, as any significant payments to the board only arise following a successful exit. These exit incentives drive a low purchase price, extensive business improvement and a high sale price significantly beyond what was initially paid.

Active Board Management

Private equity CEOs are much more likely to be fired if they cannot keep business improvement performance on track with the plan. For them, there are no incentives to pursuing an overly optimistic post-acquisition improvement plan that they can't deliver. PE investors are active managers of their boards, and if they are failing to achieve planned returns, then there is no hesitation about changing them. Sometimes the comings and goings are more consistent with Premier League football managers. Research finds that top teams are changed in about two-thirds of acquisitions (Gompers & Kaplan, 2022). Unlike corporates, family businesses are far more reluctant to make senior management changes and are more tolerant of failure.

Governance

In private equity, NEDs are normally selected due to having a background in a similar industry so they understand what is necessary to be successful. Their remuneration is predominantly in equity options, so they too are aligned with the exit objective. The proposal to acquire also must pass through a PE 'Risk Committee' that reviews each element of the deal including the due diligence. They will only sanction bids if they believe the deal can return a minimum 2.2 × original investment, plus the principal. This high bar is why few deals are approved. For them, there is no glory or benefit from large deals unless they are going to deliver significant returns.

Lessons
1. Be wary of promises made by CEOs at the time of acquiring large businesses. They frequently never materialise and remain 'jam tomorrow,' or a perpetually shifting 'hockey stick.'
2. CEOs can be confident that as time passes, market, industry and economic changes will arise which obscure whether any real integration benefits have been created, reducing the performance pressure on executives.
3. A rough rule applied by boards is that if performance is adverse then it is due to depressed markets or circumstantial issues that are beyond the executives' control. If performance is positive, then it is a consequence of executives' excellent strategy.
4. Corporates usually make major acquisitions when their own share price is high. Whether this is a result of renewed confidence drawn from the

high share price, available liquidity prompting acquisition activity, or manipulating the share price to facilitate the deal, is not known.
5. Effective governance and incentivisation are means of aligning the board's interests with those of the shareholders. Boards in which the members are significant shareholders are more effective in returning shareholder performance. In short, boards take more care when spending their own money.

References and Recommended Readings

Acharya, A., Gottschalg, O., Hahn, M., & Kehoe, C. (2013). Corporate Governance and Value Creation: Evidence from Private Equity. *The Review of Financial Studies, 26*(2), 368–402.

Baron, J., & Lachanauer, R. (2015, January 15). Surviving in a Family Business When You are Not Part of the Family. *Forbes.*

Basu, D. R., & Miroshnik, V. (2018). *Corporate Governance and Effectiveness: Why Companies Win or Lose.* Routledge Studies in Corporate Governance.

Bloch, A., Kachaner, N., & Stalk, G. (2012). What You Can Learn From Family Business. *Harvard Business Review, 90*(11), 1–5.

Burrough, B., & Helyar, J. (1990). *Barbarians at the Gate: The Fall of RJR Nabisco.* Arrow Books.

Carroll, L., Haughton, H., & Tenniel, J. (2010). *Alice's adventures in Wonderland; and Through the Looking-Glass.* Penguin Books.

Clayton, Dubilier & Rice, LLC MarketLine Company Profile. (n.d.). MarketLine, a Progressive Digital Media business.

Fernandez-Aranzubía, C., Iqbal, S., & Ritter, J. (2015, April). Leadership Lessons from Great Family Businesses. *Harvard Business Review.*

Gompers, P. A., & Kaplan, S. A. (2022). *Advanced introduction to Private Equity.* Edward Elgar Publishing.

Gottschalg, O., Acharya, V. V., Hahn, M., & Kehoe, C. (2012). Corporate Governance and Value Creation: Evidence from Private Equity. *The Review of Financial Studies, 26*(2), 368–402.

Graham, J. R., Harvey, C. R., & Pure, M. (2013). Managerial Attitudes and Corporate Actions. *Journal of Financial Economics, 109*(1), 103–121.

Gryta, T., & Mann, T. (2020). *Lights Out: Pride, Delusion, and the Fall of General Electric.* Houghton Mifflin Harcourt.

Immelt, J. R. (2017). How I Remade GE. *Harvard Business Review.*

Jensen, M. C. (1989). Eclipse of the Public Corporation. *Harvard Business Review, 67*(5), 61–74.

Larcker, D. F., & Tayan, B. (2021). *Corporate Governance Matters: A Closer Look at Organizational Choices and Their Consequences* (3rd ed.). Pearson.

Meeks, G., & Meeks, J. G. (2022). *The Merger Mystery: Why Spend Ever More on Mergers When So Many Fail?* Open Book Publishers.

Pozen, R. C. (2007). If Private Equity Sized Up Your Business. *Harvard Business Review, 85*(11), 78–152.

Tricker, R. I. (2015). *Corporate Governance: Principles, Policies, and Practices* (3rd ed.). Oxford University Press.

Welch, Jack (with Welch, Suzy). (2005). *Winning*. Harper Business, NY.

Zhou, X. (2000). CEO Pay, Firm Size, and Corporate Performance: Evidence from Canada. *The Canadian Journal of Economics, 33*(1), 213–251.

9

Case Studies

Introduction

The four case studies that comprise this chapter represent different strategic approaches to business acquisition. They are chosen to illustrate some of the major pitfalls relating to pricing, due diligence and challenging integrations. The cases include Elon Musk's acquisition of the social media giant, Twitter, subsequently rebranded as X, Rawlplug, the well known and established fixings business and the private equity-funded acquisition of supermarket groups Asda from Walmart, and the previously listed Morrisons. The final case, again a PE-funded venture, is that of Garrett Motion, a major Swiss manufacturer of turbochargers for internal combustion engines. The cases are written with a primary focus on the key strategic and M&A issues they raise, therefore peripheral details have been deliberately excluded to highlight learning points.

The perils of unrelated acquisitions, strategic diversions from core growth, market and product diversification, and strategy in turbulent and transient industries are all strong themes in these cases. The pace of technological development in recent years has meant that in industries subject to rapid change, businesses have turned to non-traditional, often innovative approaches to strategy. Global events, economic disruption and governmental responses to these are a source of continued turbulence. Increasingly, these call for an agile management response, with strategies that often run counter to financial wisdom.

Case 1: Rawlplug: Stick to the Strategy

The phone rang and it was my secretary with a call from an investment banker. 'Ok, put her through.' Investment bankers cut both ways. They have significant knowledge of corporate activity in your sector, such as who is up for sale, who is buying who and for how much, but they are also there to create corporate activity and have been known to do so by lulling people into acquisition or disposal activity which might not always be wise.

Investment bankers trade in industry knowledge, so what you say to them can travel fast and this case is no different: 'A couple of businesses are being disposed of which might interest you…'.

One of the businesses was Rawlplug—a household name in fixings, bolts, plugs, and, according to their listing, 'other fabricated metal products.' Founded in 1919, they are manufactured in Scotland and sold in the UK through a variety of channels, including builders' merchants and major DIY chain retail outlets. It had been a profitable business but had stalled in recent years and, as our plasterboard business shared a similar DIY channel presence, acquiring Rawlplug potentially had much to offer in terms of cross-selling.

At that time, my job role included responsibility for all the Groups' activities in the UK, Ireland and Nordic territories. We manufactured and distributed plasterboard systems which had guaranteed test results for fire, noise, water and impact resistance, as well as acoustic performance. Provided people used our plasterboard, metal, screws, etc. to the system specification and assembled it properly, we guaranteed that it would meet all these performance promises. By providing these performance guarantees our products would be accepted by architects and specifiers in commercial buildings. However, we did not supply specific fixings, as generic versions made by anyone could be used, providing they had passed various standard tests. One potential option was to specify Rawlplug fixings only and increase demand for their products; clearly, it would make much more sense if we owned it. I knew we could remove significant administrative costs from Rawlplug. By using our already established UK Service Centre to supply financial back office, management information, IT systems, HR safety and company secretarial services, we could operate at a much lower cost and higher quality than a company of that size would be able to achieve on its own. In addition, there was some overlap in customers which included builders' merchants and DIY channels, again a source of possible cross-selling.

Making a Decision

'Ok, I'll sign a Non-Disclosure Agreement (NDA) so you can send over the Information Memorandum.' I was well and truly on the slippery path of opportunism already, deviating from our established strategy of international expansion of our plasterboard activities. But if it worked out then why not?

I called a meeting of our various marketing, sales and financial people to discuss these plans. The consensus was that they were viable and that this was an opportunity too good to miss.

We made a bid and did some due diligence on the operations and commercial areas. A more thorough due diligence was undertaken for the financial and legal areas, which did not produce any deal breakers. The premises were old, and the plant underinvested, hollowed out by various owners over the years who, deeming the business a non-core one, had little motivation to invest. My thoughts were that we could outsource much of the production and maintain only the sales, marketing and new product development and testing departments. The name 'Rawlplug' was well known, and it had good channels to market. Provided we could do the development, testing and gain certifications then did we need to make the product ourselves?

The strategy and benefits were extensively discussed with our own management who also conducted various visits. Everyone was very positive about the acquisition and felt it was a good fit. Of course, it created interest—some saw it as a means of achieving personal prominence in our organisation, others viewed it as a way of increasing their own responsibilities, others still simply viewed the project as an interesting challenge. In fact, there were a number of personal, financial and organisational reasons why we might do this deal.

An area which we could have invested in more penetrative due diligence was the current and potential competitors of Rawlplug. These were large German corporations with a specialised focus on fixings. At the price-sensitive end of the market for more commoditised products, the Chinese manufacturers were also increasing their influence. The major manufacturers dominated the specification-led part of the market whilst the Chinese were becoming an increasing threat to the price-sensitive market, Rawlplug was somewhere in between.

The acquisition was made with an EBITDA multiple of 8, which was a little high for this business size and industry, but the deal included some property and working capital. For a business of this sort, an EBITDA multiple of 6 might have been nearer the mark, but we convinced ourselves that, as Rawlplug was already a well-established name, there was much which could be done with it.

Integration

We announced our ownership and a bright new future to the staff and management. We knew what needed to be done but there was no written integration plan, just a series of promises made to our main board to justify the business purchase, what changes we would make and the benefits which would arise. We had integrated a whole series of previous businesses, honing a team that was highly practised and well-organised. We felt sure that most of the projected savings could be achieved.

The original sales order processing system had to be kept separate as there were certain detailed requirements that the UK Service Centre could not supply. The remainder was integrated rapidly and with significant savings. The system specifications were altered to specify Rawlplug fixings throughout the existing ranges. Unfortunately, we were unable to make them stick in terms of sales, as customers ignored this new part of the specification, arguing that there was no real justification for them to change and they should continue with previous arrangements in this area. Withdrawing system guarantees was not really an option as too much of our high-margin product sales depended on the system sales.

Failed Synergies

The cross-selling with our other business simply did not work. The categories were separate and had different buyers amongst our customers so we couldn't roll them into our existing bundle deals. We could only operate as we had previously, and the fact that we were the new owners did not cut much ice with the buyers. The outsourcing of production was tested but we could not find any source who could make them cheaper so there seemed little point. It appeared that the profit levels required by the suppliers wiped out any benefit that might be gained.

From Bad to Worse

Finally, there was strong competition at both the high-end specification and more commoditised parts of the market. Enormous German producers dominated the high-performance market and were pushing the EU to increase the extent of testing requirements, effectively excluding the smaller players who could not afford the hundreds of trials. At the more commoditised end of the market, the Chinese producers with cheap energy and labour could produce at a much lower cost than us. We had the name and reputation but had to sell at a premium due to higher costs. Prices were only going one way and it was a battle to hold what we had in the market.

In short, the overhead cost benefits were delivered but outsourced savings did not materialise nor were the revenue benefits achieved.

Another Phone Call

Eighteen months after the acquisition, the Group CEO rang me. 'How is Rawlplug doing?' he asked. He knew very well how Rawlplug was doing since he received the results each month. I explained the situation honestly: the markets were more competitive than we had expected and that, whilst cost savings had been achieved, the revenue benefits had failed to materialise. 'Sell it before it loses any more value,' was his response (never a man to waste words). I knew that was the best course of action in view of the failed cross-selling strategy.

We put it up for sale and there was interest from a Polish fixings business who wanted to enter the UK fixings market. In a complicated deal, we split the land and buildings to sell separately and sold Rawlplug without the working capital that we collected. Stock was to be sold at valuation to the new owners. Together with the profits and cash generated during our brief tenure, we just about broke even in the sale. It had absorbed much effort from all involved, who effectively went unrewarded. It also provided a significant distraction from running our other businesses.

Lessons

1. Strategy and Opportunism

Most importantly, create a clear corporate strategy then identify and list targets which further the strategy. Do not be drawn into opportunist ventures purely due to business availability, nor on the basis of cross-selling integration benefits which may or may not be achievable. If an opportunity is not on the list, then do not buy it. M&A is a tool to further a clear strategy, rather than a random means of growth akin to retail browsing and shopping.

Investment bankers and other intermediaries are important to the M&A process but remember their objective is to create buying and selling activity, not necessarily to further your strategic ambitions. They will regularly offer you businesses with suggested strategies which may provide growth and some integration benefits, but which do not form part of your declared strategy. Remember they are not accountable to either your board or shareholders—you, however, are.

Whilst Rawlplug might have provided complementary products, this acquisition was still a distraction from the pursuit of our main strategy. More peripheral investments usually struggle for investment as spare cash is invested in the main core activities. Eventually, a business without serious investment will wither, and it is much wiser for it to be in the hands of someone who does include it in their core strategy.

The business was not huge by any means and was probably not worth the attention of management and the effort invested in integrating and trying to extract benefits. Acquisitions and subsequent integration require huge management time and attention; they may not be worth the resource requirement.

Cross-selling revenue benefits are rarely achieved in most acquisitions. Channels, customers and buyers often see suppliers as specific to product groups and are unwilling to vary their approach just because of a takeover. Sales forces are also specialised, and widening their portfolio easily becomes a distraction from their previous product focus. City analysts and shareholders normally discount any revenue benefits when assessing deals.

2. Due Diligence

Like many businesses, we chose to undertake the commercial and operational due diligence ourselves. This was a mistake. We did not have enough knowledge of the market to recognise the major risks. The operations people saw the acquisition as a means of driving capital investment. A more formal external approach might have thrown up the true market, level of competition and equipment risks. Realistically, the people doing the due diligence lacked objectivity; they were just as keen to acquire the business as we were, as it created more interest and a greater empire for them too.

Due diligence is often viewed as a hurdle to be overcome in the process of acquiring a business, rather than an opportunity to engage with experts in the relevant area and gain an independent view. The acquirer has made the decision to buy and all else is an impediment to completing the process. With M&A, a determination to do the deal can prevent objectivity.

3. **Integration**

We should have created a detailed plan that included a timetable and allocated responsibilities ahead of the deal's completion. This is not the same as an initial proposal to the main board. In this case, our teams knew what they were doing, and the integration went smoothly. That might not always be the case. A more detailed plan drawn up in advance might have identified the real prospects of the strategy working.

4. **Pricing**

In our enthusiasm to acquire the business, price had been largely ignored. We had accepted their asking price when it was likely there would be scope for negotiation. We did not stop to get a sense of whether there was other interest and at what price other buyers might have deemed acceptable. If PE had been interested it would have been at a lower price. The owner was not overwhelmed with bids, although they weren't about to admit that, it was a policy decision to dispose of several businesses. Being more concerned with value and using the due diligence effectively could have supported a lower price bid.

Summary

This story is not unusual and reflects many of the mistakes which corporates make when determining the costs and benefits of any deal. Having said that, the protracted process and negotiation required in acquiring a business is complex and there are many hurdles to be overcome. It takes determination to see a deal through. When acquisitions underperform, pride often plays a part in delaying disposal. Corporates don't want to admit the mistake to their own boards, nor the shareholders, and so retain a deteriorating business.

Investment bankers need to be carefully managed by giving them clear guidelines/lists of the businesses and sectors you are interested in acquiring. Otherwise, they will try and sell you opportunist strategies and business ventures which are not at the core of your strategy for growth and may not deliver benefits, however attractive they may initially appear.

'Deal heat' is, to some extent, inevitable during a deal negotiation, and enthusiasm is no bad thing. It becomes a problem, however, when the board's determination to buy a business means ignoring due diligence findings or conducting an inadequate, light-touch investigation in some areas. Excitement and enthusiasm often obscure objectivity.

Case 2: Twitter: Money-Maker or Mistake?

Elon Musk is no stranger to highly competitive markets in which the ultimate agenda is to take advantage of a competitor's weakness. For once though, he was on the receiving end as, still embroiled in his difficulties at Twitter, Meta launched a rival platform named 'Threads.' For some time now Twitter had, in effect, held a monopoly in the realm of short pithy quotes or 'microblogging'—a succinct and rapid means of reaching a mass audience with minimal effort—that worked well for many high-profile individuals. Twitter was the only platform at the time that offered this innovative brevity and reach. Indeed, global news programmes augment their broadcasts daily with Tweets from prominent politicians that encapsulate a concept or view. Donald Trump has been a great exponent of unveiling new policies and making pronouncements on the platform late into the evening; love him or hate him, Trump has done much to boost Twitter's popularity.

Elon Musk himself has become a Twitter household name through his own outspoken, often controversial opinions on current affairs. At the time of his bid, he was the world's richest person, and some have suggested the $44bn he paid for Twitter to be little more than pocket money spent in pursuit of his hobby. Elon Musk claims that, in his reversal of the move by previous CEO Jack Dorsey to ban the likes of Donald Trump, he was acting to protect freedom of speech on a global scale. Dorsey, a joint founder of the business, had significantly more liberal views than those of Donald Trump.

Paying Over the Odds

In any event, Musk committed to the purchase just as tech business valuations were plummeting and the speculation is that he paid almost twice what the business was worth. In fact, perhaps realising his somewhat impetuous bid for the business, Musk had tried to pull out, but somewhat unusually, the Board successfully sued Elon Musk into completing the $44bn deal. Once in charge, Musk promptly fired the board.

The enormous price tag he'd paid drove Musk to make major rapid changes. First came workforce reductions from 8,000 to 1,500 employees in a matter of weeks. The platform's content was therefore even less well-policed than previously and Musk's tendency towards right-wing opinions meant that, by 2023, Twitter had lost more than half its advertising accounts. These were with businesses increasingly uneasy that their adverts could appear alongside controversial views and damaging their own brand image. Further inappropriate comments from Elon Musk himself only aggravated the situation. The share option valuation in 2023 was $13bn, suggesting a loss of $31bn on the acquisition price.

Despite its reach, Twitter has never been able to monetise its popularity and, for much of its life, has been a loss-maker. The opportunistic Musk saw that the business was a virtual monopoly and that he could therefore charge users both to read tweets and post them. At the same time, he knew the business was wallowing in costs and could do a better job of attracting advertisers. In the measures that followed Musk antagonised virtually all of Twitter's stakeholders and irritated shareholders of Tesla, one of his other major investments.

Tesla the Loser?

The shareholders were right to be concerned, since the Tesla share price fell dramatically from a peak of $400 late in 2021 to just above $100 in January 2023; they felt that Musk was distracted by his new purchase at a time when Tesla's future needed his undivided attention. The major car producers were, by this stage, all launching fully electric models with comparable performance levels to Teslas. Some had much more experience in car making and greater economies of scale; a battle was set to commence in the electric car market. Adding further competition to these models was the large influx of cheap, good-quality Chinese EV's at the lower end of the price bracket. Tesla was having to cut prices dramatically to sell cars. Elon Musk's fortune dived as most was invested in Tesla shares.

Twitter had become synonymous with Musk and not everyone loved him. He may have reduced the cost base, but he had lost much of the revenue in the process. Realising that he needed to start distancing himself from Twitter for the good of future revenue, he recruited Linda Yaccarino from Xerox as Chief Executive and stepped back to a position as chairman.

Linda has enormous experience in advertising and knew and understood the advertisers' needs. She is a new face and is clearly charged with rebuilding relationships and trust with advertisers. With Twitter's rebranding, she confidently claimed that 'X will be the platform that can deliver… everything.' However, many saw her as a 'puppet' of Musk who would soon find her remit limited in scope by a chairman who would no doubt interfere.

Musk's Strategy

In a short space of time, Musk had made several strategic mistakes. If a business relies on advertising for revenue, then it needs to create advertising reach by maximising users. Charging Tweeters and those reading Tweets is not going to achieve this; in fact, many may leave altogether. Musk could have either maximised reach by offering free access to users, *or* charged the users who will not be expecting to pay for advertising; charging both makes little sense.

His introduction of subscriptions was also poorly timed; many of the countries in which Twitter operates were approaching recession. Subscriptions for content were being cut by users forced to make economies as their disposable wealth was squeezed. They were likely to take a dim view of Twitter's new charges for a service they had previously used for free, or at least only paid for with their data.

Twitter was undoubtedly heavy on cost pre-Musk; however, the extent of staff cuts left content less rigorously moderated. Problems with regulatory authorities soon arose as to the speed with which controversial material was blocked.

Threads—More Challenges Ahead

Against the background of these difficulties, Mark Zuckerberg saw the opportune moment to launch his own well-funded alternative linked to Instagram. 'Threads,' as the platform was named, was, like Twitter previously, free to users and, once it had adequate usage, funded by advertising. It is well known that there is no love lost between Zuckerberg and Musk and Meta is all set to challenge Twitter at its weakest point. In fact, Zuckerberg reported that over 10 million users had signed up for Threads within the first seven hours of its launch.

Meanwhile, Musk remains under substantial pressure to balance the conflicting needs of Tesla and Twitter. For the first time in some years, December 2022 saw Musk slip from his position as the world's richest person, largely due to the significant fall in Tesla's share price. By June 2023, however, he had reclaimed this title.

These figures are astronomical enough for me to concur with the view that Musk's strategic ventures are little more than a hobby; however, the mistakes he made in the case of Twitter serve as a valuable warning that any number of poor business decisions can turn rapidly into the proverbial albatross. Whether or not Threads makes headway, Twitter still has the problem of how to monetise its large user base.

Twitter may still have dominance in its market, but the potential synergistic relationship between Zuckerberg's other social media enterprises (Facebook, Instagram and Threads all being grouped beneath Metadata) may drive significant network effects. If Zuckerberg can entice high-profile 'Threaders' who are prepared to share opinions in the candidly succinct format previously unique to Twitter, he could rapidly attract new users. Dominant businesses that rely on network effects are difficult to unseat, primarily due to the mutually dependent relationship between users and providers. Whilst you may not bet on Threads doing well, taking these factors into account, Zuckerberg may well make progress.

M&A may have the potential to turn small fortunes into huge fortunes very rapidly, but a poorly judged deal can do just the reverse. At some point, Elon Musk may well find himself an example of this. In purely monetary terms, his excursion into social media has more than halved his investment. It has functioned as a major distraction for the remaining employees, advertisers, users and suppliers who are all concerned by what is continuing to happen in Twitter. There is little doubt that Musk has a talent for opportunist deals, raising funds and starting businesses, but we can only wait to see how well Twitter's network effects can withstand real competition.

Musk's public image may not work in his favour, and there is a strong possibility that the two social media platforms will become politically polarised, with right-wing sympathisers remaining aligned with Twitter, whilst those of a liberal disposition may turn to Threads.

Ask Yourself the Following:

- Elon Musk has created a series of businesses which are mainly manufacturing-based. To what extent did he understand social media and has this contributed to the strategic choices he made at Twitter?
- How far has hubris played a part?
- Why did Elon Musk overpay by so much?
- What is his best course of action from the position outlined in the case?
- Can Musk exit X and save face?
- Are there potential better owners for X who can add value?
- Is Threads really a threat? What obstacles does it have to overcome?
- Could or should Musk focus on Tesla?
- Engaging with the core issues:

1. Strategy
2. Due diligence
3. Timing
4. Distraction
5. Competition

Can Musk's actions be analysed in the context of the 'rules'?

Analysis: Musk's Mutating Strategy

Musk does not own any other social media activities and his understanding of Twitter is that of a user rather than an owner. There are no synergies with real developmental potential and currently no management with the proven technological expertise to develop the platform. The original strategy was seemingly to run the platform more economically, removing excess costs and monetising the large volume of users one way or another. Musk had hoped to retain and expand the advertising base of suppliers.

Charging 'Tweeters' was never going to succeed, considering much of the user base is there to follow interesting tweets from the rich and famous. These prominent, frequent commentators are a main asset and means of providing advertising reach. Instating charges therefore simply does not make sense; a reduced audience is only going to damage advertisers' takings.

Indeed this, along with the poorly-policed content of posts has led major advertisers to withdraw or suspend their contracts, reluctant to be associated with certain right-wing tweeters and their controversial opinions. Musk's new strategy has adopted a more politically persuasive leaning, emphasising the right to freedom of speech. Of course, one person's free speech is not necessarily another's, and who is the final arbiter? If the answer is Elon Musk, then it may be argued that the platform is now about propagating his own views. The cost-reduction efforts have been successful, but the reduced workforce has led to erratic scrutiny of content. In short, Twitter has turned into something of a political time bomb.

1. Due Diligence—Was There Any?

The nature of Musk's bid and enmity with the board of Twitter meant there was little inclination for deep due diligence. Did Musk really know what he was buying? Did he know how it functioned, which parts should be retained and which could be cut? Did he employ experts from that industry to undertake a review and formulate a strategy? It seems not.

2. Timing/Price

If there is anything to take away from this book, it is that timing is critical to all deals. Multiples vary substantially according to deal activity and volumes as well as industry cycles and sector sentiment. The technology sector valuations have seen something of a bubble over the previous 3/4 years. Valuation levels bore little resemblance to any metric of growth or profit. It was almost a repeat dot.com bubble of valuations as excess and cheap liquidity chased any available tech growth stock.

Unfortunately for Musk, growth rates and valuations had already started to stall before his bid and declined further still afterwards. How his valuation of $44bn was calculated is a mystery, as it certainly does not relate to the non-existent profits. After his bid and subsequent legal commitment, the tech valuations halved. It was certainly a 'full' price, and on the Twitter board sued Musk into honouring. Timing had made his bid embarrassingly high—Musk was mortal after all!

3. Improvement

Advertising is clearly an industry Musk did not understand, particularly the associative power of brands with controversial opinions. He also belatedly realised the importance of advertisers as a source of revenue after alienating many with his antics and tweets. After his initial problems, Musk realised he needed an industry expert to run some of the business and he found that in Linda Yaccarino. Musk stepping out of the industry, even temporarily, may well be a chance for the business to heal and allow Yaccarino room to make a success of it.

Case 3: The Rise of PE and the Fate of the Grocery Market's 'Big Four'

The 'Big Four'

Since the banking crisis of 2008, stock market valuations of UK grocery chains have been depressed. The subsequent recession and decline in UK living standards only acted to accelerate the growth of German discounters, Aldi and Lidl, who had arrived in the UK in the 1990s. Their limited range and sale of own-brand products created a low-cost structure that enabled them to offer comparable groceries at between 10 and 20% less than the UK's four major supermarket chains. Tesco had previously been the undisputed leader with 30% of the UK grocery market. They were followed by Sainsbury's and Asda, both with around 15/16%, with the smallest of the main chains, Morrisons, having around 10/11% share. Approximately 70% of the UK's grocery purchases were therefore in the hands of the 'big four' who were all highly profitable, with Tesco making around £8bn profit in 2006. Whilst there was some competition between the 'big four' it did not appear to affect their sizeable profits. Most of the price competition seemed to be on a limited range of own-brand, commoditised products such as bread, milk and eggs.

After the banking crisis, the commercial success of Aldi and Lidl's strategy changed this. They continued to increase their market share by targeting middle-class consumers, offering promotions on luxury products such as salmon, beef steaks and champagne.

Less Is More

Typically, the 'big four' carried ranges of 30,000 items upwards with some stores at 50,000. In comparison, Aldi and Lidl limited their range to between just 4,000 to 6,000 items, aware that large ranges drive substantial costs into most businesses. Ranges bring with them a need for large stores, extensive distribution warehousing, plus the complexity of managing and sourcing product lines with many suppliers. Fragmenting purchasing over large ranges and numbers of suppliers dissipates the bargaining power that larger volumes should present, limiting further their price leverage with big brands.

Building infrastructure to support such extensive ranges creates a level of fixed cost which cannot be reduced to the levels of Aldi and Lidl. These costs are difficult, even impossible, to address, which means the 'big four' will never be able to approach the prices of Aldi and Lidl. In short, the growth of Aldi and Lidl suggests that the public are prepared to accept smaller ranges if it means a lower premium and prices.

In the face of this unrelenting competition since 2009, the margins of the 'big four' have halved with their share prices following suit. In view of the continued expansion of Aldi and Lidl and the extensive building programmes buoyed by their success in attracting customers, suggests there is little prospect of this trend reversing. Based on December 2023 figures, Aldi and Lidl together now have 17.4% market share and the main losers are Morrisons (8.7%).

The Online Grocery Market

In many ways, online UK grocery sales is a thoroughly unattractive market for the major supermarket chains. Online ordering means each order must be individually picked, packed, and transported to customers' homes in set time windows. Compare this to customers in-store selecting and transporting their own orders home from the store and the labour comparison is evident. However, supermarkets felt they had little choice; if *they* did not service this growing market, then specialist online-only businesses such as Ocado, would.

The online market grew to around 11% of all groceries pre Covid, and the rate of conversion was between 0.5 and 1% each year. Aldi and Lidl refrained from entering the market due to the significance of added costs and reduced margins. The advent of Covid restrictions in 2020 changed this. The online market rocketed to 16% of all grocery sales, limited only by the capacity of the grocers to deliver. With shop sales so low, Aldi and Lidl were also eventually forced to enter the online market. They have subsequently withdrawn due to cost and investment pressures, instead investing in new physical stores.

In many ways, online is the worst of all worlds, considering grocery margins are already limited and the store costs remain the same, unless online shopping were to take a much greater market share. To make matters worse the major supermarket chains offer online delivery in rural areas. Consider Devon and Cornwall, in which the distance between some van drops could be as much as 5 to 10 miles. This can only lose money. Yet the supermarkets feel they need to maintain national inclusivity. Pricing must incur far greater costs than any revenue secured by the rural service.

An Industry Under Pressure: The Response of the 'Big Four'

The 'big four' responded to the ensuing discounter pressure and reduced profits by attempting mergers and reducing ranges. Supermarket aisles started notably widening to accommodate this. Any new stores were planned to be smaller or cancelled altogether as demand moved towards the discounters.

Whilst some prices were reduced, none of the 'big four' could approach the level achieved by the German duo. Various standoffs with suppliers ensued as the major chains attempted to force down the buying costs of major branded goods. However, the main branded grocery producers, such as Unilever and P&G generally had too much power and the supermarkets were forced to stock their products or risk losing customers to those that did.

Asda

The supermarket chain, Asda came into being in 1949, so named to acknowledge Associated Dairies from which it had grown. Headquartered in Leeds, it offered low-priced affordable products, and its success in the north grew rapidly.

Following a major turnaround by Archie Norman, the chain was acquired in 1999 by the powerful and globally expanding US Walmart chain for £6.7bn. Walmart soon discovered, however, that their strategic advantages such as site pre-emption, low-cost structure, scale economies and efficient operations were much harder to recreate outside of North America.

The Asda acquisition was by no means a disaster, however it failed to make the returns anticipated. In fact, most of Walmart's operations outside of North America failed to generate real value, and market withdrawals became necessary in some countries.

The Reign of Amazon

The online marketplace specialist, Amazon, was a significant player in all this, as their entry into the grocery market in the USA created major pressure on Walmart which was yet to develop an efficient online presence. With such a strong competitor, margins and volumes were bound to suffer. Walmart decided to return its focus to North America, and, in view of the continued progress of discounters, also decided to withdraw from its UK project, making Asda available to be sold.

A Failed Merger

Mike Coupe, the then CEO of Sainsbury's, Asda's competitor, offered Walmart a 'merger of equals' for the two chains in 2018. This was on the premise that Sainsbury's team would run the business, but Walmart would retain a significant shareholding in the combined business. The combined operation would be listed and then have a market share exceeding 30% of the UK grocery market. This would increase buying power, allow supplier rationalisation and create major cost savings in terms of management, systems and Head Offices.

The argument was that increased buying power and reduced costs would provide lower prices to customers (either that or increased profits). Mike Coupe's hope was that the Competition and Markets Authority (CMA) would allow the merger, albeit requiring limited disposals in areas of the country in which the combined market share was high. This had been the general approach of the CMA in previous years. However, the CMA eventually concluded that the diminution of competition was such that no element of the merger could be allowed. As Sainsbury's had haemorrhaged market share over the course of the bid, with a further £50mn lost on bid expenses, Mike Coupe had little choice but to resign.

PE Buy Asda for £7.2bn

The UK grocery market was not an attractive one to potential strategic bidders, as it was unlikely that Aldi and Lidl would alter their approach towards pricing or reduce the pace of their build programme. Consequently, Walmart had little option but to look towards private equity to offload Asda. Asda was sold to a US PE house, TDR, together with the Issa brothers who had previously made their fortune through acquiring and developing petrol stations. The shares were owned equally between TDR and the Issa brothers who would run the business.

In February 2021, TDR, plus the Issa brothers, paid £7.2bn including the debt, in a private purchase from Walmart which would retain a small stake. By this stage, Asda was a sprawling business with 342 superstores, 32 very large super centres, 207 supermarkets (<2300 square metres—convenience stores), 31 Asda Living homeware stores and 319 petrol stations. Most of the stores were owned, as were the distribution centres which supplied the supermarket stores. Typically, in the UK, distribution centres are owned by UK supermarket chains, although management is sub-contracted to third-party providers. This means that the contractors can be periodically tendered, but the specialised distribution hubs remain under supermarket ownership (these would be difficult to replace, unlike the contractors who operated them). The discount petrol stations had been introduced by all the main supermarket groups in the belief that offering cheap petrol would attract trade to the supermarket. Asda and Morrisons were normally the price leaders for fuel.

Around a year later, after various major changes, the Issa brothers claimed their stake in Asda was worth 20 times the £72mn they had invested. They believed the value of their stake had risen to £1.4bn in just one year; this raises the question as to how it was achieved and what risks and benefits may be involved. What could the PE owners do to extract value from Asda?

Morrisons

Towards the end of 2021, Morrisons suffered a similar fate to Asda and was acquired by PE. Being a public company Morrisons differed from Asda, in that any sale process would be highly transparent and anyone who was able to raise the funds could bid. This time the price was much higher as three US PE houses—Fortress, Apollo Group and Clayton Dubilier and Rice (CD&R)—escalated bids up to an astonishing £10.1bn including debt. CD&R were the victors after a final bidding round, although 'winner's remorse' might well become a more likely sentiment. Their £10.1bn acquired the chain with around 10% of the UK grocery market, TDR had acquired 15% of the market for their £7.2bn when buying Asda. Competitive bidding for a public company had driven a much higher price than a private exclusive sale of a much larger business in the same markets. Both businesses were property rich and Morrisons was believed to own 85% of its property.

In August 2017, the market shares of the 'big four' according to Kantar were as follows (Kantar, 2017):

Morrisons: 10.1%
Tesco: 27.8%
Sainsbury's: 15.8%
Asda: 15.3%

Morrisons, like Asda, had a long and rich history having originated in the late nineteenth century (1899) by the Morrisons family. The family had continued to run the business during the century to come, although a listing on the stock market significantly diluted their interest. Morrisons had grown to include 497 stores with 110,000 employees, 330 petrol stations, 12 food manufacturing sites and 6 distribution centres (all freehold). There was also a trawler and a Head Office in Bradford, the town where the grocer originated.

The PE plan involved issuing around £6.5bn of debt through bonds and commercial borrowing and undoubtedly involved a property play, though this was unlikely to deliver the usual 2.5 times the amount invested by PE. Typically, PE funding would usually be around 50% debt (either bonds or commercial borrowing or a mix), and 50% PE which might be structured as convertible or mezzanine finance. The amount of 'sweet' equity would be modest and shared between PE and top management.

2021 was the year of rebound from Covid and many industries experienced a bumper year for sales as customer savings were spent. Liquidity was still cheap and readily available. Interest rates remained low, and the outlook seemed robust.

Questions

- Why was Morrisons so much more expensive than Asda?
- What risks were CD&R running?
- If we consider our exit equation of maximising returns through EBITDA, multiple and cash, then what could PE do?
- Do you think the acquisition of either Asda or Morrisons will be successful in value creation?
- How could growth be achieved?
- How will PE exit their investments?

What Might PE Do in the Case of Asda and Morrisons?

The key question for the new owners is to what extent both Asda and Morrisons need to own all their businesses and the assets that go with them, which include:

- Manufacturing (Morrisons only)
- Distribution
- Grocery Stores (including alcohol, clothing, electrical goods, household items, phones, digital printing etc.)
- Petrol stations
- Convenience stores
- Homeware stores (Asda)

Is the sum of the parts sold separately worth more than when acquired? Do the various businesses under each corporate add synergistic value or destroy it? Both Asda and Morrisons are vertically integrated and horizontally diversified, do they need to be? Do they need to be the owners of each part? Can they sell them whilst retaining other synergistic benefits if they exist?

Are There Benefits to Owning These Businesses or the Property They Operate From?

Morrisons is the only one of the 'big four' supermarket to own some of its manufacturing. The others consider the market competitive enough to achieve low costs without. In fact, a captive manufacturer has a captive customer, isolating it from competition and the incentive to innovate; the consequence may be higher costs and less innovation.

How Much Property Do Asda and Morrisons Need to Own in Order to Operate an Efficient Business Model?

The large grocery stores have space to sell other ranges to customers visiting the site. The grocer does not necessarily need to operate the other product areas and could rent space to other operators who benefit from the flow of customers to the grocer. They may also be more innovative in their approach and marketing.

What Happened?

Within months the new management at Asda sold and leased back the property in the distribution hubs raising £1.7bn. Taking advantage of the low interest rates prevailing at the time, a commercial bond was taken out raising a further £1.6bn. The petrol stations were sold to the Issa brothers for £700mn, but the CMA later reversed the deal.

Both Asda and Morrisons had held petrol prices down across the country making an average margin of 6 pence per litre sold, on the belief that this attracted trade into the supermarkets. The new management took a different approach ending the major discounts to the market on petrol. They increased prices to create margins of 16 pence per litre.

Redundancies of 5,000 employees were announced saving around £150–200mn per year. The loss-making cafes were all shut, again deducing they did not attract more customers to the store as previous strategies had predicted.

Whilst significant attempts to reduce costs, increase prices, and sell property were implemented, the problem remains: how can they create growth in a highly competitive market with supermarkets which are too large?

Some Options to Consider

1. Selling off the convenience stores.
2. Developing convenience stores at the petrol station sites, as they are no longer believed to attract trade to the supermarkets. They could then be sold.
3. Borrowings could be securitised on the property yielding low interest rates.
4. The surplus space could be sold or rented to others who might benefit from a 'destination' such as branded coffee, Accessorise, etc.
5. Asda Living could be sold off.
6. The alcohol section could be sold off as a separate business.
7. Deferring payment to suppliers to increase positive working capital.

Risks

- The main risks are high inflation followed by increasing interest rates and reducing property valuations. The prospects of selling off anything amidst declining demand would be problematic.
- A further shift to the discounters would mean more difficult decisions around pricing and profits. Exit would be delayed by some years until liquidity improves and an appetite for acquisition reappears amongst potential buyers.
- The stock markets could remain closed to new floats for several years. An exit via a listing looks the most likely option, shorn of property and having sold the petrol stations, convenience stores, Asda Living, and the distribution property. Some of the store property could also be sold and leased back.

Outcomes for Asda

At the end of 2022 interest costs for the Asda debt were £400mn a year, although most was fixed and hedged. Markets for the resale of property were closed due to concerns over values during the recession. The Asda bond prices had collapsed to the point that the bonds were paying over 10% by the end of 2022, reflecting an increase in the business's perceived risk.

Asda managed to retain its position as the third largest supermarket, but costs increased during 2022 and the ability to pass them on compromised by Aldi and Lidl. There is a general customer shift towards the discounters during periods of hardship, which means in a prolonged recession, margins at Asda will continue to be under severe pressure.

More recently in March 2024, the Issa brothers' excessive debts have been under scrutiny, and their response predictable: the sale of assets and petrol forecourt expenditure—measures that executives referred to as 'controlled reduction' to maximise liquidity (*Daily Telegraph*, 2024).

The escalating cost of finance, reluctance of banks to continue lending and lack of market to sell the various parts of Asda is proving a big headache in this deal. However, patience is key, and timing is critical. No doubt all these negative factors will improve in the coming years.

Morrisons

The acquisition of Morrisons was another case of bad timing. As a public company, it was always going to be expensive, but it was also bought at the top of the market. With three PE houses bidding, along with the Issa brothers' comments about their equity stake being worth 20 times more after a year, ensured that the successful acquirer overpaid, which meant earning significant returns would be a major problem.

Historically, the mantra of PE was that they would not enter competitive bidding situations (higher prices). They would avoid buying public companies for which the valuations are normally higher than private companies due to multiple arbitrage. PE aims to sell when markets are high (for example in 2021) and buy when markets are low. The acquisition timing for Morrisons could not have been worse.

Why break their own rules? PE has been successful at raising money from investors who are aware of PE's focused pursuit of value creation. During 2022, they had around $3.7tn of 'dry powder' to invest. The sheer weight of such funds has forced them to take riskier bets and ignore the rules which have previously served them well—most fundamentally, a business model that depends on investing, improving and selling. There is little choice but to accept that the era of cheap money may be gone and that future returns may be more limited.

The Iceberg of Floating Debt

The banks had underwritten the debt until more permanent finance could be organised. They were to be caught with much of the debt as they had been unable to find a market for bonds as interest rates rocketed and economic uncertainty prevailed. The debt was unhedged and floating with higher rates to come. Morrisons suffered charges of £350mn and rising by the end of 2022, whilst the investment banks who held the debt may be suffering much worse. The timing also meant that selling parts of the business or selling and leasing back property is more difficult. There were rumours of selling the food manufacturing arm for £500mn and selling and leasing back five stores for £150mn. However, the financial markets were in turmoil after the policies of the Truss administration. Even when the new government introduced more stable economic policies high interest rates would prevail for months and likely years.

Morrisons profits collapsed as they attempted to hold prices up, and their market share fell to 9.2%; they were only now fully ascertaining the sensitivity of food shoppers in the UK. In 2022, Aldi replaced Morrisons as the fourth largest UK supermarket chain, holding over 10% market share.

Clearly, there are various property options, and the petrol business will have plenty of takers in view of the increased margins and profitability. The food manufacturing and distribution centres can be sold off, and the latter leased back when required. It seems likely that PE will have to hold Morrisons for much longer than originally envisaged if they are to make a return, and even that will be debatable. This was a classic case of bad timing, too high a price, and a lack of planning.

Case 4: Garrett Motion—Turbulent and Transient Industries

Introduction

Private equity investors normally identify opportunities to buy, improve and sell a business in a manner that creates value even in industries which are experiencing major difficulties. They rely on a strong grasp of strategic theory in their approach, as well as financial negotiating and change management capabilities. This case explores some of their tactics in the context of the notoriously 'difficult' European car industry and its various suppliers.

The European Car Industry

The decades following the 2008 banking crash have been characterised by major fluctuations in demand for cars. Higher interest rates and a period of depressed demand discouraged the purchase of 'big ticket' items. A decade later 'diesel gate' became a topical scandal when a number of European car manufacturers were found to be rigging official emission tests, reducing demand further still.

The uncovering of 'diesel gate' was soon compounded by research that provided a direct link between diesel particle emissions, ill health and as time has passed, even premature deaths in urban areas. The ultimate point of decline for the popularity of diesel-powered cars was the introduction of low-emission zones and congestion charges in some of the largest UK cities, most notably London.

Governments, despite having previously encouraged the use of diesel vehicles, now had little sympathy for car manufacturers who were seen to have brought this upon themselves. New tax incentives were introduced for Electric Vehicles (EVs) as well as end dates for the sale of new Internal Combustion Vehicles (ICEs). All these measures heavily impacted demand levels as buyers deferred their purchases until new policies were sufficiently clarified and EV technology more evolved.

The next blow came with the arrival of COVID-19. The period during and for some time after was characterised by high inflation and low economic growth, suppressing demand further in the industry. It had, in a relatively short space of time, become a profoundly uncertain market.

Garrett Motion

Garrett Motion is a Swiss-based developer and manufacturer of turbos for Internal Combustion Engines (ICE). With 2022 sales of $4bn and profits exceeding $700mn this is a lucrative and highly cash-generative business. Turbos drive air into the engine as a means of generating improved performance. Their sophisticated turbos have revolutionised the diesel engine, which had previously not been acclaimed for its capacity for acceleration. Not only did they create better engine performance but also contributed to greater fuel efficiency.

The original owner, Honeywell, probably saw the industry writing on the wall when listing Garrett on Nasdaq in 2018. The business held substantial market share in the car industry, developing and manufacturing turbos for BMW, VW, Hyundai and numerous other automakers. Whilst they are leaders in engineering excellence and innovation the move to the turbo-free Electric Vehicles (EVs) presents a major problem.

By the time of its stock market listing in 2018, uncertainty regarding future regulation was already rife within the ICE car market, most notably regarding diesels. Demand was dropping as diesels were widely publicised for heavy carbon particle emissions. EV's were developing rapidly but remained expensive and lacked range; there was also a lack of convenient charging stations which made long-distance travel problematic.

Honeywell chose to inject a significant amount of debt into Garrett at the listing, which, when Covid hit demand for cars in 2020, forced the business to seek protection from its creditors by entering Chapter 11. This is a form of insolvency in which the business is protected from its creditors until it can reorganise its finances. In 2021, the business was acquired by the private equity firm KPS Capital Partners with a payment of $2.1bn in return for 80% of the shares. The remainder are still listed.

Whilst highly profitable, Garrett is faced with declining worldwide markets and little in the way of products which will be suitable for EV's. Although vehicles which run on hydrogen from turbos are broadly considered 'clean,' there is a long way to go until this industry becomes significant. In effect, the ICE industry is both a turbulent and ultimately transient one, which may well dwindle altogether in the years to come. What should Garrett's new owners do?

The Theory of Turbulent and Transient Industries

Turbulent Industries

Turbulent means high fluctuations in demand and any turbulent industry therefore requires rapid adjustments of production capacity and cost levels to satisfy varying levels of output. This type of industry does recover from difficult periods as demand recovers. Industries which are cyclical may fit this model such as commodities, mining, construction industry and property all have some of these characteristics (Sull, 2009).

For the car industry, the banking crisis, 'diesel gate,' concerns about government attitudes to diesels and then Covid have all taken their toll on car sales levels. The measures required to combat major fluctuations in sales are all about survival until demand recovers: high cash piles to withstand periods of losses, portfolio cross-funding by owning businesses which are less cyclical, low overheads and outsourcing activities to share the risks with others, are all strategic imperatives.

Traditional means of dealing with demand volatility include absorption methods that require:

1. High cash piles,

2. Low overheads,
3. Portfolio diversification for cross-funding in times of need,
4. High switching costs to avoid flagging demand and price wars,
5. Becoming 'asset light' through outsourcing wherever possible,
6. Avoiding vertical integration which compounds risk.

'Asset light' is a tactical means of spreading risk which allows some flexibility in meeting fluctuating demand levels. Similarly, avoiding diversification through vertical integration is beneficial as this compounds rather than spreads risk to other parties. So, if you own your suppliers and customers then all decline together if demand becomes depressed.

Garrett may be hugely cash generative, but when Honeywell listed the business, they effectively stripped it of the potential benefits of cross-funding with the rest of their portfolio, and the business would then have to survive on its own. In terms of overheads, Garrett had been a highly successful business for many years and as with most in strong market positions, costs rise with profit as the business model thrives. That is until a strong reason arrives to address costs or alternatively private equity ownership occurs, otherwise excessive cost levels are frequently allowed to continue.

For many non-PE-owned businesses, it requires just such 'difficult' periods of poor performance for costs to again become a focus. Similarly, activities are often pursued in-house as the extent of financing and substantial profits results in activity 'creep' in which activities are allowed to expand into areas which do not offer any competitive advantage either in terms of better performance or lower costs.

For Garrett, switching costs are high due to long lead times needed for product development, and a three-year-gap between signing contracts and the installation of agreed technology for developing new models. After long periods of comfortable demand levels, the question becomes, does the Garett management have the agility and flexibility to address the cost base? Cost-cutting normally needs to be centrally driven by those who provide context and direction, it is rarely effective when instigated by divisions. There is also the matter of finding new markets.

Transient Industries

Transient industries decline over time and many eventually disappear completely, so identifying the needs of new markets as soon as possible becomes critical (McGraph, 2013). This requires great sensitivity to current industry trends as to when an industry will enter steep decline and then create rapid feedback at the board level so appropriate action can be taken. Identifying new nascent industries and rapidly developing product offerings to participate in those industries should become a priority.

Examples of transient industries are those in which technology changes or progresses quickly. If we think of music, its primary media was once predominantly in sheet format. Its storage form, once developed, was initially on vinyl discs, later replaced almost entirely by cassette tapes which had poor reproduction but could be played on portable devices. This was in turn replaced by the clarity of sound produced by Compact Discs (CDs), before online downloads and now streaming sites such as Spotify have become the most common way people listen to music.

In each case the manufacturing of both music media and playing devices changed completely. Once downloads and then streaming were introduced this changed distribution dramatically by almost entirely negating the need for retail distributors. Streaming became the dominant mode of buying music which gave services significant negotiating power to squeeze both the recording labels and the artists' fees.

Sheet music and CDs are not entirely extinct, yet vinyl has made a suprising comeback in recent years. Driven partly by nostalgia and authenticity, this reflects a wish to 'own' tangible media recordings and the information, artwork and often words of the album. In 2023, prominent musicians such as Taylor Swift released her entire back catalogue on vinyl, followed by numerous others in 2024.

Another example of a transient industry is the photography business, dominated by Kodak until digital cameras forced them into insolvency. Kodak may have been an early developer of the digital camera but had always lost money in selling products. They had made their money from film sales and developing and could not envisage another camera business model being successful. The film development model disappeared in most areas once digital cameras arrived, and the incorporation of high-quality cameras into smartphones signals further industry decline. Fuji who, like Kodak, originally relied on film development, managed to survive these technological advances by diversifying into broader reprographic services.

Transient industries overall are becoming more common in the technology arena as new advances are continually fuelling the market. Some will remember AOL or America Online which supplied dial-up internet connections. The move to broadband killed AOL, and plenty of other technology businesses are likely to experience the same.

Transient industry strategy requires several important steps (McGrath, 2013):

1. High sensitivity to changing trends in the industry with rapid feedback to the centre.
2. Curtailing investment in the old industries once major decline becomes apparent.
3. Reduce costs in the old industry as the industry may become a cost-based battle as other competitors cut investment too. As demand declines competitors may battle to retain demand levels through low pricing.
4. Transfer resources to the new industry, including your best people (or 'A team').
5. Become 'asset light' wherever possible to limit investment. Outsource to suppliers where feasible, as this reduces the financial commitment and shares the risks with other suppliers.
6. Create strong central control over cash and people to ensure they are redirected to the new industries.
7. Recruitment of new people with the requisite skills for the new industry will be necessary.

Transient industries decline over time and many eventually disappear completely. Identifying the needs of the new markets as soon as possible becomes critical. This requires great sensitivity to current trends and rapid responses at board level. Bad news often travels slowly up organisations, so structures are needed that actively survey trends, scenarios and opportunities and report directly at senior level. Identifying new industries and rapidly developing product offerings should become a priority.

Investment needs to be curtailed in the old industries, freeing up resources and transferring skilled employees to the new. That is assuming however, that capabilities required for the old industry are relevant to the new; even if they are, only those with energy and flexibility are likely to 'make the cut.' Again, this requires top level management involvement; divisional management tend to hang onto useful resources and people when they might be more productively refocused and transferred to developing areas.

Cash and skilled employees therefore need to be directed away from the old industries towards the new at a relatively early stage. Once it is seen to have limited life then investors will generally avoid a declining industry, even if it has a strong cash flow.

With minimal further development of products or technology, then the old industry should be run for cash, which means cutting overheads and other costs. Management may struggle with the transition from leading a differentiated offering and the investments in quality, design, innovation, technology and service to a cost-based product. It is very difficult for previously differentiated players to remove costs sufficient enough to compete with low-cost Chinese and other country copies when they start to become attractive once designs lose their patents (Porter, 1985).

It may be that new skills and capabilities need to be recruited and technology and know-how acquired. Moreover, the culture and attitudes of the old division may be a restraint on the new, so separate structures may also be needed and innovative developers of the new; collectively these are all potentially difficult transitions.

From Traditional to Transitional: Garrett Motion Strategy

For Garrett and its PE owners the tough part is just beginning. The traditional business, if stripped of cost and resources, should produce significant cash over many years. Whilst this will fund investment in new industries, it will also pay substantial dividends and allow some debt to be injected. The real problem is the private equity buy—improve—sell model: ultimately Garrett must be sold. But who wants a long-term declining business that has a flow of substantial but diminishing dividends? The exit multiple would be little more than that for an annuity. Growth markets must be found.

In the case of Garrett, 250 engineers have been newly recruited to work on areas such as battery cooling systems, diagnostic and security software and hydrogen turbos. Some developments are focused on better fuel efficiency in hybrid and commercial businesses.

There will need to be major reductions of people in the 'old business' and a greater drive towards plant and overhead efficiency. This is likely to involve external manufacturing and supply chain consultants. In view of the relatively long history, this may come as a cultural shock to the management.

Private equity investors tend to ignore any cultural unrest and internal opposition by creating enough forward momentum to override the potential barriers of deep-rooted traditions and inflexibilities. This may be a big assumption to make in this case, as the engineers are highly resistant to cost-driven strategies and may struggle to see beyond their immediate environment. The bigger picture of cost reduction and transfer to new technologies may also fail to suit some.

PE will receive the benefits of cash flow but may find a sale rather more demanding, given that it is dependent on some of the major new growth initiatives bearing fruit.

Management Reflections on Ownership Change to PE

In the last four years, Garrett has been a division of a large, listed business before its own listing in 2018, it then descended into 'Chapter 11' in 2020 and became PE-owned by KPS in 2021. Garrett was subject to more frequent reporting on Key Performance Indicators (KPIs) during PE ownership. PE removed the divisional structure which allowed the board greater direct access to activities, the consequence being that the board was far more involved in the business (in effect, divisional structures block off the board from direct involvement). This facilitated both faster decision-making and more involvement of the board and centre in the business. There was a much greater speed of change both demanded and achieved. Some cost-reduction measures have also been implemented.

Lessons
1. Costs in a business are often only addressed when the need arises. High industry entry barriers often result in high profits to industry participants, but costs often increase due to limited competition.
2. Divisional structures tend to isolate boards and top management from operations, limiting much direct influence on activities. Simpler structures allow more direct management, particularly when making major changes.
3. Culture can be a significant problem when transitioning to new industries and is often underestimated.
4. High levels of debt in turbulent or transient industries present a problem. Industries which fluctuate dramatically in demand need cash piles in reserve to survive.
5. Portfolios of businesses do allow cross-funding when needs arise. Shareholders are less enthusiastic as they can diversify their own portfolio of investments without companies doing it for them.
6. Strong growth prospects are necessary when selling businesses and command much higher multiples. Interest in declining industries will be limited.
7. Vertical integration is best avoided in both transient and turbulent industries as it compounds risk and magnifies losses during downturns.

References and Recommended Readings

Brady, C., & Moeller, S. (2014). *Intelligent M & A: Navigating the Mergers and Acquisitions Minefield* (2nd ed.). Wiley.
'Big four' market share. (2017). *kantar*, https://www.kantar.com
Burrough, B., & Helyar, J. (1990). *Barbarians at the Gate: The Fall of RJR Nabisco*. Arrow Books.
BUSINESS: The Big Four Take a Margins Hit. (2008). *Farmers Guardian*, p. 18.
Drucker, P. F. (1981). *The Five Rules of Successful Acquisition*.
Ghauri, P., & Hassan, I. (2014). Mergers and Acquisitions Failures. In *Evaluating Companies for Mergers and Acquisitions* (Vol. 30, pp. 57–74). Emerald Group Publishing Limited.
Gunther McGrath, Rita. (2013). *The End of Competitive Advantage: How to Keep Your Strategy Moving as Fast as Your Business* (pp. 45–47). Harvard Business School Press.
Koller, T., Goedhart, M. H., & Wessels, D. (2020). *Valuation: Measuring and Managing the Value of Companies* (7th ed.). Wiley.
Lorange, P. (2010). *Leading in Turbulent Times: Lessons Learnt and Implications for the Future* (1st ed.). Emerald Publishing Limited.
Paine, F. T., & Power, D. J. (1984). Merger Strategy: An Examination of Drucker's Five Rules for Successful Acquisitions. *Strategic Management Journal, 5*(2), 99–110.
Porter, M. E. (1985). *Competitive Advantage: Creating and Sustaining Superior Performance*. Free Press.
Sudarsanam, P. S. (2003). *Creating Value from Mergers and Acquisitions: The Challenges; an Integrated and International Perspective*. FT Prentice Hall.
Sull, D. (2009). How to Thrive in Turbulent Markets. *Harvard Business Review* (Vol. 87, Issue 2).
Teitelman, R. (2013). M&A: Where It's Been, Where It's Going. *Mergers and Acquisitions, 48*(1), 28.
The Daily Telegraph. (2024). Daily Telegraph.
Wood, Z. (2022, September 17). 'Big Four No More': Where Now for UK Grocers as Aldi Overtakes Morrisons? *The Guardian*.

Part V

Conclusions

10

Ten 'Rules' to Improve Your M&A Performance

'It was the best of times, it was the worst of times.' Charles Dickens, *A Tale of Two Cities*

A common quip in the M&A arena is that '99% of acquisitions are little more than retail therapy for CEOs.' Although something of a hyperbole, there is some truth in the statement, since, once a business is generating significant amounts of cash, CEOs often look to the acquisition trail for further growth.

This is understandable to some extent—there is much excitement surrounding acquisitions, a heady sense of anticipation, power and the ability to make something happen, not to mention having something to show shareholders and investors that the growth of the business is a priority.

There is also the prospect of having a new 'toy' to play with. Whilst part of the sentiment surrounding acquisitions might be driven by ego, CEOs are constantly under pressure to grow a business. When in mature markets, or the business is over a certain size then M&A becomes the main option to rapidly generate acceptable growth rates. However, acquisitions often go way beyond any logical strategy which might have a prospect of success. There is a tendency to overpay, and frequently under-plan the integration process itself, however it remains the part in which value is generated and synergies extracted.

© The Author(s), under exclusive license to Springer Nature Switzerland AG 2024
J. Colley, *The Unwritten Rules of M&A*, Palgrave Executive Essentials,
https://doi.org/10.1007/978-3-031-68368-8_10

Pricing

In the cold light of day, the pricing can frequently be excessive, and the integration itself can go badly wrong. Pricing is often driven by the 'Fear of Missing Out' (FOMO) phenomenon—the concern that, if the target is not acquired then it will never become available again, and worse still a competitor might buy it first. The determination to acquire can transcend any economic logic. CEOs tend to 'go shopping' when they have money available, which is at times of strong economic growth and readily available liquidity. That is when they can readily borrow, and their own profits are high. These circumstances normally coincide with strong M&A markets when high multiples have to be paid. As M&A markets subsequently decline then prices paid at the peak come back to haunt the CEO.

Integration

Culture clashes are often blamed for poor integration performance, but poor planning is usually at the root of the problem. Operational and commercial due diligence findings can be helpful when planning but are largely ignored in the enthusiasm to 'get the deal over the line.'

Integration planning is usually an afterthought that occurs once a business has been bought. Expectations regarding the integration synergies have already been formulated at the time of project approval, but the integration team may only be introduced to these expectations once the deal is complete. The result is that they end up trying to deliver benefits they had no part in determining.

As this book has explored, the nature of the strategy should determine the mode of integration, including the depth and speed. People you wish to keep need to be treated well and given responsibility and clarity regarding their future. It is easy to acquire a business for its knowledge, capabilities and technology, only then to watch the management leave. At the same time, distraction levels of all concerned frequently results in lost focus and market share.

Private Equity

Whilst PE objectives are very different to strategic buyers there is much to learn from their high levels of discipline and focus. If you operate the buy–improve–sell model to make returns, then one has to be very good at each of those operations. Discipline is needed over the timing and pricing of deals, and good use is made of any third-party performing due diligence.

PE investors work to a clear and timely improvement plan that includes finding new growth markets and carefully considering the timing and mode of exit. There is virtually always a clear strategy. Governance is effective with small industry-focused boards and a management team on the board with significant equity. Incentives are clear and only pay out on a successful exit. Private equity is active in selecting senior management—if they are failing, they are changed.

As earlier chapters have suggested, PE investors may well be victims of their own success. Their overall average returns have been of such a level that they have attracted large amounts of investor cash. Despite high interest rates and restricted liquidity, they still have to find targets, pay a sensible price, improve them and find someone to buy them at a higher price.

There are signs that identifying appropriate buyers is becoming harder and public listings may be unavailable for long periods of time. No doubt returns will be affected, but PE will wait out recessions and sell as markets improve. But can the model keep absorbing the huge amounts of available investor cash and producing the same eye-watering returns?

Governance

The consideration of a number of governance models throughout the book conclude that the public company model is far from ideal when compared to PE and family businesses. However, it may be all we have. Certainly, Non-Executive Directors could be better selected for industry knowledge or relevant specialist skills and may need to commit far more time to the job than they do at present. Time and time again the public model fails. Innumerable case studies demonstrate that boards are often furnished with inadequate information, do not ask the right questions and do not have time for a fight before the particular event has already happened. In some cases, lack of intervention can continue for years despite signs of major problems.

Conclusions

As we have seen research shows that anywhere between 60 and 80% of acquisitions fail to deliver expectations (Christensen et al., 2011; Martin, 2016). Whilst essential, M&A is often abused and rarely provides the intended outcome. After the excitement and enthusiasm of the deal comes the realisation that what has been bought is not quite what one expected, the price was too high, and the various projected benefits are largely unachievable. Add to this a difficult integration and both businesses can end up worse than before the deal.

The message of this book is that none of this needs to happen.

M&A certainly provides fertile ground for analysis and advice, as it is not hard to improve on much of current practice. It has provided a discussion of what goes wrong and explained how to avoid the many traps awaiting the unwary and inexperienced.

Contrary to popular myth, M&A is not a specialist activity for the few, but an activity relevant to many in a business. Most CEOs of businesses with over 500 employees and their boards will be expected to acquire targets. Anyone involved in strategy, and particularly integration, will benefit from such guidance. Integration involves large numbers of people, and few survive a career without either being integrated or managing an integration. In short, this is a book for the many, not the few. Whilst specialists are needed, they have to be managed in the best interests of the business. Their objectives may be very different from that of the board.

These teachings are the product of a lengthy career repeatedly calling for involvement in the buying and selling of companies, as well as managing integrations. This has featured corporates, private equity and family businesses. It has also involved considered and cumulative study of academic research, plus no end of teaching, discussing and extending knowledge with executive students as a Professor at Warwick Business School. The book is informed by both extensive practise and research. Recent examples are dissected to see what works and what does not. Few books are based on both practise and theory which makes this approach relatively unique. It does engage with theory but is based on practical approaches to making M&A effective.

As a conclusion, I have selected what I consider to be the key rules from the many lessons which arise throughout the book. I do hope this book provides you with the relevant knowledge and experience to help improve the outcome of your M&A activities.

The Rules

We know that corporate M&A is far from 'efficient' in terms of growing a business. The data is overwhelming in terms of failed expectations, destroyed value, and having to 'dump' recent acquisitions to prevent further value destruction.

This book has hopefully introduced many 'rules' or guidance which can improve performance when acquiring businesses. Those presented below are not necessarily the most important to you but are likely to be amongst the most helpful to many. They are also the ones most frequently ignored, much to the cost of the acquirer.

Some would argue that rules are there to be broken, and no doubt examples can be identified in which the so-called 'rules' have not been followed but the outcome has been successful. What we would say is that if you choose to break these rules then have good reasons. The odds are not on your side. Much of the failure is associated with strategies that don't work, lack of planning and buying and selling at the wrong times. For those indirectly involved, but affected, a rule of thumb is that if the strategy sounds either vague or like rhetoric then it has very likely been recently created to justify an opportunistic acquisition beneath the guise of strategy.

The 'rules' have been divided into three major categories: strategy, pricing and integration, research and experience which have been set out, justified and illustrated throughout the course of this book.

These 'rules' or guidance if applied rationally and strategically, should go some way to shortening your learning curve and preventing at least some of the costly education which most endure whilst building knowledge of the M&A process as a tool for growth. They are written from the perspective of the business rather than the advisor. Nevertheless, they can also assist those in advisory positions or those wishing to take on such roles.

Strategy

1. Strategic Clarity and Focus

Intermediaries such as investment banks make their money from creating markets in which to sell businesses. This may involve proposing strategies to prospective buyers for businesses which are being offered for sale. Corporate CEO's can be susceptible to flattery, suggestion and persuasion coming from highly educated 'experts,' especially if it seems exciting enough and comes from credible sources. The potential for rapid growth by such means can be seen as attractive. Such acquisitions rarely turn out well unless the list of targets is consistent with and created from the agreed strategy.

Many acquisitions are driven by opportunism. In any number of cases when a business is for sale, some sort of strategic fit can be constructed to justify acquisition. Such 'ideas' rarely work out well. Unless the business being marketed corresponds with the existing strategic direction of your business, then corporate CEOs would be wise to decline such proposals (of course, private equity investors make their money through opportunistic buying, improving, and selling, but they are in a very different game.)

2. Importance of Strategic Relatedness

Unrelated acquisitions in terms of products, markets or technology are rarely successful for corporates. Knowledge of at least one of the related elements—and preferably more—increases the prospects of success significantly. Unrelated acquisitions deliver few synergies, which means the price premium paid is unlikely to be recouped. Lacking knowledge in all three areas when acquiring is a step into the unknown in which few benefits are likely to be created. There have been successful exceptions in which portfolio acquisitions are made for investment purposes such as Warren Buffett's Berkshire Hathaway. Such acquisitions need scale and substance in their respective markets to be successful. However, many buy the capabilities and resources they need; if the new industry is too far removed, then they may struggle to assess what they are buying or to put the new capabilities to constructive use.

3. Importance of Synergistic Benefits

Synergies between the buyer and the target are important for strategic acquisitions. What can you bring to the target which will create more value than the business can generate on its own? If the extent of synergies is limited, then one cannot justify the price premium inevitably paid for the business. There need to be new markets for the products, product extensions, or better quality and increased levels of efficiency arising from the benefits. If you are buying know-how or technology, then consider carefully how you are going to exploit it on a wider scale. Saving some administrative overheads alone is not going to be adequate. A question to ask is 'who would be the best owner for the business and who could create the most value from acquiring the target?' They are likely to be willing to pay the most for the business. If you are not bringing much to a business, then why own it?

4. Relative Size Matters

Acquiring relatively large businesses rarely turns out well. Prices are often high due to relative size, there will be little prospect of benefitting from multiple arbitrage, and the integration is more difficult due to sheer scale. Multiple dilution on large deals is rarely recouped through subsequent integration benefits. Research suggests that 30% by market valuation of your own business in one transaction is the maximum one should buy. A policy of acquiring smaller businesses is much lower risk and has a better chance of success. Of course, unless there are many appropriate targets to acquire then this strategy will mean slow growth. Many firms take the view that, to pursue their strategy, they will have to accept acquisitions which do not offer medium-term financial justification. In those circumstances, it needs to be a good strategy.

Pricing

5. Timing Is Critical

Bad timing is one of the key reasons that acquisitions fail, and corporate disposals often offer poor value. Periods of strong economic activity coupled with high liquidity in the market tend to prompt strong levels of acquisition activity. These high demand levels result in increased multiples being paid. For example, the difference in global multiples between April 2022 and April 2023 saw a fall of between 20 and 30%. In reality, corporates enjoying strong trade and when liquidity is good, tend to enter the acquisition trail. When reverse conditions exist and companies are forced to re-evaluate their strategies, then disposals often ensue, usually at poor prices. The most regrettable 'buy' deals are often those made at the top of the market. The high multiples paid result in the deal being handicapped from the start often to the extent it proves a failure.

Whilst private equity investors may be driven by the extent of 'dry powder' waiting to be invested, they still attempt to buy during times of poor liquidity and exit when M&A markets are strong. Of course, the willingness of banks to lend affects PE too.

6. Plenty of Option Targets

High prices paid often result from having identified few options that are consistent with the corporate strategic objectives. A short list of targets means that corporates feel anxious to buy targets when they become available, whatever the price. High prices may result in earnings dilution which is difficult to recoup through synergies and benefits created from new ownership. Longer lists of potential targets ease the pressure to buy and strengthen the negotiating hand.

Integration

7. Determining the Key Elements of the Integration Approach

There are several major decisions to be made when considering the mode of integration. How fast to go and how deep. How to integrate a business depends on the extent of synergistic benefits available and the need to retain management.

In short, if you want to keep existing management for their knowledge and expertise (that you don't have), then don't rush the integration and limit the depth of approach, at least initially. Keep the existing management in charge and give them the relevant necessary resources to advance the business.

On the other hand, if there are major available benefits to be had then rapid deep integration is usually necessary, but this course is likely to risk or accelerate the loss of management.

The real problem arises when there are both significant benefits available and a need to retain the management team. In such circumstances, slower and progressive integration may be the key whilst keeping existing management 'in charge.' This is a difficult balance to maintain as the original management may not be keen on integrating their 'kingdom' into something they do not control.

8. Due Diligence to Inform Integration and Improvement

Due diligence is a vital opportunity to produce a detailed improvement plan and inform the integration approach taken. This is especially true in the commercial and operational areas. Deeper due diligence investigations by specialised consultants will produce more than your own people are likely to unearth and can have the potential to introduce new ideas for future strategy. It will also provide an objective assessment of the risks facing a business in document form and additionally ensure any overly enthusiastic buyers proceed with a level of realism.

9 . **Detailed Plan Available Before Deal Closed**

A key finding of much research in the area is that a precondition for a successful integration is knowing what you are going to do in terms of integration approach and actions before the target is acquired. The most detailed plan, founded on both intelligence and due diligence findings, offers a far greater chance of success. Organising adequate, experienced resources to be available immediately after the acquisition is also necessary.

10 . **Adequate and Appropriate Resource Availability**

Senior management can be inclined to treat integration itself as a low priority alongside getting the deal done. Usually, none of the negotiators and team engaged in the deal will be either responsible or involved in the integration process. This is frequently left to the commercial, operational and middle management employees, not only to get the job done but to deliver its anticipated benefits (which they had no hand in determining in the first place). Do they have adequate resources and experience to integrate the acquisition? Often, they do not have them available to a realistic timetable which inevitably results in an under-resourced project.

Worse still is the business that gets on the acquisition trail engaging a number of candidates for integration at the same time with no real hope of them being resourced.

Conclusions

Follow these 'rules' and you will increase your prospects of creating value from acquisitions and disposals. Some, such as timing, are difficult to follow. Sellers of businesses usually market them at the top of the M&A market when profits are better, and multiples are high. At such times, liquidity may be high meaning borrowing money is readily available and low cost. In these circumstances, the transaction will be readily facilitated by the business environment but at a very high price, such that you may never make a return.

In terms of integration, boards need to focus far more on planning, nature of approach and resources rather than just the deal itself. There is often an implicit assumption at the board level that the integration is for management to sort out. Integration is the process that generates value from the acquisition. It is a board concern, and the board needs to be reassured as to the resources, plan, depth and speed of integration they will be overseeing. They should ask to see the plan and be given the opportunity to contribute.

References and Recommended Reading

Brady, C., & Moeller, S. (2014). *Intelligent M & A: Navigating the Mergers and Acquisitions Minefield* (2nd ed.). Wiley.

Christensen, C. M., Alton, R., Rising, C., & Waldeck, A. (2011). The Big Idea: The New M&A Playbook. *Harvard Business Review, 89*(3), 48–57.

Dickens, C. (1986). *A Tale of Two Cities* (1st ed.). Lerner Publishing Group.

Drucker, P. F. (1981, October 15). The Five Rules of Successful Acquisition. *The Wall Street Journal*.

Martin, R. L. (2016). MA: The One Thing You Need to Get Right. *Harvard Business Review, 94*(6), 42.

Stadler, C. (2015, April 30). Four Lessons Firms Can Learn from Family Businesses. *Forbes*.

Index

A
Aberdeen Asset Management 19, 44, 157
AB InBev 9–11, 16, 18, 37, 38, 40, 61, 62, 152–154, 157
Advisors 10, 16, 42, 47, 51, 53, 66, 67, 109, 128–130, 137, 141, 144, 153, 156, 207
Agency theory 81, 160
Airbus 87
Amazon 115, 117, 184
AOL 13, 16, 47, 57
Asda 16, 137, 163, 169, 182, 184–190
Asset-based approach 132
Asset light 121, 122, 194, 196
AT&T 4, 13, 14, 16, 17, 47, 57, 62, 135
Autonomy 41, 42, 55, 56, 121

B
BAE 39
Bain & Co. 77
Ball Aerospace 39
Bankers 49, 66, 128, 170, 173, 175
Barbarians 7, 162
Bayer 9, 11, 12, 18, 27, 62, 131, 157
Beecham, Smithkline 47
Bidding wars 103, 162, 163
Boeing 87
BPB 54, 66–70
British Gypsum 63, 65
'Bulking up' 37
Business
  size 16, 26, 36, 85, 155, 171, 203
  traditional 5, 117, 197
Business model
  Elon Musk's 'X' 116, 135, 148, 149
  Reinventing 39

C
Cash flow 103, 140, 196, 197
Change management 19, 51, 57–59, 143, 191
  John Kotter model 58
'Chapter 11' 198

Chem China 11
Chrysler, Daimler 17, 43, 44
Cisco 39
Clayton Dubilier and Rice (CD&R) 90, 118, 186, 187
CNN 13, 14
Colgate-Palmolive 60
Comcast 15, 57, 132
Commodities 91, 193
Communication 64, 65, 71, 108
Comparable multiples
 consumer goods 114
 maximising 88, 187
Compass 70
Competition and Marketing Authority(CMA) 16, 184, 185, 188
Competitive advantage 8, 46, 194
Competitors 6, 8, 9, 11, 25, 27, 34, 35, 37, 49, 54, 56, 57, 60, 61, 73, 103, 105, 134–136, 141, 171, 176, 184, 196, 204
Consultants
 involvement 144, 198
 motivations 59, 101
Covenants 163
Covid-19 4, 90, 112, 118, 148, 157, 158, 183, 186, 192, 193
Cyclical 90, 107, 133, 193
Cyclical industries 121

D

Deal heat 16, 175
Deal team
 experience 102, 107
 selecting your 'A' team 65, 196
Debt 10, 14, 15, 23, 35, 38, 62, 77, 84, 85, 94–97, 100, 103, 132, 133, 135, 141, 152–154, 163, 164, 185, 186, 189–191, 193, 197, 198
Delaware court 148
Diesel gate 192, 193

Discounted Cash Flow (DCF) 132, 133
Disney 15, 131
Distraction 35, 46, 62, 70, 130, 137, 140, 141, 173, 174, 179, 204
Distributors 72, 73, 195
Diversification 8, 9, 40, 49, 94, 134, 169, 194
Dot-coms 117
Dow Chemicals 11, 15, 59
Dry powder 7, 99, 118, 190, 209
Due diligence
 and concerns 71, 153, 175
 as a price chip 105, 136
 distraction 145, 180
 external 71, 105, 109, 174
 financial 26, 53, 71, 105, 109, 131, 136, 145, 171
 independent 12, 13, 71, 174
 internal 13, 18, 105
 legal 53, 105, 109, 121, 131, 136, 153, 155
 negotiation 102, 109, 134, 136, 175
 results 102, 131, 138, 153
Du Pont 11

E

Earnouts 144
EBITDA 23, 24, 84–86, 88, 91, 92, 96, 103, 107, 127, 132, 133, 171, 187
Electric Vehicles (EVs) 41, 91, 192
Environment, Social and Governance (ESG) 91, 122
Equations 83, 84, 132, 187
Executive Director (ED) 160, 162
Exit multiple 36, 84, 86, 88, 89, 93, 96, 97, 197
 calculating 24
External parties 102, 105

F

Failed integration 65, 143, 158
Fear of Missing Out (FOMO) 103, 204
Financial engineering 85
Focus 5, 9, 16, 18, 19, 34, 41, 43, 45–48, 61, 64, 77–80, 82–85, 96, 102, 103, 107, 109, 120, 121, 130, 135, 137, 143, 169, 171, 174, 179, 184, 190, 194, 197, 204, 205, 207, 211
FTSE 100 67, 107
Fundsmith 104

G

Garrett Motion 121, 169, 192, 197
General Electric (GE) 16, 120, 149–151, 153, 154
Gillette 52, 60–62
Glaxo Welcome 47
Greenwashing 114, 115

H

Hewlett Packard (HP) 41, 42
Horizontal diversification 187

I

Incentives 16, 48, 77, 82, 83, 87, 94, 96, 97, 129, 140, 161, 162, 164–166, 188, 192, 205
Intentions 3, 13, 14, 44, 158
Internal Combustion Engines (ICEs) 169, 192, 193
Internal Rate of Return (IRR) 78, 112, 163
Internationalise 7, 8
Issey brothers 163

K

Key Performance Indicators (KPIs) 79, 80, 104, 198

Kingfisher 39

L

Lawyers 12, 49, 67, 130, 156
Leverage 7, 22, 85, 86, 94, 99, 109, 120, 122, 182
LinkedIn 17, 18, 135
Lock in 106

M

Management
  bonuses 78, 82, 148
  conflict 106, 138
  incentivising 7, 40, 82, 94–96, 147, 155, 164, 165, 205
  retaining after deal 67, 71
Management autonomy 55
Management Buy Out (MBO) 137–140, 145
Market extensions 40, 57
Marketing 7, 17, 43, 46, 61, 107, 121, 129, 141, 142, 171, 188
Market share 9, 15, 16, 19, 21, 35–37, 44, 62, 67, 79, 92, 107, 137, 153, 182–186, 191, 192, 204
Media 5, 107, 116, 128, 133, 135, 149, 156, 169, 179, 180, 195
Merger of equals 17, 26, 42–44, 54, 184
Microsoft 17, 18, 135
Monsanto 9, 11–13, 18, 27, 62, 131, 157
Morrisons 90, 118, 162, 163, 169, 182, 185–188, 190, 191
Multiple
  consumer goods 114
  increasing 91, 103, 119, 149
Multiple arbitrage 5, 20–22, 24, 25, 28, 35, 36, 60, 62, 66, 85, 89, 92, 127, 149, 153, 190, 209

Multiple of Invested Capital (MOIC) 115
Musk, Elon 116, 135, 148, 149, 158, 169, 176–181

N

Net Book Value (NBV) 132
Net Present Value (NPV) 132, 133
Network effects 5, 6, 179
Non-Disclosure Agreement (NDA) 141, 171
Non-Executive Directors (NED) 24, 81–83, 92, 117, 148–150, 152, 158–160, 162, 164, 166, 205

O

Organic growth 5, 6, 18, 37, 42, 66, 155, 156
Overpaying 35, 49, 56, 84, 152, 154, 176, 189

P

P&G 60, 61, 183
Phenomenon–deal feverDeal fever v
Pierce Global Media 128
Positive biases v
Private Equity (PE)
  business model 4
  dry powder 100, 209
  exit proceeds 96
  future of 111, 122
  strategy 78
Procter and Gamble 52, 60
Product extensions 208
PSA 43

R

Rawlplug 169–174
Raytheon 47
RBS 62, 131, 151, 153, 154
Roll-up strategy 24
Round Up 12

S

SABMiller 9, 16, 18, 37, 61, 62, 152, 155, 157
Sainsbury's 16, 137, 182, 184–186
Screwfix 39
Shareholders 10, 12, 14, 16–18, 20–22, 24–26, 28, 33, 36, 37, 41–45, 47, 48, 60, 61, 67–71, 78–82, 86, 89, 96, 107, 108, 113, 117, 129, 130, 132, 138, 147–149, 152–164, 167, 174, 175, 177, 198, 203
Sky 15, 57, 131
Splunk 39
Stakeholders 25, 37, 51, 62, 79, 81, 83, 107, 108, 113, 114, 145, 147, 148, 155, 164, 177
Standard Life Aberdeen 44
Stellantis 42
St Gobain 54, 66–70
Succession 127, 128
Sustainability 113, 114
Sustainability funds 113
Synergy Trap 47
Syngenta 11

T

TDR 185, 186
Teaser 141
Tesco's 8, 182, 186
Tesla 148, 149, 177–179
Threads 176, 178, 179
Time Warner 4, 13, 14, 16, 17, 47, 57, 62, 135
Transdigm 87
Transient 121, 169, 193–196, 198
Turbulent 121, 163, 169, 193, 198
Twitter

overpaying 25, 42
rebranding 135, 177

U

Uber 5, 6, 8, 26, 115, 116
Unilever 60, 104, 183
United Technologies 47
Unrelated diversification 8, 40, 49, 54, 120, 134
Upstream integration 102, 103

V

Venture Capital (VC) 93, 115, 116
Vertical integration 44–46, 49, 94, 194, 198
Veterinary 92, 121
Vision 15, 42, 58, 64

W

Waystar Royco 128
WeWork 93

Printed in the United States
by Baker & Taylor Publisher Services